IN COMPLETE CIRCLES:

THE MEMOIRS AND TRAVELS OF AN AGEING SCHOOLBOY

CIARAN WARD

ISBN-13: 978-1475046359
ISBN-10: 1475046359

Copyright © Ciaran Ward 2013

http://dreamingarm.wordpress.com/

For the wonderful Ms H

Contents

Author's Note

During the writing of this book I contacted a number of publishers and agents but they weren't interested, citing that they didn't think this project was commercially viable or the classic euphemism "it doesn't fit in with our current publishing schedule". So I decided to go down the self-publishing route which seems to be an increasingly popular option in this digital age we now live in. In some ways this ethos reflects the DIY spirit of the punk rock era when bands and fanzines sprung up and in many cases tasted success without the financial backing of record labels or agents. The lack of interest from publishers was something of a blessing in disguise as it meant I had complete editorial control and could write whatever the bloody hell I liked without some editor telling me what I should or shouldn't include.

The vast majority of names in this book have been changed to protect the innocent - or in some cases the guilty.

In describing my proposal to publishers I came up with the following rather pretentious blurb:

"It combines the mundane with the exotic. The action shifts in the simple turn of a page from the fields and ditches of west Tyrone to the Atlas Mountains, from dull one-horse towns to London, New York and Sydney, from the school playing fields to the battlefields of the Balkan wars, from the classroom to the boardroom. A Northern Irish memoir which isn't fixated with sectarian violence, a travelogue which sees the world through the prism of absurdity."

"An Irish coming-of-age memoir with a difference – not the clichéd idyllic rural childhood nor the misery memoir of poverty and abuse, and not set against a backdrop of conflict - but a comic and at times surreal take on the absurdities of life in a provincial town."

It's taken me almost two years to write this book. I just hope it's been time well spent.

Finally, I'd just like to thank those who helped with and/or inspired the undertaking of this work – Suma for the proof reading, my three brothers James, Diarmaid and Matthew, Mum and Dad for being very indirectly responsible for this book even though they might not like what's in it, Phil "Wear thy dope cap" Larkin for the encouragement, thanks/apologies to my many former schoolmates and teachers for either intentionally or unintentionally providing inspiration for the book – and most importantly of all – thanks to Jo for being so unbelievably brilliant.

Time for the fun to begin...

Ciaran Ward

London, April 2013

1

In Search of Times Past

Whilst travelling on the London Underground on a Wednesday evening in June 2012 I noticed the passenger opposite me, a young man in his late 20s or early 30s was playing with a Rubik's cube. This suddenly brought back a flood of memories from the 1980s when the said plastic toy was all the rage and was thought to be almost impossible to work out. I hadn't seen one since my schooldays. I'd thought the cube had gone the way of the skateboard and the mullet (short on top, but long at the back) haircut, but maybe like so many other "retro-fashions" it was making a comeback?

The rise and fall of the cube was one of many trends which came and went during my schooldays in the 1980s and early 90s, a time of great transition.

I was in the fourth form when corporal punishment was banned and teachers reluctantly hung up their leather straps, cattle prods and batons. Having said that, there were teachers who to their credit never resorted to raising their fists/straps/canes in anger, yet still managed to maintain order and discipline.

Following the law banning corporal punishment, sanctions were commuted to community work such as picking up the rubbish in the school yard or plain and simple detention.

A typical situation from the Dark Ages may have gone like this:

"What are you laughing at?" asks an irate teacher to a pupil with a fit of the giggles.

"Nothing, sir" replies the fearful pupil.

"I'll give ye nothing – here's nothing!"

(Cue swish of leather strap followed by the sound of leather connecting with flesh and bone, then a cry of pain from the afflicted party – who is no longer laughing).

Let's fast forward a few years later to more enlightened politically correct times… The law has changed and teachers are no longer permitted to impose physical punishment with the impunity they once enjoyed. The scenario may now read as follows:

"What are you laughing at?"

"Nothing, sir."

"You know what happens to people who laugh at nothing? They get taken away by men in white coats."

My schooldays also oversaw the revolutionary transformation from the traditional blackboard and chalk to the newfangled glossy laminate whiteboards and felt tip pens. And the advent of the PC – the personal computer and political correctness. Suddenly computers had mice, but you weren't allowed to make racist or sexist jokes about them.

It's funny how listening to a certain piece of music or a smell or taste can suddenly trigger off memories in the subconscious. Songs like Blur's *There's no other Way* or The Charlatans' *The Only One I Know* for me evoke recollections of Friday nights circa 1991 and dry ice, half pints of shandy soon graduating to cider and pints of lager (usually a much maligned brand of local brew named after a large stringed instrument after which a mute Marx brother was also named) and a shot of lime et al. The pub looked out over the river. Sitting by the window you could see the reflection of the streetlights on the water, the reflection on the wet tarmac of the car park on the other side, the raindrops bouncing off the concrete. On the table were the wet incomplete rings imprinted by the pint glasses, an ashtray where dog-ends were accumulating, the clouds of cigarette smoke rising up to the ceiling, while REM sang about being near wild heaven – and it seemed as if we were… Or was I just being a pretentious young idiot?

Rewind to a few years earlier and the 1980s, the time in which I had the bulk of my formative years was a fascinating decade…

The early '80s conjures up memories of inner city riots, anti-apartheid demonstrations, boycotting South African fruit in the supermarkets, skeletal, unwashed, bearded men wrapped in blankets in filthy prison cells, running battles between police and striking miners, Russian tanks rolling over Afghanistan, Americans in Grenada, warfare amidst the penguins and sheep on wind-swept South Atlantic islands and Kim Wilde singing about young people across the Atlantic. And that other song "Shut up a your face".

Moving on to the mid-80s and we have the "Star Wars" missile shield, a loud-mouthed Dubliner ranting about famine in Ethiopia, the Chernobyl disaster, BMX bikes, footballers in tight shorts with bubble perms and moustaches, Joan Collins in American football-style shoulder pads, thin leather ties, Yuppies in red braces, mobile phones the size of breeze blocks, the aforementioned Rubik's cubes, grotesque rubber puppets imitating the politicians and celebrities of the day... and "The Chicken Song" by Spitting Image - I could go on all day.

Towards the end of the decade one thinks of statues of communist dictators being toppled, the Chinese military firing on defenceless students in Tiananmen Square and Russian tanks retreating from Afghanistan. Little did we know that just over a decade later European military powers would yet again occupy the country... and the chart-topping novelty song "Star Trekkin". Whenever I hear *Crazy Crazy Nights* by flamboyant, piebald-faced rockers Kiss (which is not infrequently these days given the amount of time I spend listening to radio stations specialising in "classic rock" or 1980s music), I'm reminded of Friday nights and youth club discos with myself and a bunch of other 14 year olds clad in bleached jeans and rugby shirts (they happened to be in fashion at the time - none of us actually played rugby) high on a lethal cocktail of Coke and Lucozade swinging our arms round in a circular motion on the dance floor and screaming out the chorus at the top of our voices, the tacky multicoloured lights shining on our faces.

It was during this time I was growing up in Omagh.

There's a Facebook page called "You know you're in Omagh

10

when...", which invites its adherents to contribute snippets of regional wisdom on traffic, nightlife, local characters, etc.

To select just a few examples, the thread might run along the lines of "You know you're in Omagh when":

1   "They make a bypass for traffic calming and it's the busiest road in the town".

2   "You drive right through and there's no reason to stop, not that you could find a parking space even if you wanted."

3   "When you're allowed to park cars on the roadside on the crest of a hill, forcing the traffic to the wrong side of the road, into oncoming traffic!!!"

4   "The legend in the silver Corsa that laps around Sallys [local nightspot Sally O'Briens] playing the same BeeGees song over and over again"

5   "You're back for a reunion with your mates and have the best night of your life, followed by the fear of god of someone hitting you outside Sally's for no reason"

6   "There's no taxis on a Saturday night"

7   "Tractors are in danger of taking over the main roads..."

You also get the smart arse remarks:

8   "When you see the sign that says "WELCOME TO OMAGH""

The depressing contributions:

9   "There's a big queue at the dole office"

And everything else in between...

10   "There's wile rows (local dialect for boisterous fighting) at the bus depot and everyone tries their hardest to be up the front just to see two wee boys in 1st year slappin' the faces of each other."

11 "When you ask "What's up?" and the only reply you get is "Not much""

12 "You have nothing to do on a Sunday"

13 "When your house isn't tossed by a tsunami, you're not under constant fire from lunatic dictators and you get water from a tap. Not so bad now is it?? Price of drink is shockin' but!!"

Many of these observations could of course be applied to any small or medium-sized inland provincial town in Ireland or Britain, the type of place which isn't exactly at the top of the visiting tourist's "to do" list .

I remember one day in the late 1980s one of my classmates brought the *Mirror* newspaper into school. He was amused by a short piece in the sports pages on the now defunct local soccer club Omagh Town, who back then had big ambitions. It was something trivial like a new manager, but the idea of a small town club getting a mention in a UK-wide national newspaper was something of a novelty.

"People will be reading this and saying 'Where the hell's Omagh?'"

That's assuming that anyone even bothered to read the article.

Tragically the town's name has become synonymous with the devastating bomb that ripped through the main shopping area on a sunny Saturday afternoon in August 1998. All of a sudden Omagh had joined the ranks of Dunblane, Hungerford, Lockerbie, Columbine, Beslan and nearby Enniskillen, once quiet, little-known, unassuming places that would now be remembered for the senseless loss of life. Thanks to the resilience of the town's people and the tireless efforts of the victims' families in their campaign for justice, life has gone on.

It was the town where I spent the carefree days of my youth, where I came of age, and where every other conceivable cliché occurred.

The nostalgia industry is now a lucrative business. Not for one moment I am suggesting that I'm jumping on the bandwagon! Replica football shirts from years gone by, big screen versions of popular TV shows from the 1970s and '80s, geriatric rock bands minus half their original line-ups ditching their wheelchairs and zimmer frames to re-form for mammoth world tours, TV channels devoted entirely to repeats of old stuff - all clamour to exploit the collective memory of an ageing generation and make a lot of money out of it.

The broadcaster and writer Clive James in the introduction to his autobiography *Unreliable Memoirs* says that most novels are really biographies in disguise. He goes on to say that his own autobiography is a sort of novel in disguise. This book is a bit of both. It's mainly a memoir, although not an entirely reliable one as some of the events described are exaggerated for comic effect. And some are completely fictional. But I won't say which ones. In any case I can't rely on my own memory to be 100% accurate after so many years. But maybe that's not such a bad thing.

It's a story – or more accurately a collection of stories - which deserves to be told.

2

In the Beginning

I was born in the late summer of 1973 in a hospital which is no longer there in the Irish border town of Strabane 20 miles up the road from the town where I grew up. My new-born self was blissfully unaware of the ongoing world oil crisis, the war in Vietnam, not to mention the escalating violence much closer to home, the UK and Ireland's accession to the Common Market ...and the fact that huge sideburns, flares, platform shoes and sickly flowery-patterned ties the size of kites were still in vogue – or that Gary Glitter was number one in the charts.

I spent the pre-school years of my childhood in a rural part of northern Nigeria where my father was teaching at the time. My memories of the time are very vague, but I do remember the gang of brightly coloured lizards which used to congregate on the doorstep every morning to take in the sun. They would scatter as soon as they saw me coming. Geckos used to crawl around the walls and ceiling at night. I also remember feeding a giraffe in Maiduguri Zoo. There's a picture in a dusty album to prove it somewhere at my parents' house.

I wasn't allowed to go out of the house in my bare feet because of hookworms and I wasn't allowed to walk inside the house barefoot because of scorpions. I'm also told that I bathed in the hot springs of the Yankari game reserve, but I have no memory of this.

It would be a long time before my next visit to Africa, but if you want to find out more then skip straight to chapter 18.

I was a keen ornithologist in my youth. On family holidays to the seaside we would have the car parked at the side of the road at low tide and I would look through my binoculars and watch the various wading birds oystercatchers, curlews and sandpipers which congregated on the tidal mud flats to feed on worms and shellfish. I explained to my parents and three younger brothers that these types of bird characterised by long legs and long beaks were generically known as waders. One of my younger brothers (I won't say which one, but he was about four at the time) seemed confused by this, so he piped up with the delightfully innocent remark "But a wader is a person who serves you food in a restaurant."

He wasn't the only member of the family to get catering terminology confused with ornithology. At a similar age I had once thought that a menu was a long-necked flightless Australian bird as popularised in puppet form by the 1970s entertainer Rod Hull.

But getting back to the coastal theme... Ever since childhood I've always enjoyed walking along a beach and picking up the various pieces of jetsam and flotsam (yes, I know – but why does flotsam always have to come first? Alphabetical discrimination of the worst kind!) along the way. It's always been a bit of a delightful novelty for me to walk along a shoreline with my eyes focused on the ground, exploring the beach and the rockpools. This may be largely down to the fact that I grew up in an inland town and have never lived within close proximity of a beach, so I've always associated the coast with being on holiday and the carefree days of my youth. Limpets were stubborn little buggers at the best of times, attaching themselves to the rocks so securely that they were almost impossible to dislodge. But if you crept up behind them quietly and used a flat stone to prise them off it worked. You could then see the yellowish rubbery fleshy inside of the creature in the shell. Not that there was much to see really. After this disappointment the only course of action was to put them back on the rock to which they would then stick to like extra strong superglue. Dangling a piece of ham or bacon on the end of a string into the rock pools would attract crabs, which you could then catch easily. Once you held them by the carapace as their pincers flailed wildly around the novelty had worn off, so they would be put back to the place from whence they came.

My mother's family did however come from the Co. Down coast, an area we visited regularly during my youth. On visits to the area or on family trips to Donegal I spend ages combing the beaches for marine curiosities to take home and add to the collection in my own private museum which I kept in my bedroom. I would pick up the empty husks that had once been crabs and sea urchins, lobster claws, pieces of driftwood shaped by the relentless tides, pebbles decorated with unusual patterns, shells of all shapes and sizes, fossilised marine creatures, the occasional beached whale, unexploded depth charges and containers of radioactive waste - which I would add to my bedroom museum. Apart from the marine stuff I also had a dog skull retrieved from a rotting canine carcass found by the Glenelly River, Plumbridge in the summer of 1981, a sheep skull from the Mourne mountains and shrews and mice which the cat had caught and I had subsequently pickled in jars of wine vinegar.

My Mum was constantly complaining about the smell from the badly decomposed pilot whale and the fact that all the cats in the neighbourhood would congregate on my window sill trying to force their way in was bad enough, but when the army bomb disposal team accompanied by men in radiation suits came knocking on the door and evacuated the whole area she wasn't too keen on my museum any more.

I won't go into too much detail about my early years at primary school. This is mostly because I remember very little about it and in any case most of what did happen isn't particularly noteworthy. However one incident during my third year when I was 7 or 8 years old springs to mind. We were given exercises to complete involving a short passage on a designated topic with questions at the end. One such passage was about lions. There were questions like where does the lion live, what does it eat, etc. The final question was:

"The lion has a title. What is it?"

The answer was presumably "the king of beasts", but one bemused seven year old (who I won't name) couldn't work this one out and asked his classmates "what's the lion's tittle?" (sic).
No-one seemed to know the answer, so he wrote what he had originally suspected all along:

"A place where the milk comes out".

There were also the playground rhymes and jokes doing the rounds, which were a constant source of amusement to the average seven year old.

These would range from the puerile as in "My friend Billy had a ten foot willy..." to the politically incorrect as in "Ching Chong Chinaman went to milk a cow". On a simpler level there were the times you would be approached in the playground at random and asked

"Are you happy?"

The answer would invariably be "yes" and the subsequent punchline was "Change your nappy!" – or similarly:

"Do you want a sweet?"

"Yes"

"Smell your feet!"

Or:

"You're in trouble – you sat on the bubble!"

The jolly prankster would then go off on his merry way in search of the next unsuspecting "victim".

Then there were the more sophisticated "role-playing" games, of which the following was a classic example.

The wily japester would approach his potential victim and say:

"I found a dead rat by the side of the road full of maggots with its guts sticking out. I'll say "I one the rat" – so you need to say "I two the rat" and so on..."

Innocent Victim: I two the rat

Wily Japester: I three the rat.

This would continue in the numerical sequence until:

Wily Japester: I seven the rat

Innocent Victim: I eight the rat

Japester: You ate the rat? Euuughhh!!! That's disgusting!

He would burst out laughing and encourage his assembled entourage to do likewise, before seeking out the next target with henchmen in tow.

There's a bit of a gap in the narrative now as I fast forward to the last days of primary school.

My first proper acting experience was at primary school in a pantomime of Mother Goose. So the ornithological theme unintentionally continues. I played the King of Gooseland. He was a put-upon husband who liked a flutter and cracked the odd joke. Joe Gorman played the domineering Queen of Gooseland. The school's annual pantomime whose cast consisted of the senior boys was organised by an inspirational teacher, the late Seamus Harkin, one of the school's more popular teachers due to his jokey manner.

The rehearsals started in October and took place after school.

At the very first rehearsal Mr Harkin gave us a down-to-earth, bullshit-free talk.

"The other teachers are sitting down at home with their feet up watching the snooker. I'm here giving up my spare time. I'm not going to tolerate any time-wasters. So if you want to drop out you know where the door is".

It followed the standard panto format, but being an all-boys school it was an all male cast, so some of us dressed in drag. We occasionally got out of classes to attend rehearsals. We even got our pictures in the local paper.

We were under strict instructions not to disclose any facts to friends or family. But inevitably details of characters, jokes and songs leaked out anyway to the point that the audience knew what to expect. You could almost hear younger siblings in the audience murmuring the punchlines to the jokes in advance.

The show was held in the town hall, an ancient crumbling building which has since been replaced by the spanking new riverside Strule Arts Theatre. It was open to the general public, regardless of whether they had any connection with the school or not. But the vast majority of the audience were parents, teachers and pupils.

I wore a green furry hooded suit with a bird's beak protruding from the hood between my chin and forehead. I also had a Groucho Marx style greasepaint moustache. I didn't look very like a gander if truth be told.

On the Saturday and Sunday there were matinees and evening performances, so we did two shows in the one day. There was no point in going home during the interim, so our parents used to give us money to go to the chippy. We walked up the town with our make-up still on attracting the curiosity of passers-by.

A group of teenage girls walked past and complimented me:

"I like your moustache – it's sexy!"

During the times we weren't on stage we would watch the show from the wings sets and read the graffiti on the walls which our predecessors from previous productions had written – and we would add some of our own.

Our class teacher Mr Arthurs even let us tired actors have the day off on the Monday after the last night.

And we got to have a slap-up meal of burger and chips followed by ice cream and jelly in a local eatery when it was over. It was in a pub-restaurant called the Cosy Corner. Two unrelated events several years later remind of me of the shortness of life and my own mortality. That section of the street, including the place we'd been dining in was blown up by the bomb in 1998. Then some 26 years later one of the boys I'd been sitting next to at the meal died suddenly during the writing of this book. Although I hate to use clichés, such things really do put life into perspective.

It would be another 17 years before I appeared in my next pantomime. The London legal firm I was working for at the time put on a satirical production penned by a group of young lawyers called "Snow White and the Seven Trainees". It was fun to do, but I'll leave it at that for the time being. I'll maybe put it in a future volume of memoirs.

But getting back to my primary school days...

Our teacher Mr Arthurs was a bit of an amateur historian, a railway enthusiast, a collector, an all-round boffin. He had clearly made quite an impression on some of his past pupils. A few of them, now senior boys at the "big school" regularly came back to their primary alma mater to visit him. He would hold these lads up as shining examples for us to aspire to. And some of us did the same by paying him occasional visits a few years later.

His enthusiasm for knowledge was demonstrated by what was referred to as the "class museum". It was basically a collection of antiquarian glass bottles, sea shells, cow horns, large pheasant feathers and the odd fossilised shell brought back from summer holidays by the sea lined out on the window sills. It's difficult to imagine that sort of thing being allowed nowadays. With health and safety laws being what they are now having sharp objects in the classroom would land you a hefty fine.

I remember one time when one of the local banks in the high street ran a Christmas card competition for primary school children in the town. The best entries would be displayed in the bank's foyer. Mr Arthurs, a devoutly religious man wasn't happy that many of us had included the greeting "Happy Xmas" on our self-designed cards as this was apparently crossing the Christ out of Christmas, and therefore a sacrilege. This was despite the fact that the "X" in Xmas comes from the Greek letter Chi, which is in fact the first letter of the word "Χριστός", meaning Christ. I didn't discover this fact till many years later, but if I'd known that at the time I would have been tempted to say "So put that in your pipe and smoke it, Mr Arthurs." This would have been quite funny (or at least funny to a 10-year old) as he did smoke a pipe at the time.

Mr Arthurs had a fascination with Christian martyrs and other similarly venerated figures. He would regularly regale us with his tales of Oliver Plunkett the 16th century Irish bishop who was hung, drawn and quartered at Tyburn in London having been wrongly convicted of treason. There was also John Vianney known as the curé of Ars, a French clergyman noted for his dedicated pastoral work; and Maximilian Kolbe, a Polish priest who had been recently canonised after having perished in a Nazi concentration camp where he had sacrificed himself so that another could live - and the martyrs of Sebaste in what's now modern day Turkey who in 320 AD were forced to stand naked on a frozen lake unless they renounced their faith. All very pleasant stuff indeed.

I eventually got to see Oliver Plunkett's head in a glass case in a Drogheda church when we happened to be passing through the town during a family summer holiday. From what I remember it was a shrivelled head, dark brown in colour like the trophies once collected by the headhunters of the Amazon rainforest. Hardly the most dignified or appropriate way to commemorate a man who supposedly died for his faith, but there you go.

Then years later I saw a dedication to Vianney in a church while staying with a French family on a school exchange and it all came flooding back to me. I don't remember where exactly, but it may have been Poitiers or Angoulême – one of those towns which hosts a stage of the Tour de France every few years anyway.

The classroom also had its own mini-library which contained a generous selection of the *Jennings* books by Anthony Buckeridge. Written in the 1950s the title character was a pupil at a private boarding school with an overactive imagination who along with his friend the nerdy bespectacled Derbyshire always seemed to be getting himself into bizarre scrapes. Through these stories we picked up English public school jargon, including exclamations liked "fossilised fishhooks!" and "petrified paintpots!" as well as expressions of approval such as "jolly spiffing super whacko idea!" For a brief period we even took to referring to the headmaster as the "Archbeako". Although this privileged, yet oppressive world of the cloister and the dorm, of Latin verbs (although if we'd been born a generation earlier we would have been taught Latin at school), housemasters and food hampers, midnight feasts, matrons, cricket and rugger was a million miles from our own experience we still somehow managed to relate to them. Schoolboys are schoolboys no matter where you go.

As anyone of my generation knows many teachers fancy themselves as comedians. Educational psychologists even say that it's an essential tool of the trade to garner popularity and respect among pupils. Back in the day to maintain order and discipline you either made your pupils laugh or you struck so much fear and terror into them that they were afraid to even breathe in class - or you lay somewhere in between.

Old Arthurs was no exception. Many of the jokes he told were as ancient as ST Coleridge's ill-fated mariner or the fossils in the "class museum". For example there was the one about the boy who wasn't sure what the plural of mongoose was (mongooses or mongeese?) or the ship's captain who demanded to know where his buccaneers were. If you didn't already know the answer was "under your buckin' hat". But to us they were hilarious and we repeated them to our parents who had probably heard the very same jokes during their own school days as had their parents before them.

Mr Arthurs also told us the story (possibly apocryphal) of the Irish priest in the 19th century who by chance came across a murder being committed. The perpetrator who was caught quite literally red-handed, still dripping with his victim's blood, on seeing the priest (let's just call him Father Maguire for the sake of convenience) instantly collapsed to his knees and begged for forgiveness. Fr Maguire duly fulfilled his clerical duties by hearing the murderer's confession and granting him absolution. The murderer overcome with great joy and relief then went off on his merry way. He was then probably run over and killed by a coach and horses, but presumably went straight to Heaven, having died in a state of grace.

Meanwhile as Fr Maguire was praying over the murder victim's dead body the police arrived on the scene and promptly arrested him. He couldn't apparently protest his innocence as breaking the sacred seal of the confessional could potentially condemn him to eternal damnation in Hell – or so we were told. He was then found guilty of murder as the police needed a convenient scapegoat to make their jobs easier and was sentenced to a lifetime of hard labour and transported to the then penal colony of Van Diemen's Land.

Presumably Maguire the martyr eventually perished in a stagnant mosquito-ridden swamp somewhere under the ruthless Tasmanian sun after many soul-destroying years of breaking up rocks in a chain gang. He would however have been rewarded in the next world for his honourable self-sacrifice. He was most likely reunited with the real murderer in Heaven where he promptly knocked seven shades of shit out of him.

All this talk of the Afterlife reminds me of the time I read in a comic at the age of 8 or 9 that there's a town in Norway called Hell. As well as the standard cartoons and stories comics had amazing facts, short snippets of information to intrigue the reader's young mind. I can just imagine a foreign tourist driving around rural Norway with dangerously low petrol levels. He asks a local for directions to the nearest town and is advised to:

"Go to Hell"

And I can imagine the road signs saying "Welcome to Hell"...

As the smaller half of the Two Ronnies used to say I digress...

One day after lunchtime we were all sitting at our desks waiting patiently for our teacher to arrive and resume class for the afternoon. For some reason Mr Arthurs had been delayed in getting back to class. An extra long lunch perhaps. I persuaded a classmate, Nigel Hackett (mind you it didn't take much persuasion as such) to write "Fuck" on the blackboard for a dare. Just after he'd done the deed and the laughter ensued who should walk in but Mr Holmes the vice principal who had presumably noticed the unusually high volume of noise coming from the classroom. He saw the offending word on the board and quickly tracked down the culprit.

"Did you write that word on the board, son?" he asked young Hackett.

"But he told me to!" the boy Hackett fearfully protested, pointing in my direction, a rather weak line of defence. Whether I had actually "told" him to was debatable, but I suppose it depends on your interpretation of the verb "to tell".

Naturally I protested my innocence with an indignant cry of "I did not!" - but I didn't need to.

Old Holmesy having no doubt heard the age-old "he told me to" excuse on numerous occasions during his 20 years of teaching countered it with the old schoolmaster's cliché – "so if he told you to put your foot in the fire would you do it?"

The boy Hackett had no answer to this and was taken aside for a quiet dressing down.

It's a well known fact that nothing amuses a 10 year old boy more than hearing words like "shit" or "fuck" on TV, especially if his parents are present. It's equally well-known that young boys like

24

defacing things. This can range from carving one's initials into school furniture with a compass, drawing anatomically questionable sketches of male genitalia on the school toilet walls, scrawling obscenities on classmates' exercise books to adding comedy beards, moustaches glasses and horns to pictures of celebrities and politicians in the newspapers. Neither my friends nor I were an exception.

There was a monthly magazine called the *Far East* produced by an order of missionaries which we were encouraged to persuade our parents to fork out money to subscribe to. I remember one particular day in my fourth or fifth year at primary school. There was a picture in this magazine of some Irish bishop meeting the then Pope at the Vatican. A classmate was reading this article with great disinterest and decided to make some additions to it. He drew a third arm extending from John Paul II's torso making the rude two fingered V-sign at the bishop and a speech bubble emanating from the pontiff's mouth telling his grace to "fuck up".

My reaction was a mixture of shock and amusement. I felt guilty laughing as it didn't seem right to mock these holy men, although nowadays I would feel considerably less guilty in the light of the revelations that some of them were not quite as holy as they seemed.

In hindsight I probably admired his brass neck. This was the same boy who had thought nothing of telling crude jokes to the teacher, even during a classroom visit by the school chaplain Father Carson. Father Carson to be fair to him took it quite well. Now this boy's doing rather well for himself.

****

I remember the day bushy eye-browed Soviet president Leonid Breshnev died. Mr Arthurs, a fervent anti-communist said that he would probably go to Limbo first and then on to Purgatory. Limbo was the afterlife destination for those who had not been baptised. It's since been abolished by the Vatican – or they've at least acknowledged the possibility that it may not exist. So was

Breshnev fast-tracked to Purgatory once the Pope waved his magic wand to make Limbo vanish? We'll probably never know.

Old Arthurs would set us a weekly essay, the only homework he ever really gave us. This ranged from the monotonous such as "What I did during my Easter holidays" to more imaginative titles like "As I turned the corner..." or "I heard a noise..." We also had a book of photographs and were often given an essay based on one of the pictures. Most of the time I regurgitated material from the comics and books I read at the time – mostly serial fiction like the Hardy boys, Nancy Drew, the "Alfred Hitchcock and the Three Investigators" series (which contrary to the prevailing beliefs of school boys at the time weren't actually written by Hitchcock, but a mere franchise which shamelessly cashed in on the great director's name) and Willard Price's adventure novels of two brothers who travelled round the wild parts of the globe to capture animals for the world's zoos. Invariably the stories I wrote featured schoolboys stumbling across a den of thieves by accident and managing to outwit them in the end.

It was usually a tall thin boss with twirly moustache aided by a fat stupid henchman whose incompetence would often be the downfall of the villainous mob. The influence of the comics I read at the time was very much in evidence here.

Based on a picture of a young child in a pushchair I wrote a story called "The Micro-chip Kidnapping" set in the year 1986, two years into the future. Young Harlem J. Hachenbacker IV, the three year old son of Silicon Valley multi-billionaire Harlem J. Hachenbacker III who had amassed his fortune through computers had been kidnapped by a gang of thieves who demanded a massive ransom. Harlem Junior gets rescued by an 11 year old boy and his BMX bike who receives generous reward from Hachenbacker Senior.

Mr Arthurs was sometimes open to persuasion to the title of the essay. We suggested he give us "My Favourite TV Programme" as a title and he accepted this. Almost everyone in the class (and I'm ashamed to include myself) wrote about *The A Team*. One boy I believe chose *Knightrider*. I was a relatively late convert, having only started watching *The A Team* quite recently. Nevertheless I wasn't immune to peer pressure at the age of 10.

The A Team was a rather mindless, formulaic and highly implausible series in which the title characters, a bunch of Vietnam veterans on the run from the military police having been wrongly accused of a crime eked out a living as a trouble-shooting paramilitary unit who always helped the underdog triumph over the big baddies. Despite being wanted men they travelled around in a distinctively marked transit van with an attractive female journalist who supplied them with classified information when they needed it. It was effectively an urban western or a modern day version of Robin Hood and his outlaws with the skyscrapers of downtown LA replacing the trees of Sherwood Forest.

Almost every episode culminated in a pitched gun battle usually on a patch of wasteland behind a warehouse and featured a series of spectacular and totally unnecessary explosions. Top notch entertainment for the average 10 year old. However the producers were naturally keen not to have a negative effect on young children. So despite the extreme violence no-one ever seemed to get killed. A shed would be blown to smithereens, yet its occupants (under constant machine gun fire as well) would manage to stagger out unhurt except for a few minor scratches. We looked forward to Friday evenings with dizzy anticipation of the team's latest adventure.

In hindsight the show was probably meant to be tongue-in-cheek, but the irony was lost on our 10-year old minds.

Like many other small screen action thrillers of the 1970s and '80s *The A Team* has succumbed to a 21st century cinematic makeover. In the updated version Vietnam has been changed to Iraq and all the cast have been replaced by contemporary actors with Liam Neeson taking on the role of team captain, the cigar-chomping silver-haired fox John Hannibal "I love it when a plan comes together" Smith as played previously by the late George "I was in *Breakfast at Tiffany's* with Audrey Hepburn you know" Peppard. Come to think of it I'm surprised that the *Six Million Dollar Man*,

Wonderwoman, *The Fall Guy*, *Knightrider* or *The Professionals* haven't been remade for the big screen, despite endless daytime repeats on ITV37½ + 1 keeping hungover students and welfare scroungers entertained.

Another picture in this essay book was of an old man sitting on a chair outside what appeared to a hardware shop, on the window of which was engraved the name A. Litvak. The name sounded Russian to me so I came up with a story of a refugee from the war.

In the playground at lunchtime running games were played where two teams would run back and forth towards a wall and try to catch members of the other team. I generally didn't participate, preferring to indulge in role-playing adventure games with my own separate clique. However once we got to grammar school these games suddenly stopped. Lunchtime now consisted of milling around the yard or staying rooted in one spot talking with your mates – or if you were prone to the weed – having a smoke round the back of the temporary classrooms.

As well as meaning back to school after a seemingly endless two month summer holiday autumn marked the chestnut season.

Gangs of schoolboys would descend on the local park to plunder the chestnut harvest. At the risk of sounding like a Seamus Heaney poem there was a certain delight in finding these small hard shiny brown spheres freshly fallen on the ground inside their split spiky green casing. The best of the crop were then taken home to have a hole bored though them and a shoelace inserted through the hole and ready for battle in that age-old schoolboy game which involved flicking your chestnut (or "chessie" as it was known as in the local schoolboy dialect) at another in an attempt to crack it.

There were various myths as to how you could make your chessies harder. Apparently putting them in the freezer or the hotpress or (bizarrely) soaking them overnight in vinegar would do the trick. I once mischievously told one gullible individual that soaking a chestnut in urine overnight was the best way of fortifying it for competition. To give my story an air of credibility I invented some bollocks about the chemicals reacting with the chestnut's outer casing to force its molecules to pack more tightly together. He fell for it hook, line and sinker. The story goes that he pissed into a plastic cup and put the chestnut into it, then left it overnight. On the floor of his bedroom in the corner of all places. He apparently got up in the middle of the night (ironically to go the toilet) and accidentally knocked the cup over spilling its contents on the carpet. His mother noticed the smell the next morning and accused him of having wet the bed. His room must have smelt like a dark alleyway in the town centre on a Saturday night. Somehow word of this incident got out and spread like wildfire and this unfortunate individual was mercilessly slagged off by his classmates for weeks afterwards. I don't know what happened to the chestnut though.

Much later on I explained to him that I'd been taking the piss. Pun very much intended. But if I was reading this joke out as part of a live stage show I can just imagine the prolonged deathly silence and the swooshing of tumbleweeds punctuated by the distant clanging of a funeral bell which would inevitably follow.

Autumn was soon followed by winter. If there was snow and ice on the ground Mr Skeffington the headmaster wouldn't allow us to go out into the yard to play as normal at lunchtime. Instead we were forced to sit quietly at our desks and wait for class to resume. Naturally we resented being cruelly denied the pleasure of indulging in snowball fights, making snowmen or sliding down icy slopes using those large thick plastic fertilizer bags as makeshift sledges.

"I bet when oul' Skeffers was young he used to like playing in the snow. He just hates to see us enjoying ourselves" came the anguished cries of resentment from naive young minds. Yes, I'm sure old Skeffers was partial to the odd snowball fight during the carefree days of his youth, but in those days you didn't have the litigation culture. In the modern age if a child slips and ends up with a slight bruise on his knee his parents go straight to a solicitor and attempt to sue the school for negligence to the tune of a few dozen grand. In Skeffer's day if you came home to your parents on crutches, balancing on your one remaining leg with shrapnel wounds and blood dripping from every part of your body after a particularly adventurous escapade in the school playground you'd get a clip round the ear from your mother for ruining your good clothes and sent to bed early without dinner.

It was on one of these snowy days (or it may have been raining) when we were stuck inside during the lunch break and one of the masters was patrolling the classrooms to make sure no misbehaviour was occurring. At the exact moment he entered the classroom I was committing the serious criminal offence of being out of my seat. As it happened I'd got up to put the crisp packet I'd just finished into the bin. But I still got a slap with a bamboo cane for this "misdemeanour", even though I protested my innocence, citing the perfectly good reason for being out of my seat. Although it was hardly on the scale of the Birmingham Six or the Guildford Four or the incarceration of Nelson Mandela or Aung San Suu Kyi, I saw this as a gross miscarriage of justice.

Among the extra-curricular activities were the regular internal gaelic football tournaments which would usually feature six teams selected at random from two different year groups. The school didn't have its own pitch so we used the playing fields of the local secondary schools which were a good 15 minutes walk away. This to our great delight ate up a large chunk of the school day. We used to pass a builders yard secured with wrought iron gates where a dog used to stand guard and bark noisily at anyone who walked past. When passing we used to kick the gates or bang them with our kit bags so the dog got even more wound up and started to bark all the more vigorously - much to our great delight.

We played in old manky jerseys that didn't get washed after the games and probably hadn't been washed for years and were usually caked in mud and sweat to the extent that they were almost rigid. Someone was assigned to carry the bag of jerseys, but didn't always do so with due care and attention.

I remember one occasion when the bag containing the jerseys wasn't properly sealed and a couple of them fell out just as we were on the bridge across one of the town's main thoroughfares. I

30

could see two jerseys floating down the Strule. No doubt they eventually ended up in the Atlantic, possibly in the stomach of a whale or maybe washed up on some West African beach.

The playing fields were across the road from a mill which made animal feed and is now long gone. The smell was quite distinctive and not altogether pleasant.

The pitch seemed to be either rock hard or like a marsh. There was no happy medium. There always seemed to be a crater-shaped brown patch of bare soil at each goalmouth which was permanently indented with countless stud marks. After heavy rainfall the crater became a large puddle so when we talked about "dirty players" it effectively had a double meaning.

I must have played in about six tournaments at primary school between the ages of 8 and 11, but was only on the winning team once. Each league had a theme on which the team names were based. I had originally been a full back and had made a defensive error in one particular match which led to the opposition scoring a goal. The team manager Mr Skeffington made me goalkeeper as a sort of punishment for this. Almost as soon as I'd taken up my new position I managed to block a potential goal and it then emerged that I wasn't such a bad keeper. From this point on I was always selected to play in goals, which frustrated me as it meant I could never score.

I remember playing in torrential rain once. Matches were usually called off in such conditions, but this game was already well under way by the time the rain started coming down in sheets. Skeffers decided to adopt the classic Magnus Magnusson "I've started so I'll finish" approach as seen on the high-brow TV quiz *Mastermind*.

"Don't be afraid to dive in the muck!" he shouted to me from the sideline. By this stage the goalmouth resembled a small lake. We won this match, thus sealing our place in the final.

In this particular tournament held during the autumn of 1984 (or possibly'83 – I'm not sure) the teams were named after cars. The final, by contrast was played on a gloriously sunny October afternoon when the Corollas (us) took on the Sunbeams for the ultimate prize. The game was tight and I remember conceding a virtually unstoppable goal when a cannonball shot glanced off my hand and across the imaginary line into the imaginary net between the real posts. But to quote classic footballer speak (aka bollocks) at the end of the day it was a game of two halves and we scored more than them. So our Japanese precision engineering and high tec efficiency won the day for us. We lifted our captain Shane Rogan (more on him later) up into the air as he held the trophy aloft glinting in the autumn sunlight.

In my very first tournament I played in at the age of eight, the teams had been named after TV and comic book super heroes. So there were the Hulks, the Batmen, the Supermen, the Fall Guys and my team the Spidermen. This league was won by the Condormen who were named after the hero of a long-forgotten film of the day starring Michael Crawford, an actor more famous for his portrayal of a man with apparent learning difficulties who bore the hallmarks of an autism sufferer (although this was never officially confirmed) in the popular 1970s sitcom *Some Mothers Do 'Ave 'Em.* We would often pretend to be super heroes in the school playground as well as on the football field. Duffle coats with only the top peg buttoned and with your arms outside the sleeves would make excellent Superman cloaks. Woolly hats pulled down over your eyes would make you like Spiderman – or more realistically a junior member of one of the local alphabet soup of terrorist organisations. While we're on the subject, it's always baffled me as to why Spiderman could do the things a spider could do – ie spin webs and dangle from threads, but despite his name, Batman couldn't even fly let alone harness the powers of echo-location.

The last football competition during our final year at the primary school featured teams alliteratively named after North American cities and large cats – so we had the Toronto Tigers, Chicago Cheetahs, LA Lions and my team the Baltimore Bobcats – although a bobcat is a type of lynx and therefore not officially a "big cat" . Naming the teams after small cats would have been interesting though. We could have had the San Francisco Servals,

Omaha Ocelots, Calgary Caracals and the Montréal Margays. The standard this time was lower than usual as only the boys who weren't good enough to play for the school team participated.

The Bobcats had quite a good team and were one of the favourites to win the league. Sure enough we reached the semi-final fairly easily and could have won it, but for a goalkeeping error. The ball was rolling slowly towards me and posed no threat. There were no opposing players anywhere the goalmouth, so all I needed to do was either pick it up and whack it down the field with the greatest force I could muster or pass it to one of my defenders. But rather than doing the sensible thing and pick it up, take a few steps forward and drop kick it down the field, I decided to take a run at it and kick it along the ground when it was rolling. Somehow I missed it and the ball rolled past me into the net – or more precisely over the goal-line as there was no actual net. We lost the match by a single goal. Whether we would have got to the final and won it had it not been for this monumental cock-up of mine I'll never know.

I feared retribution from my team mates, but thankfully it never materialised. Mr Holmes our team manager was wise to this and mentioned it during line-up that lunchtime – "Someone on my team did make a mistake. But I don't want anyone blaming anyone else for what happened. Anyone can make a mistake" he pronounced firmly. It seemed to work.

*   *   *

1984, as well as being the year of Orwell's "Big Brother" and the LA Olympics was the year I sat the 11 plus exam. It was a mixture of verbal reasoning and mathematical problems. And there were considerable pre-exam nerves among many of us.

"Sir, is it true that this is going to be the hardest 11 plus ever?" one boy asked Mr Arthurs.

"They say that every year" he replied dismissively.

This reassured me, as I was getting quite nervous about sitting the exam, but I found it difficult nonetheless.

A week or so later the headline on the front page of *Belfast Telegraph* screamed "MISTAKE IN 11 PLUS SAY TEACHERS!" – or words to that effect. This particular question which was multiple choice had come near the end of the paper. By this stage I was running out of time, so rather than use up valuable time trying to work out the answers I simply guessed them and randomly wrote down c, a, d and b for each one – or a sequence to that effect. The story went round that as there hadn't been enough information provided to work out the answers you would be marked correctly for any answers you gave. Not sure if this was true, but it gave me a great deal of satisfaction.

Mr Arthurs had a morality speech about the futility of cheating in exams which he uttered on numerous occasions when he'd really go off on one...

"You're not cheating me, you're not cheating Mr Skeffington, you're not cheating the cat, you're not cheating the dog, you're not cheating your granny, you're not cheating Rudolph Hess...at the end of the day you're only cheating yourself..."

One boy came into class one morning and made the announcement:

"My mum says if I pass the 11 plus she'll get me a new bike".

Such was the overhyped prestige associated with this accursèd exam coupled with the pressure to get one's children to pass it.

On arriving home I duly asked my mum what I would be getting if I passed,

I received the sensible answer "nothing" qualified with the caveat "isn't passing it in itself enough of a reward?"

There were two papers, the first of which we sat on the morning of Friday 12th October 1984, the day the IRA attempted to assassinate Margaret Thatcher and her cabinet by bombing the Brighton hotel in which the Conservative party conference was taking place. It was also just a few weeks before the assassination of Indian prime minister Indira Gandhi by her own bodyguards on Hallowe'en day. The morbid assassination theme continues with the second and final 11 plus paper which my classmates and I completed on 23 November, the day after the 21st anniversary of the fatal shooting of President Kennedy. The distinctive thing I remember about this exam is that it was printed on pink paper rather than the usual plain white. Maybe the printer was a *Financial Times* reader.

We had fifty minutes to complete the exam. It was a nerve-wracking experience, not helped by the long three-month wait between the ordeal itself and the arrival of the results, but for me it all came good in the end.

By late February 1985 the results had come out and we now knew where we were going in September. Those of us fortunate to have passed would be going to the local Christian Brothers grammar school. Our knowledge of the "big school" came mostly from the older siblings, cousins or mysterious "friends of friends of friend, friends of friends", etc of classmates. I was certainly in a position to gain some inside information having a father who taught at the school, but I was never going to get the real lowdown that came from big brothers who were at the school. Though having said that older siblings and cousins, etc tended to exaggerate.

"There's this master in the grammar school called Loopy Lenny and he's a real psycho!"

There was indeed a teacher called Lenny, or more accurately, Raymond Leonard. There was also a different teacher who had the unflattering nickname Loopy. No-one was quite sure what his real name was. One was quite beefy while the other was virtually anorexic, and they taught different subjects. Neither of them was particularly psychotic. The mysterious Loopy Lenny was no doubt the product of a fevered imagination, an exaggerated composite of two very different individuals.

"They have initiation ceremonies for the first years. The second years hold you upside down and stick your head down the toilet then flush it. And the teachers just stand there watching and they don't do nothing about it. They just laugh"

"Aye right! I'm sure they do!" we sarcastically dismissed this story – but secretly felt a little scared that there might just be some truth in it.

This story of course turned out to be a complete fabrication. Not that any of us had really believed in it in the first place – or if we did we would never have admitted to it.

During the last days of primary school things got more laid-back now that there was less pressure on teacher and pupils alike. We had a female student teacher in for a few weeks. She must have found us hard work.

If I remember correctly during the last few weeks Mr Arthurs, now free from the burden of coaching his young charges for the most important event of their primary school career got into the habit of taking us to mass almost every day. This was good for us, but not for religious reasons or anything to do with spiritual well-being. Although the Sacred Heart church was but a two minute walk from the school, the mass nevertheless ate up a reasonable chunk of the school day. Sitting (or kneeling) in a church and daydreaming, vegetating, poking each other with pencils, discreetly whispering jokes, half listening to the dull well rehearsed dronings of a pious old man or surreptitiously reading comics was preferable to sitting in the classroom - where we'd usually be... daydreaming, vegetating, poking each other with pencils...and oh well never mind. The presence of the whole class in the church during a week day morning mass effectively quadrupled the congregation, the rest of it being composed mostly of elderly women with shopping carts on wheels.

The church's distinctive twin steeples dominate the town's skyline and are a popular postcard image of the town – yes, you can buy postcards of Omagh!

Winston Churchill once famously referred to the "dreary steeples of Fermanagh and Tyrone". But the Gothic architecture of the church's steeples is far from dreary. Although I'm not terribly religious these days I can still admire the exquisite architectural design of great churches, mosques, synagogues and temples as well as faith-inspired artwork

The Sacred Heart church is located close to the town centre in the appropriately named Church Street, as are the Church of Ireland, Presbyterian and Methodist churches all within a stone's throw of each other. My younger ecumenically minded self used to wonder why there were so many places of worship all beside each other when it would be much more cost-effective to build one big church. Little did I know...

Just off this thoroughfare are Mosque Street and Synagogue Street where the town's Sunni, Shia and Hasidic Jewish communities worship. This part of the town...

You had to pause to think that through didn't you? Had you going there for a second or two! OK, probably not. I seem to be getting predictable now.

As you may have guessed Omagh in the 1980s wasn't exactly a cosmopolitan multi-cultural melting pot. Although we had a few boys at the school of Asian origin, the only ethnic minorities you generally saw around the town were doctors at the hospital from South Asia or the Middle East, Indian traders who sold clothes or electrical goods at the weekly market, the staff at the Chinese takeaway or the occasional black soldier from the army barracks.

I remember one incident where one of my contemporaries (I'll call him "Dick Head") was in town on one Saturday with his mates hanging around aimlessly as teenagers do. There was a black man on the other side of the street and they started shouting "Apricots and bananas, man!" at him in a comedy Caribbean accent. I wasn't there, but one of our teachers Mrs Galvin happened to be in the vicinity and gave Head a bit of a bollocking in class the following Monday. Ironically the same tossers who dished out this idiotic abuse probably had posters of black footballers and boxers on their bedroom walls.

As previously noted my fascination for the coast is probably due to the fact that I grew up inland. In the same vein my fascination for train journeys may be largely due to the fact that I grew up in an area without a railway network. Tyrone used to have a railway network, but by the time I arrived on the scene the trains were long gone from the county. The railways in Tyrone were dismantled in the 1960s, but there are still remnants of the tracks in Omagh as well as a residential street in the town called Railway View. Train journeys provide a sense of freedom that you just can't get on a bus or aeroplane. More on that later.

The town is littered with other remnants of its long dead past reflected in the names of places. Jail Square oddly enough is the former site of the town's 19th century place of incarceration. Similarly Gallows Hill is where executions once took place, Castle Street probably once had an aristocratic residence, Abbey Street was many moons ago the home of a religious order and High Street is where the local opium den used to be. But that's enough of a local history lesson as I'll give. There are others more knowledgeable than me who could give a more reliable account, so I'll leave to the experts. Yet again I digress...

The town has certainly changed over the years. It's even changed considerably since the days of my youth. You no longer hear the constant whirr of army helicopters from the town's military base overhead. The barracks has now closed down, a consequence of the improved "security" situation. The current plan is to turn the site into a multi-school educational campus. And while I'm on the subject of education...

3

Christian Brothers in Arms

The Ireland correspondent of a well-known London-based daily newspaper once wrote a short travel piece on Northern Ireland, in which he stated:

"Places to avoid include almost all of Co Tyrone, which has so many non-descript, grim one-horse towns you can hear the collective hooves clop from across the border in Donegal. I have found next to nothing to see or visit in that county."

Despite having the distinction of being to County Tyrone people what Salman Rushdie was to Islamic extremists, this journalist is clearly not alone in his views.

He will also no doubt have any interest in the fact that I grew up in the largest of the county's so-called "non-descript, grim one-horse towns".

Omagh could be described as a "passing-through town" where people simply enter and leave en route to the more tourist-friendly destinations of the Fermanagh lakes or the Donegal coast. The comedian Tony Hawks passed through the town during his famous hike around Ireland with a fridge, but didn't stop to take a look. Travel writer Paul Theroux stops briefly in the town in his book *The Kingdom by the Sea*, describing the place as "funereal", but this was probably on a wet Sunday afternoon.

My grammar school had a large catchment area which covered much more than Omagh's urban sprawl. The surrounding hinterland is a largely rural region covering a lot of ground – fields, mountains, lakes, valleys, boglands, woodlands, and no-man's-land.

The area from which pupils were drawn stretched over a distance of about 40 miles from Strabane in the north of the county on the Donegal border to the Clogher Valley in the south close to the border with counties Fermanagh and Monaghan – and from Aghyaran in the north-west to Ballygawley in the south-east.

The staffroom seemed to be dominated by what I'll call the "golden generation", those born in the 1940s who were roughly the same age as our parents and had been the first cohort of ordinary folk to go to university following the introduction of free third level education. Most of this clique in particular were from the local area and had been pupils at the very same school back in the day. Some of them would often reminisce on their own school days many moons ago. There were in fact three generations of teachers at the school. Some of the elder statesmen of the staffroom had taught a number of the golden generation. The golden boys in turn had taught a few of the younger teachers back in the day.

I recently had a look at my old school's website. I was relieved to find that about half a dozen teachers who were there during my time are still on the staff list – a fact that doesn't make me feel so old now.

Needless to say the school didn't have a website in my day. Younger readers will no doubt be thinking at this point – "Here he goes again" – and expecting me to launch into an embittered tirade of how difficult life was in the dark days of the 1980s compared with how easy things are for the youth of today. In fact things weren't so bad really. OK, even though we had to walk 20 miles to school every day in our bare feet through fields which the evil absentee landlords had scattered with shards of broken glass and all we had for lunch was a stale piece of mouldy concrete and a glass of raw sewage and got flogged within an inch of our lives for so much as breathing in class we were still deliriously happy. Tough love didn't do us any harm. It made our generation what we are today – ie a bunch of bitter, cynical and twisted, overweight middle-aged wretches struggling to pay off the mortgage, the loan on the kitchen extension, the bill for the house insurance, car insurance, the insurance on the insurance policy itself and moaning about how much better things were for our parents' generation.

Around two thirds of the pupil intake came from outside the town. The majority were from just over a score of villages situated roughly within a 15 mile radius of the town – Beragh, Fintona, Drumquin, Dregish, Castlederg (which was apparently just outside Aghyaran), Loughmacrory, Dromore, Trillick, Ouagadougou, Sixmilecross, Augher, Clogher, Carrickmore, Gortin, Mountfield, Newtownstewart, Clady, Greencastle, Plumbridge, Sion, as well as the town of Strabane plus a few other places, or the various townlands in between these villages. There was a bit of a tribal divide between the town boys and the country boys – or the townies and the culchies as they were called in the local parlance. Ironically when us town boys went to university in the big city, we were now the culchies as far as the streetwise Belfast and Dublin students were concerned.

My form teacher in first year, Mr Donal Hennessy, one of the more popular members of the teaching staff was known to his pupils simply as "Donal" – although not directly to his face. He was one of a handful of teachers who didn't have a nickname as such, but were referred to by their first name or variations thereof. He taught us both Irish and history and was particularly passionate about saving the local townlands.

"Don't let the townlands die" he urged the rural pupils as he encouraged them use the local name in their address rather than the "artificial" name of some road which bore no relation to the local character of the area. At the time new suburban housing developments were springing up on the edge of town with meaningless estate agent-friendly names like Ashvale Rise, Ferndale Court, Summerfield Drive and Berkeley Close. They were names more suited to a sleepy commuter village in the Kent or Surrey stockbroker belt (the kind of places where you could pin a blue rosette on a donkey and put it up for election as the Conservative candidate and it would still get elected as the local MP) than in semi-rural West Tyrone.

Being a town boy who lived within twenty minutes walk of the school, I felt I was missing out on the mischief and tomfoolery that occurred on the school buses going to and from the satellite villages of Omagh's rural surroundings every morning and evening. These shenanigans ranged from throwing missiles around the bus, or out the windows, flashing bare bums out the windows, dangling legs out the windows, setting up betting syndicates concerning who was about to be thrown off the bus, conducting dangerous chemical experiments at the back and all manner of other things.

In the aftermath of one such incident, the exact details of which escape me, Donal gave the class a stern talking to.

"I don't care if it's the Strabane bus or the Fintona bus...or the Timbuktu bus, I'm not going to tolerate this kind of behaviour!"

At this moment I contemplated coming out with a smart remark to the effect of:

"But sir, Ulsterbus doesn't run a service to anywhere in North Africa. Their cross-border service is patchy enough, but anywhere south of the Sahara would be technically outside their jurisdiction. And anyway their tyres aren't designed for crossing desert terrain."

But sensibly I chose to keep my mouth shut on this occasion. Donal, although he had a good sense of humour at the best of times was in no mood for joking at this time. But I did then envisage an imaginary conversation following an incident of horseplay on the fabled Timbuktu bus.

"There was a wil' bit o' hooley on the Timbuktu bus yesterday! Duffer brought a camel on to the bus and it went berserk! It crapped everywhere and ate Paul Mulroy's homework – or at least that's his excuse!"

"Who's Duffer?"

"You know Duffer – the big tall fourth year with the frizzy hair, sometimes wears a towel round his head. What's this his name is – aye - Djibril Mohamed Sissoko Touré McElduff – you know who I mean?"

"Oh aye, him."

"And then the camel bit Cathy Gallagher on the arm and she screamed the place down. The driver stopped the bus at the Ballygawley roundabout and made the camel get off."

"The driver must have had the hump, then."

Cue eerie silence followed by howls of highly sarcastic laughter.

"So Duffer got off as well. Had to walk all the way home."

"Did he get back alright?"

"Well the last thing I heard was he got a lift off a lorry driver who was going as far as Dungannon. He probably got the bus to Taoudenni from there and then probably hitched a lift off a bedouin trader who would have got him as far as Araouane, which is still a good couple of hundred miles from Timbuktu, but if he legged it – and the Duffer's a handy runner – he could have got home by about midnight allowing for a stop at the oasis. Come to think of it, I didn't see him in class this morning, so he might not have made it back yet."

"And what happened the camel?"

"The driver wouldn't let him take it into the lorry. He had to leave it in a field. The local farmer must have been confused when he found that one of his cows had a long neck and a hump."

This was even less funny than the previous joke – or more precisely - would have been less funny had this conversation actually taken place.

Then I woke up. Donal had finished his rant and was now talking about the Battle of the Little Bighorn. A quarter of a century later I would meet someone with a family connection to Timbuktu, but more on that later. Or if you can't wait till then you can go straight to the chapter on Morocco.

43

Another time during a history class when the industrial revolution was being discussed, the role of the city of Liverpool as a major port and manufacturing centre got a mention. On hearing the word "Liverpool" a boy from Greencastle let out a cheer in reference to the city's eponymously named football team who were doing quite well in those days. How times have changed.

Donal came back with the classic response:

"Do you think people over in Liverpool cheer when they hear Greencastle being mentioned?"

As form teacher he would regularly give the class philosophical pep talks in the mould of a general preparing an army for battle or a football manager addressing his team before the big game.

"You go through this school in a flash" he would say.

"You're only wee fish in a big pond now, but before you know it you'll have a mortgage and a family..." or words to that effect.

"I see wedding pictures in the paper. There's wee Sean Farragher who got married – and I remember when he was just sitting down in first year – seems like yesterday".

A well-worn cliché, but one that reminds us of our own mortality and the passage of time. It was almost like a version of Robin Williams' inspirational "carpe diem" speech in the film *Dead Poets' Society*. As the film didn't come out till three or four years later you couldn't have accused Donal of plagiarism though.

For me the seven years of my second level education seemed to go quite slowly. However, looking back and considering that triple that amount of time has passed one does indeed wonder where the time has gone. To an 11 year old half an hour seems like ages. To an adult twenty years can be a mere drop in the ocean. Time is like alcoholic who went down to the pub for a pint and never came back. During my final year at school for me it couldn't end soon enough. Not that I didn't enjoy it – for the most part I did, but I felt stifled amid the parochialism and monotony of small town life and yearned for the bright lights of the big city. Ironically I now find myself living in one of the world's major metropolises, but sometimes wish I was back in Omagh...

But just sometimes, mind.

Although my secondary education during the mid-1980s to the early 1990s from the age of 11 to 18 was formed at a Christian Brothers school, even during my time there weren't many of these brothers left on the teaching staff. The order has come in for much criticism of late in the wake of the major abuse scandals which rocked Irish society. But like any other sub-group in any society it was swings and roundabouts. There were good brothers and bad brothers. And mad brothers. By the time I had left the school there were only two or three of them remaining on a teaching staff of almost 50. For the last 20 years the headmaster has been a layman, but during my time it was one of the last "CBs" in charge, Brother Daniel O'Loscan. He was known to the pupils as "Corky". This may have been due to the mistaken belief that he came from Cork. He actually came from one of its neighbouring counties in the deep south – Tipperary or Limerick most probably. But as far as many of us northerners were concerned, if you drew a line across Ireland from Galway in the west to Dublin in the east, anywhere below that line was so far south that it might as well have been Antarctica. An alternative explanation for the "Corky" moniker may have been the equally erroneous belief that he was fond of his wine. He probably enjoyed the odd sip of transubstantiated communion wine, but he generally wasn't a drinking man. Or more simply the most likely explanation was that someone back in the swirling mists of time had thought that he bore a resemblance to the cartoon cat of the same name.

A Google search took me to a discussion forum in which a couple of past pupils took part jogged my memory of the PLO – the short-lived Pupils' Liberation Organisation. The PLO was a group of fifth formers who had decided to rebel against what they saw as an oppressive administrative regime within the school. As a protest statement they attached a poster to the school noticeboard. It was a photocopied A4 page which bore the legend "OFFICIAL PLO BULLETIN" below which was a picture of a man in a guerilla-style military uniform holding a machine gun with Corky's head disproportionately superimposed on to the body. The large head and small body made him look like a cartoon character - much to the amusement of the pupils (and no doubt to the private amusement of the odd teacher).

The guilty parties were summoned to his office. I'm not sure what exactly their punishment was, but all returned to the school.

The Christian Brother is a curious beast. He dresses in similar attire to a priest, but lacks the same rights and privileges. If he was an animal he'd be on the critically endangered list. Maybe he'd be a wolverine – a creature with a fearsome reputation which is exaggerated and largely undeserved. In fact some of the lay teachers were just as violent as their brotherly colleagues if not more so.

Following the retirement of the previous principal Brother Sinarms, it was announced towards the end of my first year at the school that the notorious Brother "Corky" O'Loscan would be taking over from the beginning of the new academic year in September. He already had a bit of a reputation before coming to power. There were rumours circulating that he was going to impose a totalitarian regime and would commit the ultimate act of tyranny against 1980s schoolboy fashion by banning white socks and trainers, or that anyone with hair resting more than half an inch past the collar would have it publicly cut off during school assembly.

The rumours became more wildly exaggerated as time went on.

"He's going to make us wear top hats with gowns and monocles."

"He's not going to allow red hair. Any boy who comes into the school with red hair he's going to make them dye it grey".

"He'll make us get tattooed with a serial number so he'll be able to tell us all apart."

This idle gossip not surprisingly proved to be untrue – apart from the story about the tattoos. Getting mine done was quite painful as I recall, but now as look in the mirror and see 98765433W on my forehead in black ink I remember my schooldays with fondness.

But there were also rumours that he had a giant hamster wheel behind a secret wall in a hidden compartment in his lair office which he would get the vice principal to spin around while he revolved inside it as a way of venting his frustrations on the world. This in all likelihood was probably true as well.

There was however a new rule introduced that dark footwear had to be worn. This rule was ambiguous as it didn't explicitly state whether dark brown or navy blue shoes counted as "dark" or whether black trainers with white stripes or swooshes on them were acceptable. One teacher was particularly anal about this rule to the extent that he would make any boys wearing such foot attire cover the white parts up with black tape. Not surprisingly he was ridiculed for it – by teachers and pupils alike.

Also the much-maligned blazer, the perennially unfashionable item of school attire now had to be worn at all times. In previous years the blazer had played second fiddle to whatever the latest fashions in leather, denim or sportswear were. It was something you wore on the first day of term in September, hung it up inside your locker, then retrieved it the following June. Bizarrely the school uniform rules specified "charcoal grey" trousers, but almost everyone wore black trousers. Despite the drabness of the black trousers and blazer we had the most colourful tie of any school in the town. It was an electric kingfisher blue with shiny narrow red, green and gold stripes running diagonally across it.

In our first year at the school we had of course yet to go through puberty. We still had high-pitched voices and smooth faces which had yet to experience the cut of a razor. Some of the deep-voiced senior pupils by contrast had the beginnings of moustaches, which would usually disappear after a few days. The gap between an 11 year old and an 18 year old male (both physical and psychological) was huge. This gap was glaringly obvious to us naïve young freshers back in '85. The odd senior boy sometimes even sported a

47

full moustache. They were popular among young men back in the mid-1980s for some reason. This much maligned article of facial hair typically sported by tyrannical dictators such as Hitler, Stalin, Saddam Hussein, Des Lynam and Tom Selleck has since largely gone out of fashion. There were allegedly even boys who drove their own cars to school.

Some of the older boys also had what was known as "designer stubble" a look perfected by Don Johnson of the then highly popular US cop show *Miami Vice* which was basically two or three days growth of beard that was for some reason considered cool. The shiny silvery suits with the sleeves rolled up and worn over white t-shirts had to wait till after school though.

At the risk of sounding like one of those essays on "My first day at the big school" that English teachers tend to give their new intake of young charges and some of which inevitably end up in the school magazine - it was a whole new experience. Instead of just one teacher we now had about a dozen of them, which added a bit more variety to school life.

It was a balmy day in early September 1985. I must have been the only boy of the new intake of about 120 not wearing a jumper. I was an early trendsetter by choosing to go jumperless and wore my blazer directly over my shirt. After all it was quite warm.

As I came from one of the larger primary schools in the area there were naturally many familiar faces at the new school. There were also a few other familiar faces which I hadn't seen for some years. I'd spent the first year of primary education at a school in Strabane just before the family moved to Omagh. Moving to a new school, a new town and a new neighbourhood, losing all my friends, bearing the stigma of being the "new boy" and having to make new friends was from what I recall a highly traumatic experience for my six year old self. Alright, put the violins away, this isn't a misery memoir.

I was now suddenly reunited with four of my old classmates from

Strabane six years since I'd last seen them. Although I hadn't seen them since we were five year olds I was still able to recognise them. At least one of them also recognised me and was able to recall the time I won an "Action Man"™ doll in a class raffle.

The four form teachers of the new classes 1A to 1D - one of whom was my dad - assembled us in the yard and called out the list of who was to be in their class. I breathed a sigh of relief when I found out that my dad wouldn't be teaching me. No disrespect to the old fellow - I'm sure he was a great teacher, but the discomfort and awkwardness would not have been pleasant for me.

Being a teacher's son I ran the risk of some flack. But by a bizarre coincidence (or maybe by design?) there were two other teacher's sons in my class.

Most of the school yard was taken up by the gravel "all-weather" football pitch. On wet days the rainwater would react with the gravel to form shallow milky puddles. These were the days before the long overdue school extension. The first year classrooms back in the day were temporary mobile huts adjacent to the pitch. These huts had fragile interior walls. Any kind of horseplay which involved contact with the walls or even closing the door with any degree of force would result in holes in the walls. One small hole was created by the door being slammed into the wall. Inevitably it got enlarged over time and more hols followed.

"This class is beginning to look like a sieve!" Donal remarked.

The majority of pupils ate hot (or invariably lukewarm) school dinners in the canteen, but a minority of us brought in our own sandwiches which we would eat in the classroom. Then we'd go out into the yard. At lunchtime a group of senior boys from the sixth form headed by a lad called Rankin, but universally known by the unfortunate nickname Ranker, (a natural derivation of his surname – and very convenient for rhyming with, as illustrated below) would congregate on a corner of the pitch to have a smoke. As Ranker and his two mates Ollie and Foley huddled together to light up against the chill wind a group of us would run towards them and ping fistfuls of gravel at them, then run away, shouting "Ranker's a wanker!" or "Ollie's a wally!" or "Foley's a [insert whatever term of abuse sprang to mind on this particular day – usually depending on what new words we'd learnt from the fat paperback thrillers in the school library or whatever American gangster film we'd seen lately]!". Puerile, childish behaviour of course, but we thought it was funny at the time. To their credit Ranker and co rarely rose to the bait. Had they pursued us however and given us a good kicking, it would have been thoroughly deserved.

During the 11 o'clock break a group of sixth and seventh formers used to assemble under a tree just outside our classroom for a smoke. Fortuitously for us this spot was just below the classroom window and within easy missile range. There was a metal grille attached to the outside of the window to prevent it from being smashed. This was obviously a limiting factor to what we could throw. We usually just projected screwed up pieces of paper at them for no other reason than as we would say in the local dialect "pure badness". One boy poured half a bottle of coke out the window which not only wet the senior smoker's hair and made it sticky, but also extinguished his cigarette. He was none too pleased and promptly raced around the corner, burst into the classroom, still dripping with the fizzy brown liquid, the wet Benson (or maybe it was a Hedge – I never could tell the difference) still between his fingers and yelled:

"Right, which one of you assholes chucked that out the window?"

There were about 15 of us in the room and unsurprisingly no-one admitted to it. Not even the boy holding the half empty bottle. We just looked at him blankly and shrugged our shoulders innocently.

The extension to the school was still a few years away, but my year group never got to see it. As science teacher Jim Thompson who bore a passing resemblance to Sean Connery said "You won't get to see it unless you come back here to teach". Although a few of our year group did become teachers none of them returned to the school to teach.

50

-4-
It wasn't just Zammo

It was the early autumn of 1986. I was starting my second year of secondary education. For the first time in their history Tyrone were in the All Ireland senior football final against the mighty Kerry. There was much excitement, and the school could claim a few past pupils among the Tyrone players. On this occasion it was not to be, but we were still given the afternoon off on the Monday after the final. Seventeen years later the long watched day finally came - eleven years after I'd left the school. And yet again the (this time victorious) team could boast some former pupils among its players and backroom staff.

In the summer of '86 I'd spent three weeks in Donegal at an Irish language college, supposedly learning the niceties of the lingo, a rite of passage for many Irish schoolchildren. We'd be encouraged by Donal, himself a veteran of the summer *Gaelscoieanna* to apply. Local people earned a bit of extra income by putting up the students in their houses. I shared a room with three characters from Greencastle and Carrickmore called Bradley, Teague and Hughes. The place was called Magheroarty and was situated in the rugged remote north-west corner of the county. You could see Tory Island in the distance - the island whose name bizarrely became the alternative moniker for the Conservative party. How ironic that the political party of the British establishment, a club of Old Etonians and aristocrats should be named after a windswept treeless island off Ireland's rugged Atlantic north coast. But stranger things have happened apparently.

The *fear a ti* (man of the house) was a fisherman who would go out each day and come back that evening with a bucket of crabs the size of dinner plates. I'd never seen crabs that big before.

Each house had a young supervisor or *cinneara* who was in charge of its inmates. Our *cinneara* was a Belfast lad called Dermott in his late teens or early twenties, probably a veteran of five or six summers at the place. I took a liking to him at first as he seemed quite easygoing and a good laugh. But by the end of the three weeks I hated him.

His catch phrase was *"Na bí ag caint* fucking *Bearla!"* (Don't speak fucking English!), which he would scream in frustration whenever he caught us conversing amongst ourselves in the dreaded Saxon tongue. It was therefore highly ironic that he used a classic Anglo-Saxon swear word in policing our use of language. In fact for some of the less academically able inmates this was probably the only Irish phrase they actually learned during their time here. On reflection, it's also likely that they also remembered the Irish word for "word", *focal*, pronounced "fuckle", the source of much classroom amusement. Some years later there was even a hit song in the Irish charts which shamelessly pounced on this rather cheap innuendo.

We were confronted with the idle threat of being sent home in disgrace on an almost daily basis for speaking the wrong language – a threat which was never enforced. Expecting 12 year olds away from home who had only been learning Irish for a year to be speaking *as gaeilige* (the little that they knew) among themselves was frankly unrealistic.

There was a lighthouse just off the coast whose powerful beam would revolve around at night so for a few seconds at regular intervals each night the bedroom we were sleeping in would be bathed in bright light. These of course were the days before GPS and sophisticated satellite tracking systems when boats relied on lighthouses to guide their passage through dark and stormy seas.

Every night there was compulsory ceili dancing at the main hall. I didn't like this as I was a crap dancer with no co-ordination on my feet - and still am now. Everyone else seemed to enjoy them though.

Singing traditional Irish songs was also a regular activity. I wasn't a great singer either and was often told by the young women supervising the singing to *"oscail do bhéal"* (open your mouth), which I didn't really want to.

There were bawdy versions of these well-known songs which had been presumably handed down by generations of amused school children summer after summer.

For example there was the lively *Oró Sé do Bheatha 'Bhaile* :

Oró Sé do Bheatha 'Bhaile (**Translation**: Oh-ro you're welcome home,)
Anois ar theacht an tsamhraidh (Now that summer's coming)

Which became:

"Oro she's the best of value
Especially on the sofa"

Similarly the poignant romantic ballad:

A stór, a stór, a ghrá (My darling, my darling, my love)
An dtiocfaidh tú nó an bhfanfaidh tú? (Will you come with me or settled be?)

became:

"I stole, I stole a bra
I stole a pair of knickers too." (No translation required).

I googled the crude versions of these songs out of curiosity and found out through online discussion boards that they had indeed been sung by subsequent generations of schoolchildren in summer colleges throughout Ireland.

The college director didn't like it. Not so much because the lewd content, but more because it was supposedly making a mockery of "our cherished native tongue".

At the time we hadn't a clue what the real lyrics meant. For all we knew we could have been singing "Stick a pink elephant up your left nostril on the second day of every third month".

Then there were Irish words which sounded rude in English such as the word for "Bank" which in the definite article is "*an bhainc*" (pronounced "wank").

Positively side-splitting.

This phenomenon is of course replicated in other languages. One of my classmates once asked Christine the French assistant what the French for seal was. The answer "Phoque" (pronounced "fock") which for obvious reasons is amusing to the average school boy. Christine also saw the funny side eventually. Years later I was to discover that the Romanian word for carp is quite amusing in English. If you can't wait to read about it you can flick straight to the chapter about Dracula's castle.

The Gaeltacht experience is also an opportunity to pair off romantically. All the good-looking girls seemed to be in the 15-18 age bracket and therefore unattainable for us 11 and 12 year olds. Or at least that was my excuse. There were however a few extra-curricular activities which I did enjoy. Sports competitions were organised. We had a five-a-side soccer tournament on the beach which my team won. And with all those miles of coastline and sandy beaches a dip in the sea was inevitable at some point. The icy waters of the North Atlantic are still bloody cold even in the height of summer, but rather invigorating.

At the big ceili on the last night, which was held at a local hotel for which a bus was laid on there were many moist eyes. I was glad to be going home though. Three weeks was after all along time to be spending away from home at that age.
I must have enjoyed it enough as I vowed to come back the following summer. But a year is a long time for a 12 year old and a hell of a lot can happen and I changed my mind and decided not to go back.

****

One of the big chart hits that year was the anti-drugs song "Just Say No" by the cast of the then popular TV series set in a London

55

secondary school *Grange Hill*.

I watched the video on Youtube recently for the first time in over 20 years and found it to be so embarrassingly cringeworthy – the hairstyles (mullets for the boys and poodle perms for the girls), clothes, the music - it was almost painful to look at. At least it was all for a good cause.

One of the show's leading characters, a likeable rogue called Zammo had become a heroin addict, as part of a storyline devised to discourage young people from going down the same route. His desperate face adorned the campaign posters warning impressionable youths of the dangers of drugs alongside the slogan "IT'S NOT JUST ZAMMO – JUST SAY NO" – or words to that effect.

I even got to meet the boy who played Zammo and his screen girlfriend Jackie when they visited the local leisure centre as part of the town's annual arts festival. I was the proud owner of another celebrity autograph to add the collection alongside that of former Dr Who actors Peter Davison and the late Jon Pertwee (who I'd written to via their agents – so whether their signatures were genuine or not I have no idea) as well as that of international soccer goalkeeper Pat Jennings. Jennings made an appearance at a paint shop in the town as part of a commercial publicity stunt shortly after the 1982 World Cup in which Northern Ireland had pulled off a shock victory by defeating the hosts Spain. If you bought a tin of paint you'd get a free football and if you were prepared to queue up the man himself would sign it for you. It was one of those dirt cheap light-as-a-feather balls that would burst if you so much as sneezed in its direction.

I also had the signature of Kerry gaelic football legend Jack O'Shea who visited the local GAA club – even though I have no idea of where that particular scrap of paper is now. And for the record the Pat Jennings-signed ball got accidentally kicked into a clump of bushes and was never found, despite a thorough and painful search through the foliage which incurred several cuts and bruises and a few peck marks after a confrontation with an angry robin.

There was even a boy at school nicknamed Zammo in honour of the character. I don't know what became of him, but I'm sure he didn't follow in the footsteps of his TV namesake.
Grange Hill was in fact one of the most popular TV programmes among schoolchildren at the time. An entertaining mix of drama and comedy which often dealt with controversial social issues such as racism, bullying, teenage pregnancy, abuse and inappropriate pupil-teacher relationships it was compulsive viewing for pupils of my generation – and even the odd teacher.

In a third year geography class our then form teacher Mr Martin Walsh had asked Zammo, whose real name was Jason McEldreen a question relating to the lesson. But he seemed to have dozed off into a world of his own.

"How does the organic layer of a soil profile get formed? Jason?"

"Don't know, sir."

Marty tried to prompt him.

"Ok, then what happens to you when you die?"

"Don't know, I haven't died yet".

Walshie was losing his patience.

"OK, what will happen to you when you die?" he asked exasperated.

"I'll go to Heaven". Zammo just didn't care any more.

"What's up? Were you up late last night watching Clint Eastwood?" asked Marty.

A similar line had featured in a teacher-pupil confrontation during a recent episode of the TV school drama. This caused the entire class (except for myself who had missed that particular instalment) to suddenly erupt into a chorus of "Ha sir, you were watching *Grange Hill!*"

Not entirely surprising as he had children of school age who in all likelihood watched the show which was broadcast at around 5 pm just when teachers usually arrived home after a hard day's graft and put their feet up with a cup of tea. And before anyone writes in – no I don't mean they literally used the cup of tea as a foot prop – you know damn well what I mean.

Martin Walsh used to brush his hair forward in at the sides the Napoleonic style and wore ties with prodigiously large knots in them. One day for a laugh the whole class brushed their hair forward and tied huge knots in their ties.

"Isn't it great to be jealous?" came the response.

If one is to take the expression "imitation is the sincerest form of flattery" at face value he did have a point.

Out of school fashions for formal occasions such as family weddings or christenings included shiny flecked suits and wafer thin leather ties with the obligatory footwear of black slip-on shoes and white socks, the sort of dress which would nowadays make anyone with any sense of taste cringe.

Argentina were the newly crowned world soccer champions in Mexico, having beaten the Germans in the final, following Maradona's infamous "hand of God" goal against England in the quarter finals.

Breakdancing was all the rage. The hip-hops sounds of the African-American ghettoes of New York and LA had reached the wilds of West Tyrone. Shiny tracksuits, baseball caps and fluorescent socks featured among the out-of-school fashions of a certain section of the younger generation down at youth clubs up and down the county.

This was the age of the CD and MTV. These shiny metallic discs which you could apparently eat your Sunday dinner off, then put it back in the machine and it would continue to play and still be intact were at the cutting edge of technology. Having said that I've never actually used a CD as a dinner plate. For a start there would be the danger of food leaking out through the hole in the middle.

Live Aid was still fresh in the memory. The big stadium rock bands like U2, Dire Straits, Queen and Simple Minds were popular with the younger boys. The yuppie culture was in vogue. *Brothers in Arms* had just come out – one of the great (albeit much derided by the cynics) rock albums of the '80s with its iconic sleeve design featuring a guitar in the sky. Mark Knopfler and his rather anonymous fellow band members have come in for a lot of criticism. There's the old joke "Dire Straits – with 'dire' being the operative word", but I've always had a soft spot for them. They were the quintessential '80s yuppie band of the genre popularly known as "coffee table rock", the preserve of the upwardly mobile young professional.

And groundbreakers in that they were one of the first bands to use computer graphics in their videos and their bestselling album *Brothers In Arms* was one of the first albums to be released on CD. In fact the very first album I bought at the age of 12 was one of their early works *Making Movies* – but on cassette tape as I (or more specifically my parents) didn't have a CD player back then. I chose this one because it was cheaper than their current offering *Brothers In Arms*. Shortly afterwards I was able to get Paul Mimnagh to do me a copied version for free (less the cost of the blank tape of course). I'm not sure if he'll thank me for reminding him that he was a Dire Straits fan in his youth though. The Straits were one of these artists of the day just like Phil Collins who were phenomenally successful, but were generally sneered at and dismissed as populist rubbish by a cross-section of pseudo-intellectual rock hacks and trendy comedians - (although to be fair Collins probably deserved most of the flak he received). For anyone who's interested there's an excellent parody of the Dire Straits hit *Money for Nothing* from the satirical comedy show *Spitting Image* on Youtube.

I didn't buy another Dire Straits album for another 25 years. It was from a charity shop in Sheffield, where I was at a conference presenting a paper on political blogging in Northern Ireland. It was a CD of their 1982 offering *Love over Gold* which was ironically cheaper than the cassette I had bought a quarter of a century earlier.

There was a time when I was branded a yuppie by classmates for wearing one of those waxed coats with the corduroy collar and chequered interior lining – a gift from Aunt Mary. I didn't quite go the whole hog and have the red braces, round-rimmed Versace specs, the breeze block-sized mobile phone or the filofax or go around sipping cappuccinos and eating ciabattas with basil and mozzarella filling for lunch – or I would have run the risk of getting beaten up – and probably justifiably so.

These were eventful times...

The Cold War was rapidly beginning to thaw as evidenced by Reagan and Gorbachev, the US and Soviet leaders having a face-to-face meeting in Reykjavik. In the quarter century since then an Icelandic volcano erupted and its banks collapsed. So at least three newsworthy events have happened in Iceland during the past 100 years.

Closer to home we had this thing called the Anglo-Irish Agreement, an accord between the British and Irish governments which some people weren't too happy about as it gave the Republic of Ireland's government a say in the affairs of the North. At the age of 12⅓ I kept a "secret" diary, inspired by Adrian Mole. My entry for 3rd March 1986 recalls the day of the general strike organised as a protest against the Agreement. I had walked to school through a deserted town centre past numerous road blocks. There were 17 out of 30 pupils in class.

Posters bearing the slogan "Ulster Says No" had been put up all over the place by those who opposed the Agreement. At least this was one thing that Ulster allegedly had in common with the kids from *Grange Hill*.

A typical entry from my 1986 diary reads as follows:

"Got up. Had breakfast. Went to school. Went swimming after school with my friends Obasanje Mkomwe from Greencastle and Mazuki Yashimoto from Fintona. We got a bollocking from Ken Blow-Torch the pool attendant [more on him later] for splashing in the deep end. We had competitions to see who could stay under water the longest.
Came home. Had potatoes with bacon and cabbage for dinner. Did homework. Watched some TV. Read a book. Had fight with brother over the meaning of the word "prat". Fed cat. Went to bed."

This pattern continued for some years. In fact if you substitute the word "school" for "work" in the above paragraph that's more or less how things are for me nowadays. I jest of course. I don't do homework and I don't have a cat anymore, nor do I see much of Obasanje or Mazuki these days.

My diary was sometimes a mix of international news events and school life. Take the following entries for 14 and 15 April 1986 for instance:

"Yet another hateful wet Monday. We got a new temporary maths teacher called Mrs N. She's covering for Brother Skaramasov who's about to retire. Sent away for an entry form for a World Cup Mexico '86 "Spot the Ball" competition.
Simone de Beauvoir, author of *The Second Sex* died today."

****

"The Americans bombed Libya today. Reagan said it was

in self defence.

I have been selected as corner back for 1C in tomorrow's first year league match against 1D. The match probably won't go ahead unless the weather improves.

Roll on summer.

Mum says the cat looks pregnant."

****

And sure enough the match was postponed due to the continued wet weather. And not long after that the cat had kittens. Sometimes life is predictable after all.

At this time one of the major scare stories was a new disease called AIDS which was apparently gripping the world by stealth. There was a major awareness campaign in the media. Public information broadcasts were being aired at the most inappropriate times.

On the local BBC station Radio Ulster over breakfast, just before I was about to head off for school I heard the announcer advising listeners to use a condom if they were having "casual sexual intercourse" with more than one partner. I didn't know what a condom was (or at least I thought I didn't), but was beginning to hear the word quite a lot at the time on the news. You could hardly blame me for being curious. So purely to satisfy my curiosity I consulted the dictionary to spare the embarrassment of asking my parents what it meant and discovered that it was a "protective rubber sheath used for contraception named after the 18th century inventor" or words to that effect. It then dawned on me that I'd known what condoms were all along but just hadn't realised it. Up to this point I'd known them in more colloquial schoolboy terms as "frenchies" or "rubber johnnies". This terminology was often a source of amusement in the classroom. There was a boy in my class called Johnny who was inevitably on the receiving end of lewd jokes if anyone wanted to borrow his eraser to correct a mistake.

"Lend me your rubber, Johnny!" would be said loudly enough for the teacher to hear.

This wasn't the only example of side-splitting hilarity involving classroom accessories. We also had plastic non-shatter rulers, which surprisingly were decorated with the legend "NON SHATTER". I have no idea why, as plastic tends not to shatter anyway and as far as I know there is no such thing as a glass ruler on the market.

One imaginative pupil Richard Kenny discovered that you could scrape off certain letters with a coin, so that the ruler now described itself as "NO   SH IT". This caused endless amusement. One of us would say to another "Look - my ruler's hard, it takes no shit!" We all split our sides laughing.

Around the same time there was a French international rugby player called Jean Condom. In his native France this was a perfectly normal name. To the French the other Condom was simply the man who invented the *preservatif* or the *capote anglaise*. However a player with a name like that wasn't going to go unnoticed within a sport dominated by English-speaking countries.

A few years later I was to unexpectedly find one of these rubber sheaths in the side pocket of my school blazer. Some joker had obviously planted it there for a cheap laugh. Or maybe he was dropping me an unsubtle hint. I never found out who the culprit was, but at least the offending item was still intact in its silver foil wrapper and thankfully unused.
Richard Kenny was less fortunate though. One day he was tucking into a packed lunch only to bite into his sandwich and find something rubbery inside. I only heard about this incident second hand, but I hope for RK's sake that the surprise sandwich filling hadn't been used for its specific purpose.

That was the Question
There was a brief flurry of excitement towards the end of my first year at the big school when two boys from the sixth form appeared

as contestants on the popular TV quiz show for schools *Blockbusters*. They didn't do terribly well, but being on TV didn't do them any harm. The coveted Blockbusters sweatshirt given to all contestants is now I'm sure a collector's item on e-Bay. I was reminded of this when the show's legendary host Bob Holness passed away during the writing of this book. A few years later I would even appear in a TV quiz show myself...

I've been on TV a few times, but only in a silent capacity– twice as a spectator at football matches, once during my university days as a spectator at a lecture by the then Northern Ireland secretary of state Sir Patrick Mayhew organised by the student politics society at Queen's.

But my first (and to date my only) "proper" TV experience happened at the age of 15 in a new BBC Northern Ireland inter-youth club quiz called *All Square* hosted by Mike Edgar who was then a fairly locally well-known fresh-faced presenter of trendy youth TV and radio shows. A quick Google search reveals that he's now Head of Programme Production at BBC Northern Ireland. Now there's a successful example of climbing up the corporate ladder if ever there was one. It was also through Google that I found out that one of my fellow contestants in a different round had been a young Stephen Nolan, now a well-known local broadcaster in the "shock jock" tradition - but thankfully our paths didn't cross.

This was the first and last series. I was already a veteran of the local youth club quiz circuit thanks to youth leader Terry Patterson who organised the club's team.
Along with team-mates Fabian McGlone and Anne Hunt I represented Omagh Youth Centre having reached the televised stages through a preliminary heat. The format was simple enough – a quickfire buzzer section with a number of "activities" rounds as the filling in the sandwich in which the junior member (ie myself – being the youngest team member I had little choice) had to complete a jigsaw by placing sticky cardboard pieces onto an allocated space on the wall. From what I remember we spent a whole day in the studio rehearsing before the actual recording that

evening. There were also a few scenes which needed to be redone.

We got through to the final, but lost to the superior knowledge and buzzer speed of a youth club from North Belfast. As runners-up we received a personal stereo (or Walkman as they were known as) and an Adidas sports bag (with this being the BBC, other global sports brands were presumably available).

Apparently this had brought me some local attention. Classmates would approach me with the line "There's a girl at the youth club who fancies you". I wasn't sure whether to take such stories at face value or with a pinch of salt. In any case they quickly fizzled out when I began to further investigate the matter. For some strange reason a second series of *All Square* was never commissioned.

Nerds of Steel
Among other extra-curricular activities was the Doctor Who fan club (or the more sophisticated sounding "appreciation society" as we preferred to call it) chiefly organised by an older boy called Mark Johnson, a martial arts enthusiast, and an amateur photographer/film-maker, who in a few years time would go on to forge a successful reputation as "DJ Marco" on the local disco and hospital radio circuit. His highly original nickname was "Doc" – presumably after the original lexicographer Dr Johnson and not because he was a Doctor Who fan. Nicknames, not surprisingly followed a general pattern. If your name was Des O'Connor you would most likely also be referred to as Doc. If your name was Brian O'Donnell you'd be called Bod. If your name was Seamus O'Connor you'd be referred to as Soc and so on. If you were called Conor O'Kane, however you could potentially be lumbered with a rather unfortunate nickname - depending on how popular or unpopular you were. There's a chance that your nickname would be Junkie, given that your name be written as "C. Okane". If your name was Murphy, you'd be known as Smurf or Spud. And for some unknown reason anyone whose name was Damien was universally referred to as simply "D". But most nicknames simply just involved adding a Y or an O to the individual's surname – so

we had the likes of Quinny and Murpho.

Nicknames could also derive from the place you came from. Some lads hailed from remote villages or townlands in rural areas which often amounted to little more than a row of houses along a road in the middle of nowhere, so they were in some cases the only native of that particular area at the school. We therefore had lads simply known as Dregish or Glebe or Galbally. I felt sorry for a fellow called Ronan Durridge though. He came from an isolated village in the Sperrin Mountains called Twat-Faced Dickhead.

Another Doctor Who club member was an anarchic lad in the same year as Doc called Brendan Bankfield, whose highly imaginative nickname was Fieldy. He had an explosion of upstanding hair and was studying art, drawing inspiration from the morbid, gothic imagery of heavy metal album covers. He showed us one of his masterpieces. As homework the art teacher had set the class an assignment entitled "Back to school – an environmental study". Fieldy's interpretation of this theme was a boy in school uniform hanging by the neck from a tree, with his tie as the noose. At least you couldn't fault him for originality.

Our Dr Who club meetings were held Friday afternoons after classes had ended in the school lecture theatre. We would watch old episodes from the 1970s of very dodgy quality. These generally came from a friend of a friend of a friend an uncle of a colleague of a friend of a "contact" who knew someone who worked in the BBC archives department and had smuggled out illegally copied videotapes of old serials. So what we were watching was effectively a copy of a copy of a copy of a copy (etc) on videotape. These were the days before digital recording technology, DVDs and downloads of course. Or alternatively if you had penfriends in Australia which was several years behind in the episode schedules they could send you tapes.
We would have debates on who the best Doctor was, quizzes where we would impress each other with knowing who the second boom microphone operator on *Terror of the Zogdats* broadcast on the 12th of March 1967 was - or which famous transvestite appeared as an extra in episode 3 of *The Skeletons of Badness*, only

to be corrected and told that he/she had actually appeared two minutes and 21 seconds into episode four of *Tomfoolery of the Greepos*. We were basically a bunch of nerdy 13-year olds who attracted much derision from our classmates. Looking back in hindsight this derision was probably wholly justified. But to quote our glorious leader Mark "The Doc" Johnson it did stop you from smashing up the town.

It should be noted that *Doctor Who* in those days was not the big budget, highly popular and successful phenomenon it is now. Back then the original series was dying a slow painful death and was considered very uncool. But part of me enjoyed being on the receiving end of the derision. Part of me revelled in the nerd tag. I felt I was part of an elite minority. It would take a few more years to realise how deluded I'd been. It certainly wasn't the sort of hobby you could hope to meet girls through. However, one of the main attractions of *Who* from an adolescent male point of view through the years has been the high quality of the lead character's young female assistants. The girl in the role back then was certainly no exception. She was a whiney American called Peri who often wore tight low cut tops exposing curves and ample amounts of cleavage. A pathetic and cynical ploy on the part of the production team to boost the already flagging ratings of a washed-up TV show in terminal decline no doubt. But we weren't complaining.

We once had a stall at the annual model and hobby exhibition held at the local leisure centre. In among the collection of model aeroplanes, vintage cars, football programmes and stuffed animals we had our curly Tom Baker wigs, long scarves, miniature cybermen, inflatable daleks, plastic TARDISes, countless books, posters and a TV screen with the Dr Who titles and theme music playing in a continuous loop.

One particular teacher who was a bit of a sci-fi fan took an interest in our club. He would occasionally pop his head around the door just briefly to lend us some moral support and encouragement, impressed that we were doing this through our own initiative and without any outside influence from teachers or parents. But he would deliberately keep his distance so as not to be seen to be interfering.

The late PA Maglochlainn was a colourful character to say the least. He was one of the last of a dying breed, the genuinely eccentric teacher. I suppose every grammar school must have had one or two of them back in the day. Dressed in an old man's cardigan, (even though he was only in his early 40s) and flared trousers which had gone out of style a decade ago and with his trademark beard and glasses he cut a unique presence both within the school and the wider local community. We knew him ostensibly as a French teacher, but he seemed to have taught nearly every other subject at some point. Being something of a renaissance man he ran the school chess club, was involved in local politics, worked as a part time life guard at the local swimming baths and was an occasional actor with the town's drama society as well as being a bit of a computer boffin.

PA once challenged the whole class to a bet about the occurrence of cannibal chickens in battery farms, which were fitted with special tinted goggles to prevent them from eating their fellow poultry. His wager was that such a phenomenon – although for us it seemed hard to believe – was actually true and not just some nonsense that he had made up. He subsequently won the bet and pocketed his winnings. He proved it by showing us the relevant entry in an agricultural book from the school library. I had sensibly chosen to believe him so didn't forfeit anything. He had nevertheless instigated a clever double bluff by trying to make us think he was bluffing us.

He was a regular visitor to Eastern Europe in the days of the Iron Curtain and one of his claims to fame was that he was one of only two people in the town who could speak Polish. Since the expansion of the European Union and the movement of labour from east to west I'm sure the town has at least a few dozen Polish speakers these days.

He had an endless repertoire of stories, jokes, anecdotes and amazing facts about almost everything under the sun which he would impart to us during class and relate in a variety of theatrical voices and accents – often with only a very tenuous link to what he was supposed be teaching us. Some of us would try and take advantage of this by asking him a question at the beginning of class with a vague connection to France, such as the Channel Tunnel on which construction had just begun, in the hope that he would spend the whole lesson talking about it. He rarely fell for this and would simply say "ask me after class". But not surprisingly no-one did. His breadth of knowledge and generosity in sharing it taught the pupil as much about life and the world as the subject being taught.

After his retirement from teaching he relocated to Belfast and became chair of the Northern Ireland Gay Rights Association where he used his position to work tirelessly for equality and tolerance. An interesting career move if ever there was one - and something of a surprise to many of us. During my student days in Belfast I used to bump into him occasionally. He always had time for people and never forgot his old pupils.

One boy, a curly haired fellow by the name of Otis McAleer, but better known simply as Curly (I've no idea why) once asked him the meaning of the Irish expression "*Pog mo hon*", knowing damn well that it meant "Kiss my arse". Generations of parents and older siblings throughout Ireland must have urged their gullible offspring or younger sisters/brothers to ask their Irish teacher the meaning of this phrase . Dozens of tacky Irish pubs the world over have also named themselves after this phrase without people knowing what it means. A certain London Irish popular beat combo who specialised in a unique fusion of punk rock and traditional folk music even named themselves after this time-honoured "greeting". But on discovering its meaning the record company allegedly forced them to shorten their name to the less offensive "Pogues".

PA, with a completely straight face replied to Curly's question saying that it was a reference to anyone in a white collar, a respectable form of greeting reserved for priests and Christian brothers. Curly said it anyway to Brother Skaramazov, one of the more benign of the school's brothers and got a clip round the ear for being cheeky.

Although he didn't use it on this occasion Skaramazov's rather ineffectual weapon of punishment was a length of rubber which was probably cannibalised from a car window. He would slap it down on the palm of your hand with the minimum of force. And if you pulled your hand away at the last minute he'd let you get away with it. It was an ineffective punishment - as if he couldn't bear to do it, but had to pretend so he would command some respect.

There were certain teachers who were known to be a soft touch. This was especially true of the supply teachers, who were filling in for the permanent members of staff on sick leave, study leave or maternity leave. They generally tended to be young, newly qualified and inexperienced, a status we would often take criminal advantage of. Some of them couldn't handle us. Some were just too incompetent to land a permanent teaching post.

Taking advantage ranged from smoking at the back of the room during class to all-out riots using anti-tank missiles and rocket launchers. On one occasion Tony Philips hid in a locker with a recorder which he occasionally blew on throughout the duration of the class. The teacher in question could hear the notes, but had no idea where they were coming from, so he decided to take his frustrations out on a totally innocent party.

Such teachers often resorted to ineffectual threats such as:

"Right, I'm reporting you to your form teacher! Who is your form teacher?"

"Mr Squawkelofocacus"

"Right I'll be telling Mr Squawkelofocacus all about you! Wait a minute, you just made that up! Who's your real form teacher?"

"Mrs Getoutthatfeckindoorandgiveyournoseagoodrubinthedirt".

"I don't believe you. What's your name?"

"Baron Octavius H.Von Schweinsteiger IV of Lower East Saxony"

"WHAT'S YOUR NAME?"

"Er…Paul Mulroy"

"Right, Mr Mulroy, your name's going into the book!"

At the point the entire class burst out laughing – that is except for the real Paul Mulroy who was not best pleased at this blatant identity theft.

And so on... I'm sure you get the picture.

Getting back to the late great PA Maglochlainn, (I only found out what those initials stood for many years later after reading his obituary on the *Irish Times* website – for the record it was Patrick Anthony) such was his influence on a generation of pupils that the former head boy "Cheese" McArdle at the 1993 prize-giving night paid tribute to "our swimming French teacher who has since followed in a different dimension".

Ideal Holmes Exposition
I first became seriously interested in Sherlock Holmes at the age of 14 or 15 in early 1988 I think when the centenary of Conan Doyle's character was being celebrated through various TV and radio documentaries, newspaper articles and the like. My unhealthy anorak-like obsession with *Doctor Who* was coming to a natural end (after all this was during the era of Sylvester McCoy when the show was at all-time low point) and the more mature and rational Holmes became the natural replacement. I would get the books from the school library and devour Silver Blaze, The Yellow Face, The Solitary Cyclist, The Engineer's Thumb and The Hound of the Baskervilles with relish.

Several years later I would eventually visit Baker Street. Holmes' address 221b is now a museum. Inside were a young Mrs Hudson and a Dr Watson – but no sign of the great detective himself.

Maybe he'd been arrested for wasting police time after asking them whether he actually existed.

I remember having an argument when aged 8 or 9 with a schoolfriend called Joseph Gorman over whether Sherlock Holmes had been a real life character. I contended that he was purely a work of fiction, but young Gorman insisted that there had been a real Holmes at some point in time. In an attempt to settle the argument he advised me to pop down to the local police station and ask them to verify the past existence or otherwise of the great detective. I was confident in my assertion, so didn't bother to take him up on this. But over a quarter of a century later I often wonder what the officers of the Royal Ulster Constabulary (RUC) as they were then known at Omagh's heavily fortified police barracks would have made of a 9-year old making such an enquiry. As police stations throughout Northern Ireland were liable to come under attack in those days, getting into one would have involved quite a rigorous security vetting. Assuming I'd successfully got through security clearance I can just imagine what would have happened...

What comes to mind is the image of a tall ruddy-faced desk sergeant with a moustache (a lot of them had moustaches back then) impatiently enquiring of me:

"And what can I do for you, son?"

"I'd like to see the case files of Sherlock Holmes please."

"Are you trying to be funny?"

"No."

"Well fuck away off then, son and don't be wasting my time!"

No doubt if this had happened in more recent politically correct times the officer would have been disciplined for using abusive language towards a minor. But as this incident never actually happened that's neither here nor there. This fictitious scenario has stuck in my head and provides many an amusing moment on these

72

cold dark lonely winter nights. In fact it's becoming a rather tiresome running joke – as certain nameless individuals will be able to testify.

I won't go into the time I had another argument with the same boy over whether God was real and he challenged me to go to the parochial house and ask the parish priest to confirm.

Purely by chance I found myself sitting opposite the very same Mr Gorman on a London underground train almost three decades later. I hadn't seen him for a few years at the time. It was one of those one-in-a-million situations which happen to everyone on a number of occasions during their lifetime.

But there's more… A few years ago on my way back from work, I stopped off at a supermarket to do some light shopping. I won't say which supermarket it was, but it shares its name with a well-known pint-sized Belfast musician who has a reputation for being grumpy and with the late lead singer of a popular American 1960s rock band who had a famous hit single about promoting pyromaniacal tendencies who popped his clogs while in the bath and is now buried in a famous Parisian cemetery.

Anyway, I only had a few things to buy, namely a four-pack of tomatoes, a three-pack of small tins of tuna, a French loaf and some oranges. The total bill came to £4.11. I had notes in my wallet, but wanted to use up the spare change in my pocket if possible. I fished around in my pocket for the change and found I had exactly £4.11, not a penny more, not a penny less. An amazing coincidence – or maybe not depending on your point of view. Probably not a particularly interesting anecdote, and for that matter, probably not even worth writing about. But there you go.

Then on another occasion in the summer of 2005 I was on a train returning from a conference in Harrogate when I noticed a passenger who bore an uncanny resemblance to Pink Floyd's Dave Gilmour. The very next day it was announced that Pink Floyd would be reforming for a one-off appearance as part of a star-studded concert to raise awareness of the environment. Former band member Roger Waters would bury the hatchet with his ex-colleagues and briefly reunite with them after years of bitter feuding. Maybe there had been a Waters lookalike in the next carriage. A year later the band's original vocalist Syd Barrett died. Ironically he'd once sung a song in the late 1960s containing lyrics about surviving till 2005.

-5-

Apples, Oranges and Handball

Of the few remaining Christian Brothers during my time at the school was one who taught maths called Brother Heffernan. He was a bit of a character, something of a Jekyll and Hyde personality - not a natural sadist like some of his brotherly colleagues and in fact quite good-humoured most of the time. But if you got on the wrong side of him he could turn quite vicious in an instant and administer severe punishment which was often disproportionate to the crime committed. However, he would usually manage to nip any rowdiness in the bud with his immortal catch phrase:

"Now there's a time and a place for all that, and it's not here and now".

A funny thing happened during a maths class where we were tasked with working out a simple algebraic equation

The sum to be worked out was $3x + 2y$. As any algebrist (if that's the correct term – not that I've come across any specialists in algebra – for some reason there doesn't seem to be much demand for them) knows you can't add the two figures as x plus y doesn't add up. So the answer wasn't 5xy as we had initially thought. As Bro Heffernan explained by way of analogy

"If you had three apples and two oranges you couldn't call them five apples-oranges".

One bright spark, Johnny Brannigan (now a teacher himself) piped up with the classic remark:

"But brother could you not just call them five fruits?"

On this occasion old Heffernan saw the funny side: "Oh we're very smart, aren't we?"

A younger brother of mine one Christmas quite recently recounted another funny story about algebra involving one of his former

75

classmates (who for convenience purposes I'll call XY) and a maths teacher who for convenience purposes I'll call Mr Fitzpatrick. This happened a number of years after I'd left the school.

"Sir, what's the point of algebra? When are you ever going to use it? It's not like if you're building a house you're going to call one wall x and the other wall y?"

"If that's your attitude you might as well go looking for birds' nests in Carrickmore [a reference to XY's home town]" came the bizarre response.

XY then proceeded to get up from his desk and was about to exit the classroom.

"Where are you going?" roared the Fitz.

"I'm off to Carrickmore to look for birds' nests, sir"

"Sit down!"

Algebra is of course an Arabic word. Many other terms beginning with the pre-fix "al" are also of Arabic origin - alcohol, alchemy, alkali and Al Pacino to name but a few.

On another occasion we were going through the answers to the previous day's homework with Heffernan. It was the morning of April 1st.

"Is there anyone who didn't get that right?" he asked after having shown the working of a particularly complex equation.

Johnny Brannigan's hand went up.

"Well?" old Heffo enquired as to how he got it wrong.

"April Fool, Brother!" came the reply.

"Get up on your two hind legs and come up here!" Heffers barked sternly, apparently not amused.

Johnny walked to the front of the class and stood in front of his mentor who shot him a vicious look.

"You'd think you would have made the effort to clean your trousers!" the Heff said contemptuously.

Johnny looked down at his trousers to find they were perfectly clean.

Wily old Heffernan smiled as if to say "got you there!"

It was Bro Heffernan who introduced us to handball. For the benefit of anyone unfamiliar with the game I should point out that this was the ancient Irish game played by striking a ball against a wall with the palm of the hand (what a cynic might call "poor man's squash" - not to be confused with the Olympic team handball game which resembles a cross between soccer and basketball and involves two teams trying to throw a squishy ball into their opponent's net).

Ironically the two games which most resemble handball are Eton fives and Rugby fives, played (as their names suggest) almost exclusively within elitist English public schools, although there is also a variation called pelota played in the Basque Country – a place I would visit a quarter of a century later – but more on that in due course. Or you can go straight to that chapter if you're already bored. If you haven't already thrown the book down in disgust by now that is. If you're reading this on Kindle then I hope you haven't.

I wasn't very good at football, but wasn't completely crap at sport either, so I found my niche in this more genteel non-contact game. We would go to the town's leisure centre to play on Friday afternoons after school and again with the local club on Saturday mornings. The school didn't have a handball court (or alley as it was also known – the correct term is open to dispute) since the old one had been knocked down to make way for the "imminent" extension which we never got to see during our time at the school. Several years later the extension was finally completed with a spanking new handball court. But by this time we were long gone. That mysterious legislator Murphy along with his colleague Sod has a lot to answer for.

Nevertheless handball at the school took off spectacularly even in the absence of proper facilities, with every available wall in the yard being used every breaktime and lunchtime and even in the mornings before classes started. Any kind of small rubber ball would suffice. On one occasion a group of chancers even tried to play the game using a golf ball (painful) until Bro Heffernan firmly intervened expressing his concern about the fate of the windows.

A rather sadistic and violent variation called "killerball" evolved from this. One advantage it had over its less harmful relative where only two or four (ie singles or doubles) could play at a time, there were no numerical limits on who could play killerball. This was however the game's only redeeming feature. About 20 boys would stand beside the wall. One would then throw the ball against the wall with the greatest force he could muster. The object was to avoid getting hit by the ball on the rebound, so everyone would then make a mad dash to avoid making unintentional contact with the ball. If it hit you on the rebound you would get a kicking from all the other participants. It was the element of living dangerously that appealed, something that many of us would get addicted to over the coming years. But that's another story altogether...

The recipient of the beating then threw the ball against the wall with equally great force and the cycle would continue until the bell went – or until a teacher came along and happened to witness this sado-masochistic spectacle before putting a stop to it with a few stern words. I should make it clear that participation in the game was purely voluntary. No-one was forced to take part. Having said that the legal doctrine of *volenti non fit injuria* probably wouldn't stand up in court. If you didn't take part you were branded a yellow-bellied chicken, but that's neither here nor there.

In a similar tradition to killerball was the birthday bumps. If word got around that it was someone's birthday (and somehow it always did, even though you kept very quiet about it), the celebrant would be grabbed by about ten boys and held face up by his arms and legs before being tossed up into the air as many times as the years he had spent on the planet. As my birthday was during the summer holidays I tended to escape this. However this didn't stop rumours circulating on any given day that it was my birthday, which my classmates conveniently chose to believe.

Another similar practice was the "christening" of shoes. If a boy came into class wearing a pair of shiny new shoes his classmates were dutybound to "christen" them in an initiation ceremony which involved the unfortunate items of footwear being stamped on by 30 pairs of feet – while the owner was still wearing them of course. This sort of carry on was just one step up the ladder from putting a "kick me" sticker on the seat of someone's trousers.

Anyway, getting back to the subject of handball – a group of us would occasionally club together to book a court/alley the odd evening after school.

It must have been a Wednesday or Thursday evening after school when myself, Shane Rogan, Noel McGowan, Vladimir Zanetti and Brian "Squire" Maguire had gone to bang rubber balls against walls for a couple of hours. The council run leisure complex was still relatively new at the time and was kept to remarkably high standards of cleanliness. That is until we polluted it with our presence.

We only had the use of one court as the other was being used for squash. Only four of us could be in the court at the same time, so we rotated it around on a winner-stays-on basis.

Squire meanwhile had gone off to the pool to check out any hot female tottie modelling the latest bikini range, but came across something completely different.

Squire interrupted our game to announce the breaking new "Guess who's in the pool? Loopy, Lenny and Corky!"

As well as two off-duty school stormtroopers the Fuhrer himself was in our midst, even though "Loopy, Lenny and Corky" sounded like a bad comedy treble act from a forgettable 1930s slapstick Hollywood B movie. We rushed through the rest of our game and dashed towards the poolside spectators' gallery. Sure enough O'Loscan was there in a pair of baggy bright orange trunks with his two cronies doing lengths of the pool. If I remember correctly it was the backstroke. I wondered if they'd all arranged to go swimming together or if they'd come together purely by chance. It was a well-known fact that Lenny wasn't exactly on the closest of terms with his boss. Unless of course unbeknownst to us the vice principal was retiring and Lenny was angling for promotion.

We starting shouting from the gallery – "Corky's a simian-faced troglodyte!" as he did his back stroke up and down the pool. We used varying terms of abuse which also included "cream-faced loon", a quotation from *Macbeth*.

Every time he looked up to see where the shouting was coming from we put books in front of our faces and pretended to be reading. How brave we were. This went on for a few more minutes until a member of staff kicked us out. Inevitably it had to be Ken Blowtorch, the officious little twat that he was. He was apparently so-called due to his fiery temper. No-one seemed to know what his real surname was. Every time he opened his mouth it seemed that flames issued forth. And the fact that his nickname sounded similar to James Bond's adversary Blofeld was somehow appropriate. But he was not so much an arch-villain as a mere henchman like a less threatening version of Odd Job or Jaws, where his whistle and grating voice would take the place of the metallic teeth or hat with blades inserted into the brim. We'd had a few run-ins with him over the years. He seemed to have a vendetta against schoolboys regardless of whether his wiry frame and trademark red moustache were reluctantly behind the reception desk, routinely patrolling the changing rooms, enforcing non-existent rules in his own whistle-happy manner by the poolside and even when he was crunching numbers in the back office. Maybe he was just bitter as he seemed to have ambitions towards getting into senior management, but instead seemed to be stuck as a general dogsbody in a lowly jack-of-all-trades-master-of-none role. He would patrol the poolside in his ill-fitting tight shorts and take great pleasure in telling off seven year olds for splashing.

On another occasion we'd been playing handball and the adjacent squash court was free. As there were more of us than there was room for in the handball alley a few of us decided to make use of the squash court. OK, technically we weren't entitled to do this as we were using a facility we hadn't booked or paid for. But as it was unoccupied it would otherwise have been an empty space going to waste – an empty unused space which the local rate-payers (ie our parents) had funded. Nevertheless, the irritatingly unmistakable high-pitched voice of Ken Blowtorch the incorrigible jobsworth announced over the intercom system:

"Could the handballers please vacate the squash court...NOW!"

Shane Rogan glared at the CCTV camera that was positioned above the balcony behind us and shouted:

"Could Ken Blowtorch go and stick his fucking head in the oven...NOW!"

We carried on playing for a few more minutes to see how long we could get away with it.

Blowtorch was just one of a number of public hate figures for schoolboys in the town. There was also the grumpy newsagent who would get irate if you browsed through comics on the shelf with no intention of buying anything. How unreasonable! And the dour cafe owner who didn't like students overstaying their welcome in his establishment – but more on him later. The irascible woman at the library with the permanently surly look on her face would stamp your books without saying a word. The only time she did speak was to violently shush you for making noise. The only time she ever seemed to smile was when collecting a fine for an overdue book. There were even stories circulating that she pocketed the proceeds of the fines for herself and was now living in a huge mansion on the edge of town having financed through 30 years worth of ill-gotten gains. The fact that the fines system for overdue items had only been introduced a few years earlier placed considerable doubt on this less than convincing story.

And not to mention the barman who refused to serve you unless you had ID proving you were over 18.

We also sometimes got to go to the leisure centre during school hours as part of PE. PE was almost always football or basketball, but occasionally it involved a trip to the centre to play handball, squash or to swim. The complex was a good 15 minutes walk from the school. But if we took our time returning to the school this could easily be trebled. We made our way back as slowly as we could, going round in circles and making sure to take the longest route possible. On our way out of school we took every conceivable short cut of course – even if this meant trespassing on private property. But then apparently all property is theft anyway as a learned man once said.

On the way there we took a short cut through a large branch of a well-known chemists chain. Coincidentally two policemen were also walking through the shop and no doubt watching our every move.

As schoolboys are prone to do when confronted with the forces of law and order some of our number began to grunt and squeal like pigs in an attempt to wind up the uniformed enforcers. Judging by their reaction it obviously worked a few dozen grunts later.

"Have you got a problem?" one of them eventually said angrily.

We all laughed at this outburst, and went on our merry way triumphant that we'd provoked him into reacting. However, I was almost tempted to say:

"Yes I have got a problem, officer. I wanted to determine the real life existence or otherwise of Sherlock Holmes. So I asked one of your colleagues a few years ago, but he was rude to me and didn't give me a proper answer."

But I thought better of it.

I hadn't actually joined in with the porcine grunting as I considered myself to be above this puerile schoolboy behaviour. Funnily enough there were many aspects of schoolboy behaviour which I refused to participate in as I considered it to be beneath me. Yet in my infinite hypocrisy I would actively encourage others to engage in it as I found it highly entertaining – just as I had "persuaded" Nigel Hackett to write the F word on the board back in primary school.

Inevitably we were late in returning to the school.

There were various well-rehearsed teacher-pupil scenarios which arose as a result of tardiness – such as:

"Where were you?"

"Sir, I was at lunch."

"Lunch finished five minutes ago!"

Or better still:

"You were at lunch? I'll lunch you!"

I've often wondered what the hell this was supposed to mean.

Or:

"Sir I missed the bus."

"You shouldn't be throwing things at the bus!"

"No, I mean the bus was late, sir."

"So you had to go to a funeral service for the late bus?"

Our PE teacher Mr Gareth Sheehan (known to us as "Hairy Gary" on account of his beard which seemed to cover most of his face – probably grown to compensate for his premature baldness) used to give us long lectures at the end of every game of football or basketball we played. We would all be made to sit down in a circle on the gravel pitch or on the floor of the gym with Gary in the middle who would always give a brutally honest assessment of our performance.

"Right lads, that was a crap game. That's not how you play gaelic football/basketball/volleyball/ Russian roulette [delete as appropriate depending on the occasion]. If any of youse want to play for the school team in the McRory Cup youse are gonna have to do a hell of a lot better than that."

In classic PE teacher tradition he addressed his pupils by their nicknames. I'm not sure if he was trying to be chummy or if he just didn't know what our real names were. I suspect it was the latter as he used to address Shane Rogan as "Jim" for some bizarre reason.

He would single out the more promising players for apparent mistakes they had made.

"Quinny – see that time you fisted the ball to Murpho across the face of the goal? That was a rubbish pass. What was all that about?"

It was always a rhetorical question. He would then continue turning to the goalkeeper:

"Spud, what kind of a kick-out was that?"

By this stage a few of us used to drift off and start staring at the ground, playing with the gravel, waiting for the bell to sound. This pissed Gary off. He would pause for a few seconds so that everyone's attention was diverted to the daydreamer in a world of his own who was flicking pieces of gravel up in the air.

"SWIGGSY, ARE YOU LISTENING TO ME?" he would bark.

As he rubbed his hand over the top of his smoothly shaved head he would conclude with a cliché like:

"Skill and co-ordination – that's the name of the game!"

The previous week "stamina" had apparently been the "name of the game" and the week before it had been "determination". It was as if "the game" had a different name every week.

He would become more passionate as he went along.

"Give yourself a mark out of ten for each game. Then you can compare this to your next performance"

We would be desperately trying to hold in the laughter by this point.

These lectures were completely irrelevant to those of us who were

84

never going to play on the school team. We were never going to get any better.

The boys who weren't very good and tended to get picked last were usually dumped in goal. Getting hit full blast on the thigh with the ball on a frosty winter morning was not pleasant. The stinging sensation lasted all day. But it could have been worse.

Although I didn't play for the school team I occasionally went to matches to cheer them on in the local provincial schools tournament the McRory Cup. The school colours were maroon and white, apparently the legacy of a Christian Brother from Galway back in the swirling mists of time who had decided to kit the team out in the colours of his native county.

On the bus journeys to matches the songs of the traveling support could occasionally be entertaining. One song that was sung to the tune of the "This old man" line of the "Knick-knack Paddywack" song and seems to be shared by many other sports teams around the world who wear white.

"We're maroon, we are white,
We are fucking dynamite!"

I don't remember how the rest of the song went, but it didn't go down too well with teachers sitting at the front of the bus. Another popular bus song was "They're all a pack of wallies at the back" sung to the tune of "She'll be coming round the mountain", although "wallies" was often substituted for more offensive words. Among the more puerile ditties was "Stop the bus I want to wee-wee" sung to the tune of "Glory Glory Halleleuia".

I remember one match against the famous St Pats of Maghera which was played at Derrylaughan on the shores of Lough Neagh on a freezing cold February morning. It was the first time most of us had seen this vast inland sea, the largest lake in both Ireland and the UK close-up. But on this occasion a large swathe of the lake's foreshore was frozen over. Boys were throwing stones on to the ice. They slid away into the distance with a long way to go before hitting the unfrozen water.

It wasn't the only time I walked on thin ice…

6

The Class Struggle, Urban Myths and Rural Legends

When I talk about class war or class solidarity in this book I'm not referring to the manifestos of Karl Marx or the latest campaign by some left wing socialist workers' organisation. I'm in fact alluding to the daily rivalry between 1C and 1D or 4A and 4E which formed a major part of my school days. There were the legitimate forms of inter-class competition such as football, debating and quizzes. A quarter of a century later and I still feel gutted at being on the losing 1C side in the final of the first year league which 1B narrowly won by a single point on a very wet and muddy pitch. I wasn't in the best of shape having had my fingers badly bruised after accidentally getting them crushed by two shot putts during athletics practice a couple of weeks earlier, but still managed to get on the scoresheet.

Two years later I was on the 3C debating team who lost to 3A on the motion "This house believes that integrated education is the way forward", which we were proposing. The following year I was on the defeated 4E team in the fourth year debating final on the motion "It's a man's world", which again my team was proposing.

But being an all boys school of raging hormones there were also the unofficial class conflicts. If a fight broke out between two boys from different classes the unwritten rule was that you supported the one from your own class, a bizarre state of affairs given that we had no say in what class we were put in.

If a brawl didn't get resolved in the classroom or the yard, if the two combatants were rudely interrupted by the bell or the intervention of a meddlesome teacher it would often be rescheduled for after school with a neutral territory as the venue. One such fight had been arranged to take place in the large public pay-and-display car park beside the school which hundreds of school boys and girls passed through daily on their way home. The two opponents on this occasion were Skins Fallon and Cheese McArdle. At this stage of the book I've run out of names given that there were so many Seans, Shanes, Pauls and Michaels (or variations including Mick, Mickey, Micko, Mike or Mikey) during my time at the school, so I've had to resort to using fictitious nicknames.

No doubt the school boys of today film fights on their mobile phones and post the footage on Youtube and Facebook, but back in the day we had to rely purely on memory and eyewitness accounts of varying degrees of accuracy and exaggeration. Young people reading this (ie anyone under 30) could be forgiven for thinking we were living in some kind of primitive dark age back then. In many respects we were. This was a world without e-mail, Facebook, Twitter, Spotify, blogs, i-pads, i-pods, Skype or Google. Back then an i-pad was a surgical dressing which you wore if you had an infected iris. Blackberries were still fruits that grew on thorny bushes at the side of the road. Androids were something out of *Doctor Who* and a wiki was a small metal implement used to open a small door or padlock. An app was what you took when you were tired.

Although I know I'm getting on a bit now that I'm in my late 30s, I don't consider myself to be particularly old. I draw some consolation from the fact that I'm still young enough (in theory at least) to be a goalkeeper at a top Premier League club. It's a lonely position to play in at the best times, but I often wonder how ageing goalies must feel being the oldest player on the team and surrounded by young lads half their age. But I'll leave this discussion for another time.

The fight started in classic style with a bit of pushing and shoving and the odd insult thrown in.

"So do you want a fight, McArdle?"

"That's what I'm here for, Fallon!"

"Is that right?"

"Oh, you think you're smart do you?"

"So what are you going to do about it?"

It was as if each party was playing for time by deliberately prolonging the dialogue.

A substantial crowd had gathered. Things were about to kick off as the customary pushing and shoving had started, when a traffic warden – or more accurately the council-employed jobsworth with the peaked hat whose task it was to check if the car owners had paid and displayed with those annoying adhesive square stickers you put up on the inside of your windscreen - intervened. He was a small chubby man with a moustache.

"This is a public car park!" he screamed. "You can't get up to this kind of carry on here!" It was probably safe to assume that he had an MBA (Master of Busybody Administration) from the "Ken Blowtorch School of Management". Naturally his interference wasn't exactly welcomed with open arms, especially when a bunch of exuberant schoolboys had been looking forward to a bit of entertainment.

The Fallon-McArdle bout fizzled out and attention instead turned to the developing confrontation between Mr Pay & Display and a big lad from the fourth form called Barry Bennett. Bennett was none too pleased that his rights as a spectator to this feast of gladiatorial action were being curtailed by a small man in a uniform.

He squared up to him eyeball to eyeball and asserted himself, being a few inches taller than this uniformed killjoy.

"And what the fuck are you gonna do about it, mister?"

Pay & Display Man was quite clearly getting very nervous and could only repeat his previous words, but this time in a much higher voice, as if a lobster had somehow crawled down his trousers.
"This is a public car park, you can't..." he squeaked only to be cut off in mid-sentence.

89

"So you think you're the big man do you? This is nothing to do you with you!"

"I'm going to report you, you know. You won't get away with this!"

Bennett ignored this empty threat and continued his campaign of intimidation.

"Go ahead. Go and put a ticket on some poor bastard's car while you're at it!"

The council employee backed down, humiliated at being made to feel small by a schoolboy. The crowds of school boys and girls cheered and continued on their way to the bus station via the town centre. McArdle and Fallon were even seen joking amiably with each other. The car park incident inevitably became the main topic of conversation throughout the whole school over the next few days. Everyone claimed to have witnessed it, even the boys who lived in the opposite direction to the "crime scene" and didn't take that route home. Not surprisingly the reports became grossly exaggerated and distorted. Even though there had been no actual physical contact there were rumours that Barry Bennett had left Pay & Display Man lying on the ground in a pool of his own blood.

"My sister Sinead's a nurse up at the hospital and she said he had to be treated for concussion and head injuries and needed 20 stitches. You shoulda heard the roars of him! The doctor said he was this much away (the storyteller at this point – not a medical expert by any stretch of the imagination - demonstrated a tiny gap using his finger and thumb) from getting his jaw broke. Bennett just done it for badness, like."

Another "roving reporter" expanded on this account:

"Sure the cops came round and cordoned off the area. I seen them doing it. The forensics boys had to take blood samples away with them. There was a big queue of traffic all along the Kevlin Road for two hours. The cops lifted Barry and took him round to the nick for interrogation. They roughed him up a bit just for badness, but he still never told the bastards nothin'. He gave them as good as he got".

In an alternative narrative the traffic warden had actually attacked Bennett with a taser (or an Uzi sub-machine or machete depending on who you chose to believe) and forced him into retaliating with his fists.

Not that I'm condoning thuggish behavior, but as the accounts of that day became more and more distorted Barry Bennett became a bit of a legend after that, a Robin Hood character fighting injustice. Nothing could have been further from the truth. Just like a few other (but by no means all) events described in this book....

Urban Myths and Rural Legends

In our early years at the school the weekly supervised class trip to the school library would throw up the occasional surprise. Hidden within the shelves were thick paperback thrillers or horror novels which contained strong language and sexual content. One particular individual Richard Kenny had a knack of finding these racy passages and even took the trouble to go through them with a highlighter pen so the next generation of pupils could find them easily.

Not even the supposedly great works of literature were immune from this treatment. *Oliver Twist* was one of our set texts for GCSE English literature. There's a minor character, a young boy in Fagin's den of juvenile delinquents called Charlie Bates. Dickens regularly refers to him in the text as "Master Bates". Our teacher Mrs Gallagher would get us to take turns reading chapters from the book. When the scenes involving "Master Bates" came up, the inevitable giggling ensured. Mrs G angrily demanded to know what we were laughing at, but no-one would come clean about it. Now, did Dickens intend this as a deliberate innuendo in the hope of shocking (or perhaps slipping it innocently over the heads of) a prudish Victorian readership? I can't help thinking that this was the case. The evidence certainly points this way in terms of the inconsistencies in the narrative. The title character, for example is always referred to by Dickens as Oliver, but never "Master Twist". This gave rise to the puerile schoolboy joke:

"You know that boy Charlie Bates out of *Oliver Twist*? He was a bit of a wanker!"

Pathetic schoolboy innuendo was rife at the time – like "how was your French oral? Did you find it hard?" And the references to writing "French letters" to our Gallic pen-pals goes without saying. It was like the cast of a "Carry On" film on acid.

Fourth year French classes with our unfortunate temporary supply teacher Mrs Gallagher became innuendo city. Some of my classmates were filthy-minded little thugs. Even *quoi* the French word for "what" could sound suggestive if pronounced in a lecherous Sid James voice as "Quawwwwgggghhhh!"

I'm reminded of the children's cartoon series *Captain Pugwash* - which the followed the adventures of a bunch of pirates on the high seas - and the infamous urban myth that it featured a character who shared a title with the aforementioned "Master Bates" as well as a crewman called Seaman Staines. Pugwash creator John Ryan was apparently a devoutly religious man. He was naturally furious when he heard these scurrilous rumours and even apparently took legal action to force the Sunday paper which had published these allegations to retract them.

While we're on the subject of urban myths one of the more common forms of this was that some famous celebrity had died either unexpectedly or as the result of some bizarre happening. There was a widely believed rumour in the mid-80s that Gary Coleman, the young actor from the American comedy series *Diff'rent Strokes* (famous for the catchphrase "Whatchoo talkin' about Willis!") was dead. Some years later around 1989 there was a much more localised, short-lived rumour that Axl Rose, lead singer with Guns N Roses had died of a drug overdose. This story was then rubbished by an "insider" who claimed that it was actually Slash, the band's guitarist who had snuffed it. But just how reliable the inside information of a spotty 15 year old from Killyclogher was remained to be seen. Without internet access or 24 hour rolling news (which was still over a decade away) you had no way of verifying these stories.

At the time of writing both Slash and Axl are still very much alive, although they have since gone their separate ways.

Mr Bangang, the Deston Invasion of Earth and other Long Stories

My brothers and I used to create fictional characters with alarming regularity during our early childhood. The most enduring of these characters was a young boy called Mr Bangang. The story around him gradually built up over several years and even into adulthood. For some reason he didn't have a first name. He was basically a spoilt brat, the son of a multi-millionaire confectionery tycoon who had amassed his fortune through the Bangang Sweets corporation. Young Banagang was also multi-talented. He was the captain of a highly successful soccer team, Inter High School (a bit of a misnomer as it was a football club not a school) who played at the ultra-modern Inter Avenue stadium as well as being the lead singer of the fictitious punk band Nuts. Nuts recorded experimental albums which involved spending several weeks at a time in the studio recording hours of highly complex layers of silence. As part of their stage act they catapulted live mice and hot tea bags at the audience.

He lived on a diet of junk food which was nutritionally modified to make it healthy – notably vitaminised hamburgers. However things weren't all sweetness and light for the boy Bangang. His life was under threat from the Anti-Mr Bangang Gang (AMBG), a terrorist group whose sole *raison d'être* was the assassination of Mr Bangang. But somehow they never achieved their goal. Given his high profile existence as a footballer and rock star who didn't employ security guards you would have thought he was an easy target. The AMBG must therefore have been the most incompetent terrorist group in history. Having said that, the motive behind their aim was never clearly established. There was also a rival organisation, the Anti-Anti-Mr Bangang Gang Gang (AAMBG) whose only objective was to eliminate the Anti-Mr Bangang Gang. Don't ask why though. There was really no logic to it.

When we got older and our sense of humour became much more cynical, we decided to send up the Bangang legend by inventing a riches-to-rags story in which he had become a homeless alcoholic, having gambled away the bulk of his fortune and blown the rest on drink and drugs or ill-advised investments including a supposedly "highly lucrative" banana plantation in Greenland.

To raise funds for their former captain's rehabilitation the Inter High School club had organised a charity benefit match at Inter Avenue, in which the fallen Bangang was due to play. However he turned up in an advanced state of intoxication and got into a fight with his former team mates, then called the club's supporters a "bunch of fucking losers" over the intercom system, a chain of events which sparked off a riot and ended up with Bangang setting fire to the stadium. Inter Avenue subsequently burned to the ground and the club went into liquidation. The land on which the stadium had been built was sold to a local sheep farmer for £1.58.

It then transpired that this version of events was a propaganda myth concocted by the Anti-Mr Bangang Gang to make themselves look good. While they hadn't succeeded in their aim of killing Mr Bangang they decided to take the credit for the next best thing – ie having reduced him to a pathetic penniless wretch. It emerged that Bangang had in fact become an eccentric recluse who now spent his time writing obscure and incomprehensible philosophical tracts having voluntarily given his fortune away to the camp TV presenter Dale Winton. I came up with the alcoholic story while my brother James invented the Winton version.

However it was debatable as to which version of events was

gospel, as there was no legal ruling on who held the rights to the official Mr Bangang canon. The legal battle continues to this day.

Other less famous characters included an unscrupulous bank manager called Jehosophias P Staybacksir and a furry rodent called "Jeremy The Hamster", who despite his name was in fact a gerbil. As stated above such fantasies rarely followed the basic rules of logic and reason.

There were also rival arch villains Wibble Wogan and Peeny McQuacket as well as the mysterious Mungo Beansprout, although no-one seems to know who he was or what he did.

Like many children of my generation I spent my formative years reading comics. This may have had some role in the inspiration behind Mr Bangang. I started on the likes of the *Beano* and *Dandy* (as had my parents before me) and followed the implausible weekly adventures of Desperate Dan, Dennis the Menace, Minnie the Minx and the Bash Street Kids (and their canine equivalents the Pup Parade), children who never seemed to age. Although this was the 1980s the comics seemed to have a quaint outdated 1950s view of society. The teachers wore mortarboards and gowns, and would whack disobedient pupils on the backside with a cane. All the dads sported toothbrush moustaches, Bobby Charlton style comb-overs and pin-stripe suits and would threaten their children with a slipper if there was a hint of insurrection in the air, while the mums wore aprons and had curlers in their hair. Characters would flee in terror as soon as their mothers told them it was bathtime. For some reason cleanliness and hygiene were frowned upon.

I later graduated to more mature and gritty publications like *Eagle*, *Battle Action Force* and *2000 AD* and *Roy of the Rovers*. The latter was a collection of idealised football stories. The title character Roy Race was captain of a successful club which had its share of ups and downs. A typical scenario would have Roy's team in the FA Cup final trailing by five goals to nil against the mighty Arsenham City, with two minutes remaining. Suddenly spurred on by their inspirational captain the Rovers would stage a remarkable comeback to win 6-5, with the winning goal being scored in the very last second of injury time, usually a freak shot from the goalkeeper's downfield clearance.

I even started my own comic "Scrap" while at primary school and sold copies to classmates at 10p each. It was a combination of humorous stories, sport, action adventure and science fiction and included a gaelic football version of Roy of the Rovers which followed the fortunes of a fictitious West Tyrone club called Kildrum. Although the comic was called "Scrap" the letter S at the beginning was in hindsight probably surplus to requirements.

Scrap was one of many creative enterprises I immersed myself in during my youth with varying degrees of success.

I've done quite a lot of writing during the (almost) four decades I've spent on the earth. Most of it has remained unpublished – and in some cases justifiably so. Until now that is. I kept my first diary in 1982 at the age of eight. I didn't buy the diary till half way through January though, which meant there was two week's worth of blank pages at the beginning. As I couldn't remember what had happened during this time I decided to fill in the space by writing a story. I recently re-discovered this diary in my parents' loft, so here is the unabridged story of the Swamp Monster (I had scant regard for punctuation and paragraphing in those days):

1982 January
4 Monday
Week 1 (4-361)
BANK HOLIDAY IN SCOTLAND

"I am writing a story because I can't remember what happened these days". (sic).

Swamp Monster. Part 1
Out of the swamp came a huge monster. He had big green eyes. And his hair was made of swamp weed and his body made of hard turf. He walked a thousand miles

96

until he came to a city. He stamped his huge green foot. And the ground opened up. Sky scrapers collapsed. The bridge collapsed. Fighter planes crowded the sky. The creature breathed poisonus (sic) gases. All the pilots died. The planes were on fire and they crashed. A man was on fire! The monster stamped on him unaware. Army lorries came with fire throwers. All at once the lorries shot fire throwers at the monster. He was on fire. I forgot to say that the

Tuesday 5
5-360) Week 1
Monster's nose was covered in limpets. Meanwhile in Belfast three giant robot scorpions who were controlled by the monster were blocking the traffic. A scorpion's tail smashed the window of a bus. It hit the driver in the eyes blinding him. A man fired a grenade at the scorpion. The robot scorpion was destroyed. The monster (who was still on fire) hurled himself into the sea. On the News the newscaster said a huge monster has come into Roggum City [a fictitious place possibly inspired by Batman's Gotham City] and caused a lot of damage. He stamped his foot and the ground opened up. The monster walked to New York. He blew very hard and there was a wind all the skyscrapers fell down. The skyscrapers were on fire. Two million fighter planes and tanks fired bombs at him. A swarm of giant

6 Wednesday
Week 1 (6-359)
EPIPHANY

Killer bees crowded the sky. Two bees ate a plane. The monster breathed poisonus (sic) gas at the planes. The bees shot acid at the tanks. A bee was eat the Empire State Building (sic). A man fired a bomb at the bee. The bee turned into dust. An android monster was fighting the real monster. A giant robot crab grabbed the real monster's leg and the real monster fell down. The weed slowly turned to stone. The monster rose up and ripped the android monster open. He bit the android monster in half. Then the android monster turned into dust. The monster began to eat

The story stops abruptly here. I suspect my mum was calling me for dinner at the time or something good came on TV or some similar distraction had ensued. As a result the pages between the 7th and 15th of January remain blank. To this day I still have no idea what it was the monster had begun to eat. In hindsight the story reads suspiciously like Ted Hughes' *The Iron Man* fused with *King Kong* fused with *Godzilla* and the various killer bee movies (in both senses of the term) and other monster/disaster films of the era.

Swamp Monster was by no means the only piece of science fiction I wrote. I was 11 when I (very ambitiously) attempted my first novel during the very wet summer of 1985. It was the weird transition zone between primary and secondary school and it seemed to rain every day. In fact it had been the wettest summer in living memory. But that's neither here nor there.
I don't remember giving the novel a name, but for convenience purposes I'll call it *The Destons*. It was a sci-fic epic about a reptilian alien race called the Destons. Their home planet VarLeck 37 was a decaying world ravaged by centuries of internal nuclear wars and its fuel resources were due to run out. In order to acquire further energy sources the Destons from their base on the Moon were plotting an invasion of Earth to steal its coal and oil supplies

so their planet could be given a new lease of life. I'm not sure why they didn't think of investing in solar power, tidal or wind energy, but then it's not the sort of the thing an 11 year old would consider.

Destons was heavily influenced by *Doctor Who* and the works of people like Arthur C. Clarke, Isaac Asimov and John Wyndham. Although it was set in the near future of 2035 it was both of topical and local interest and also had an ecological message behind it. At the time a lignite seam had been discovered near Lough Neagh's western shore. There was talk of mining the area, a proposal which met with a great deal of local opposition. The Destons had somehow caught wind of this lignite mine and under the command of their leader President Zarnod of the Morkongholoid race planned to launch their invasion in County Tyrone, so they could enslave the local population and force them to work in the mines. The hero was a 12-year old boy called Harry Crayfield who comes across their spaceship while out walking his dog on the bog. He tries to alert of the world of the imminent invasion, but the adults refuse to believe him. I don't think I had a clear idea in my head as to how the book ends, but it was probably something along the lines of young Harry saving the world by thwarting the Destons' plans just in the nick of the time.

I have no idea where the original manuscript for "Destons" is – that is if still exists, but from memory its opening lines were something like this:

> "Never again would the cry of the curlew be heard above the bog. The peaceful silence of the heather would be soon be shattered by the mechanical sound of bulldozers and diggers now that the area had been earmarked as a mine to provide a new source of energy. But someone else had other plans…"

I think this must have been partially inspired by a TV commercial for that much-maligned local beer I referred to earlier.

The novel fizzled out towards the end of the summer and was never resurrected. Until now that is. In any case the plot was totally implausible. I mean the idea of a foreign empire invading a territory in order to plunder its energy resources? A war fought over a fossil fuel? No-one would buy that. Joking aside I can now look back in retrospect and take the view that my unfinished novel would have worked quite well as a contemporary political allegory. I did however submit a short story spin-off involving the Destons for the school magazine during my first year at the new school. It didn't get published much to my annoyance.

I stopped reading comics at the age of 12. Ironically a few years later I went back to reading comics – or more specifically *one* particular comic. I first came across that disgusting (yet sometimes incredibly funny) rag called *Viz* at the age of 15 or 16 when a copy (owned by a chap called Declan McKillop who would later join me on the school magazine editorial committee) was doing the rounds of the fourth year classrooms.

The idea that a comic could contain bad language, extreme violence (albeit rather surreal cartoon-style violence), biting satire and "adult" humour (although adolescent or schoolboy/student humour may be a more appropriate description) was a novel one. Another major appealing factor was that I'd read more traditional children's comics of the day like the *Beano* and *Dandy* in my youth, but *Viz* went a step further by employing a similar style, yet creating grotesque parodies of these familiar characters.
We're misleadingly brought up from an early age to believe in a sense of natural justice and that good will always triumph over evil. When we get older the sense of disappointment on learning that this isn't true hits us like a tree blowing down in a storm. *Viz* hits the nail on the head here, as unlike in traditional children's comics where despite many setbacks the underdog triumphs over the bully in the end, there is often no sense of natural justice as it's usually the underdog who suffers a cruel fate at the hands of his oppressor.

The comedian Billy Connolly, when questioned about his style once said words to the effect of "I'd like to think I'm 'dangerous' - I'd love to imagine there's a 14-year old somewhere listening to one of my tapes, but he's got the volume turned down low, because he doesn't want his parents to know". In many ways I was that

14-year old, as were many of my contemporaries, although I wasn't a huge fan of Connolly. It was a similar illicit thrill with *Viz*. Smuggling copies into your bedroom under the noses of your parents was all part of the adventure.

It was during that time of life when there are certain things you can't legally do. So buying *Viz* at the newsagents was like the thrill of getting served alcohol on licensed premises or being admitted to an 18 cert film when you're still only 17¾.

I'm not sure if I should be admitting this, but over 20 years later I'm still an avid reader.

7

Metalmania

At the tail-end of the 1980s heavy metal, which had for years been a rather marginal genre was now becoming mainstream. Bands like Guns N Roses, Iron Maiden, Metallica and Poison were storming the charts. At the other end of the scale were Bros, Brother Beyond (probably now residing in the proverbial "Where-Are-They-Now?" File – otherwise known as the dole office) and the highly irritating American boy band New Kids On The Block (or as a classmate used to call them "New Dicks on the Cock"), the Antipodean pairing of gay-icon-to-be Kylie Minogue and washed-out hasbeen-to-be Jason Donovan, cashing in on the success of the trashy Australian soap *Neighbours* which for some bizarre, inexplicable reason was incredibly popular at the time. If you liked any of these bands you were labelled "gay". Presumably it was officially OK to like them if you were actually gay, but with homophobia being more widespread than would nowadays be acceptable, particularly in an area where other prejudices like racism and sectarianism thrived, no 15 year old would have dared come out.

Talking of which, Queen's penultimate Freddie Mercury-fronted album The Miracle had just come out. I hesitate to admit that I was a Queen fan back then. They had gone out of fashion years ago and listening to Queen alongside the likes of fellow stadium rockers such as U2, Dire Straits and Genesis was considered very uncool.

Then there was Marillion whose ex-lead singer the hefty balding, mullet-haired Fish wore a fish-shaped ear-ring and wrote pseudo-intellectual lyrics reminiscent of sixth form school magazine poetry to accompany the elaborate artwork on the sleeves. Around this time Fish was leaving or about to leave the band. One rock magazine described them as the band who inspired a whole generation of nerdy, girlfriendless, provincial university students to bad poetry and bedsit angst. Although I still like Marillion some 20 years later (albeit with considerably less enthusiasm than during my idealistic youth), I will concede that this description isn't completely inaccurate.

Fish was replaced by Steve Hogarth who never had the same commercial success as the Piscean one, but managed to remain in the band a damn sight longer – 23 years and counting.

I even used Marillion lyrics in my A-level English literature exams. I passed them off as my own words though rather than ascribing them to Marillion as I don't think the examiners would have been impressed by me quoting an unfashionable prog rock band from Aylesbury who they probably wouldn't have heard of. As I type these very words the speakers of my computer are blasting out Marillion's latest offering *Sounds That Can't Be Made* – although some of you may be thinking that *Sounds That Shouldn't Be Made* would be a more appropriate title. So 23 years after experiencing my first Marillion album (a CD borrowed from the library which I copied to a blank cassette tape) as a 16 year old in my bedroom studying for my GCSE exams and fantasising about imaginary girlfriends I've gone around in complete circles – an ageing schoolboy listening to a bunch of ageing rockers…

I actually had quite diverse tastes in music depending on the mood I was in. I liked both Enya and Guns N Roses for instance. Enya's ethereal mysticism and Celtic dreamlike easy listening qualities contrasted nicely with the bad boys of LA metal and their politically incorrect songs about crack whores and motherfuckers. While Axl and co were busy cavorting in hot tub jacuzzis and snorting coke through hundred dollar bills from the naked bodies of glamorous groupies, Enya was probably happy to sit in quiet contemplation in the conservatory over a cup of mint tea and an organic oatcake. Each to their own I suppose.

I didn't have long hair or go around wearing a denim jacket with the sleeves cut off or a studded leather codpiece or any of that. I merely observed the metalmania phenomenon from a safe distance in between learning about osmosis, evapotranspiration, photosynthesis, coastal erosion, the chemical properties of industrial solvents, isosceles triangles, Seamus Heaney's poetic tales of frogs on bogs, pregnant cows and drowned kittens, how to order a kilo of tomatoes if you were ever in Salamanca and a dozen other long-forgotten concepts.

I still had a fascination from an anthropological point of view for the tribalism and culture based around the genre. Tattered copies of the industrial journals *Metal Hammer* and *Kerraannggg* (sic) would circulate around the classrooms smuggled inside copies of Macbeth or GCSE Biology. The centrefold pull-out poster usually featured heavily tattooed young men with bleached blonde shoulder length hair in sleeveless tops and ripped jeans (also invariably bleached) (for some reason discoloured jeans with holes in them were highly fashionable back then) clutching a bottle of Jack Daniels, the other arm around a topless young woman. It all seems rather tame by today's standards, but for testosterone-fuelled 16-year olds in pre-internet time when real porn was hard to come by, especially in a smallish provincial town in a very socially conservative society where newsagents generally didn't sell top shelf material - or if they did it tended to be kept under the counter (or so I'm told) – it was often the next best thing. Although the real thing did occasionally circulate around the classrooms. One particular individual who shall remain strictly nameless had a bit of a reputation as a purveyor of such material. He would bring his "wares" into the classroom – until (or so the story goes) the incriminating publications were found by his mother under his bed while she was cleaning his room. As a result of this unfortunate discovery he was apparently put under virtual house arrest for the next six years until his twenty-first birthday and banned from going out in the evenings. Although this story may have been exaggerated for dramatic effect. Another equally nameless and rather unfortunate individual was apparently caught "in flagrante delicto" watching a dodgy video by his mother who had come home from work unexpectedly early. I wouldn't like to speculate about what happened next.

And then there were the two eejits (again whose names I won't mention) who spent one lunchtime going around the travel agents in the town looking for brochures on sun-kissed Mediterranean resorts in the pathetic hope of finding pictures of nubile women sunbathing topless. For the benefit of any young people a travel agents was a place you went to book your holiday or flight before the internet was invented. Ok, I'm just being patronising so I'll stop now.

There was a notorious American heavy metal act called HÖRNETS who played a gig in Belfast around 1989, on the European leg of the tour to promote their new album *Decapitated Corpses*. A bus from Omagh was laid on specially organised by the local record shop. On board was a motley crew of local schoolboy metalheads.

As well as being the name of a brightly coloured insect with a sting in the tail the name was also apparently an acronym as it was spelt "H.Ö.R.N.E.T.S" on the album covers in upper case with a dot between each letter and a superfluous umlaut over the O to give the band a Gothic Germanic feel. However no-one was quite sure what the letters stood for. It was the subject of an early morning classroom debate before lessons began.

The band members were renowned for their "bad boy" image along with their sordid on-stage antics, raunchy videos and sexually explicit, expletive-laden lyrics, facts which naturally became grossly exaggerated by school boy fans.

"They rape live hamsters live on stage. And as part of the encore they eat human entrails!"

"I heard the drummer spontaneously combusts at the end of every gig!"

"So what does HORNETS stand for anyway?"

"Harbingers Of Rage-inducing Narcotics Enslaved To Satan."

"Does it shite! It's Hell-spawned Onanists Revelling in Never-Ending Torture."

"But that just spells HORNET."

"What's an onanist?"

"Dunno. I think it's somebody who sells onions."

"Like them French boys with the berets and the striped jerseys?"

"Aye, I think so. Anyway, it stands for Homicidal Objects of Retribution, Nothingness & Eternal Terror"

"That still spells just HORNET."

"I know. They just added the S at the end to confuse people."

"Actually, it means Holocaust Of Ruin/Nazi Everlasting Tyranny Squad"

"Well I read an interview with them in the latest issue of *Satanic Moshpit* and they just said they used the names of each band member – Henry, Oliver, Robert, Nigel, Earnest Together in Stereo."

"How could it! The lead singer's called Whitey Uncontrollable for fuck's sake!"

"But his real name's Henry. Henry Uncontrollable. They all have day jobs you know. One works in a bank, the drummer's a civil servant – and the bass player's a librarian..."

"Has anyone heard *Decaffeinated Corpses* (sic) then?"

"No, I only drink real coffee".

And so on...ad nauseam.

Legend has it that that the band's frontman was asked in an interview what the name stood for and was alleged to have said:

"I'm HOnestly Really Not Exactly Totally Sure".

A fight broke out at the Belfast HORNETS gig and made the late night local TV news. But it was more likely to have been due to a combination of alcohol (and possibly some less legal stimulants), exuberance and testosterone rather than sparked off by an argument over what the band's initials stood for. In this case "Heavily Orchestrated Rioting – Not Entirely Trouble-free (Sigh)" would have been appropriate. Apparently the rioting spilled out of the concert hall and on to the streets. Police were pelted with bottles and cans. On the positive front however this was a rare example of politico-religious harmony between nationalist and unionist youths. The two rival tribes had on this occasion happily set aside their differences and found a common bond in their mutual love of heavy metal and violence. How refreshing it was that they had got together to attack the cops rather than each other for a change. And there wasn't even a single mention of Sherlock Holmes - in an existential context or otherwise.

The gig had taken place on a school night. Some boys didn't make it into class the following day. Their absence didn't go unnoticed, especially in Mr Horgan's biology class. Apparently a lot of alcohol had been consumed on the bus to and from the venue. The unfortunate driver had been forced to stop at several points on the way back to let the passengers empty the contents of their bladders and stomachs. I don't envy the poor sod who had to clean up the bus.

Heavy metal music has long been criticised by authority figures from priests to politicians to parents for allegedly exerting a bad influence on young people and encouraging wayward youth to indulge in devil-worshipping. We did have a few would-be Satanists at the school, but in reality they probably didn't know the difference between a pentagram and a pentathlon. In fact the nearest they got to witchcraft was the time they made that pointy hat for their younger sister to wear at the Hallowe'en fancy dress party down at the youth club.

One member of this coven, in order to prove his obeisance to the forces of darkness wrote "Satin Rules" in felt tip on his schoolbag. I suppose he had a point. High lustre weaves with glossy surfaces made from silken filament fibres do tend to be of superior quality to similar weaves derived from cotton or polyester.

Inspired by HORNETS and their ilk a plethora of schoolboy heavy metal bands suddenly sprang up in the town with names like Psychosis, Sanatorium and Savage. But there was no danger of them upstaging the town's best known musician, a down-and-out "busker" (I use the word advisedly) known as Arty G who had seen better days. Arty was one of the town's best known characters, who would play the guitar, usually with a few strings missing, and sing badly in a slurred voice in the main shopping area between the bank and the supermarket, a bottle of extra strong cider and a small dog always by his side. Although he cut something of a pitiful figure who had clearly had happier times in the past, he was generally liked by the townsfolk and revered as a local institution. Various urban myths about his colourful past abounded – that he had once been a highly successful musician and had played alongside the likes of the Rolling Stones and toured Japan with Deep Purple in his youth. After Arty passed away in 2007 he received one of the biggest funerals the town had ever seen. There's now even a plaque dedicated to his memory in the town. His wide bulging eyes and unruly mop of fuzzy afro-style hair were a familiar site in the town centre for many years. You can now even see footage of him on YouTube. He even got a mention on BBC Radio 4's weekly obituary slot *The Last Word*.

I remember one geography A-level class when we were studying the concept of industrial and economic development in less favoured regions. Government subsidies known as "Regional Development Grants" – or RDGs (which sounds a bit like "Arty Gs") – were available to these areas. This caused a few titters although it went above the teacher's head as she wasn't a local.

The Summer of '89

Just like the summer of 20 years earlier as experienced by Bryan Adams, the summer of '89 also seemed to last forever. But this was largely because I had far too much time on my hands. By the time I started looking for a summer job it was a bit too late as most of the few jobs available to school boys had been snapped up already.

In a pathetic attempt to get in with the metal crowd I even bought a ticket for the Anthrax gig in the rather incongruous setting of Omagh GAA. Even now the idea of an internationally famous rock act like Anthrax playing in a backwater like Omagh - and at the local GAA club of all places - seems nothing short of surreal. Despite rumours from classmates that anyone with short hair attending a heavy metal gig would get beaten up I went anyway – or at least went to the venue. A record shop called Top Pop in Bridge Street, which is now long gone and I believe (but could be wrong) is now a health food shop – perhaps anyone from Omagh old enough to remember could verify this. The ticket was a rather dull yellowish-brown piece of cardboard, not like the glossy silvery multicoloured tickets you get these days.

When I arrived at the venue I decided I didn't really want to go, so decided to cut my losses and sell the ticket at a profit for £11. I had been about to sell it to Brian Corry for its face value, but then got a better offer from a well-fed older lad. I even remember the details of the £10 note he handed me. It was a Scottish banknote with the Victorian explorer David Livingstone and some African slaves in chains. If I remember correctly Brian got in free in the end by virtue of playing for the gaelic football team, so it was happy days all round. 20 years later I found out that himself and his mate Mike Cathcart had got to meet the band after taking the back lane into the premises, but were eventually chucked out by Anthrax's security staff. Something to tell the grandchildren about I suppose.

I'd got the last laugh. It was my first and to date only experience of ticket touting. I suppose to a 15 year old in those days £3.00 would have been considered a not unreasonable sum – it would have bought you half a cassette tape album or two *Viz* comics.

Apparently Anthrax complained about being spat on by the audience and vowed never to play in Ireland again. At the time this practice known as "gobbing" I believe was a common occurrence at heavy metal gigs at the time – but have no idea why. Anthrax's loss was Ireland's gain. And now some 23 summers down the line they're still very much on the go and up there in the "Big Four" of thrash metal alongside fellow elderly rockers Slayer, Metallica and Megadeth – but they're unlikely to return to Omagh any time soon.

8

Retreat from Reality

There are various urban myths (and probably a fair few rural myths as well) in Northern Ireland relating to how you can tell the difference between a Catholic and a Protestant. Among the more ludicrous ones relates to the distance between one's eyes, though I'm not exactly which tribe is supposed have their eyes further apart. Another, which is partially true relates to the pronunciation of the letter H. Those of the reformed faith will apparently say "aitch" with a silent H, whereas adherents of the Roman church will say "haitch". There is however one day of the year when you can definitely spot the difference. Every Ash Wednesday there would be a morning mass in the school to mark the beginning of Lent. The school chaplain would anoint the foreheads of pupils and staff with wet ashes. It was supposed to be the shape of a cross, but as the priest tended to do it quickly as he had a whole congregation to go through it would invariably be more like a formless blob. So every Ash Wednesday you would see people walking around the town with big brown smudges on their foreheads. In a place where religion is a form of cultural expression and identity and where creed, culture and politics all blend into one and are often used to have a go at the "other side", people would wear their ashes with pride, in much the same way as poppies, Easter lilies, shamrocks, Orange sashes or football jerseys of either one of two well-known Glasgow clubs would be worn. Having said that, poppies and shamrocks are not necessarily worn exclusively by one community, but that's a whole different kettle of ball games, which I have neither the time nor the inclination to go into.

The symbolism behind the Ash Wednesday anointment – that we're all mere mortals on a short journey through life and will end up as ashes - is reasonable enough in itself. But walking around with a big smudge on your forehead does seem to be taking things a bit far. Some of the more rebellious boys were of this opinion and would go into the toilets as soon as the mass was over and wash their ashes off.

There's an old joke told once by a relatively well-known local comedian (ie relatively well-known within Northern Ireland, but unheard of anywhere else) that the shipyard workers in Belfast used to be let out early on Ash Wednesday (or "Spot-the-Taigs Day" as they called it). They would allegedly walk the streets with a hammer behind their backs and approach unsuspecting anointed Catholics with the question:

"How did you get that bruise on your forehead, mate?"

"It's not a bruise, it's the holy ashes!" would come the indignant reply.

"Well it's a bruise now!" the shipyard workers would shout as they produced their hammers.

From an early age we were encouraged to give things up for Lent. This would usually mean abstaining or at least trying to abstain from sweets for 40–odd days.

I remember my mum complaining about TV ads for confectionery during this period of fasting and abstinence. "They shouldn't have ads for sweets on during Lent" she said.

I can just imagine the directors of Nestlé, Cadburys and Mars (other confectionery manufacturers are available) sitting around the boardroom table with the head of the Broadcasting Standards Agency at a specially arranged EGM.

"OK, following a motion from Mrs Ward of Omagh we propose to suspend all advertising of confectionery products for a period of 40 days every spring. All those in favour raise your hand."

I can picture a number of bemused looking executives exchanging worried glances, as if to say "Has he gone mad?", one of whom probably has a brown smudge on his forehead in the form of a misshapen cross.

Whether you're religious or not, the concept of giving things up for a set period of time, a practice common to many religions is a noble one. Spiritual matters aside, self-denial and self-discipline are useful forms of character building. And with all due respect to Mum, she was missing the point in that banning such advertising would defeat the purpose of Lent – ie if the temptation is no longer there, then you're not really resisting it, and therefore the concept of self-discipline becomes effectively redundant. In any case banning the promotion of chocolate products in the run-up to Easter would be commercial suicide.

There was however one day of the year when we were allowed to break Lent - St Patrick's Day – presumably this concept evolved from the adult practice of what was known as drowning one's shamrock every 17th March – ie having a drink or three or thirteen on the national day. Adults who had given up the booze for Lent could hardly be expected to remain dry on this day of all days. In any case it was so inconsiderate of St Patrick to die during Lent. Having lived in England for several years now I find it ironic that this day is a bigger event on the eastern side of the Irish Sea than St George's Day, which has always been a fairly low key event. Poor George killed an evil dragon (something the Welsh weren't best pleased with), yet Pat just kicked a few harmless snakes out and gets all the credit. Despite the fact that dragons never existed and there never were any snakes in Ireland to begin with – unless while he was at it he got rid of all the snake fossils on the island. Come to think of it Paddy is the only patron saint of our Hiberno-Britannic archipelago to have a bank holiday in his honour in the respective jurisdictions.

March is often a strange time of year. Easter eggs are already in the shops, having been there since early January. Daffodils set the countryside alight with colour and pubs throughout England's green (and yellow) pleasant land celebrate a famous British saint adopted by Ireland – and I don't mean Jack Charlton. In a convenient tie-in with the Six Nations rugby (now what clever marketing executive came up with that idea?) the cardboard shamrocks are hanging on the wall, the Guinness balloons are out and the silly leprechaun hats have rolled off the production line. Many of the pubs around London (and not just the Irish ones) already have the full regalia hanging outside. Come March 17th these establishments will inevitably be packed to the rafters with punters, plastic paddy or otherwise in tacky leprechaun hats and false red beards singing and dancing (or at least attempting to) along to the Dubliners, the Pogues or whoever. The beer and whisky flows regardless from Boston to Buenos Aires, but those with a real cause to celebrate are no doubt the directors and shareholders of Diageo plc.

Some years ago I remember the latest Paddy's day gimmick in the supermarkets was Guinness flavoured marmite. I enjoy the occasional pint of the black velvet devil's buttermilk (responsibly and in moderation of course – well most of the time anyway), but marmite was never a regular dietary feature of mine. I vaguely remember Guinness flavour ice cream coming out back in the swirling mists of time, then vanishing without a trace. It looks like the black and creamy spread went the same way. What will it be next – Fosters flavour vegemite? Magners flavoured apple crumble? Cheese and onion flavour crisps? The mind boggles.

Anyway, getting back to my schooldays after that digression - being a religious school, retreats were compulsory. They served little practical purpose though. Sending a bunch of unruly adolescent boys oozing with hormones on a residential course of supposed spiritual renewal was a recipe for disaster. Although their purpose was supposedly to provide sacred reflection in the tradition of the school's ethos, they were in reality, a complete waste of time – a view that I'm sure many of the teachers would even share. These retreats were usually chaired by an earnest young priest who liked to think he was in touch with the angst and frustrated minds of the modern youth. On one such event held at an old priory in the historic village of Benburb, the site of the Battle of Benburb of 1646. The youngish priest presiding over this supposed course of spiritual renewal happened to be German. For convenience purposes let's just call him "Father Von Schumacher". The cringe-worthy events which ensued were like that famous episode of *Fawlty Towers* where the concussed hotel proprietor ends up insulting his German guests. Cue Basil Fawlty style Nazi jokes, goose-stepping around the grounds, Nazi salutes, etc.

There was a totally pointless group session in which pupils would get into pairs and ask each other what their favourite food was,

114

what deadly disease they would compare themselves most to and how would attempt to solve the famines, diseases and wars of the world armed only with a blunt pencil and a plastic carrier bag. The findings of these "questionnaires" would then be reported back to the group.

One cringeworthy session went as follows:

Q: Where would you most like to live?

A: The Berlin Bunker

Q: Favourite film?

A: "Sink the Bismarck"

The next day the entire class was hauled before the teacher in charge who had a few stern words to say. Given the troubled political situation of the time he said he could understand why we were "angry young men", but why did we have to take it out on a harmless German priest? He had a point I suppose.

I would bump into Fr Von Schumacher again a year later when the same priory was used for an A-Level French immersion weekend attended by students from all over the north-west, who were considerably better behaved than the previous year's retreaters. I don't think he recognised us though. He greeted us in French.

The following year – my last year at the school the retreat was residential. It was around March or April of 1992. The master in charge of our entourage was a small, but firm no-nonsense man called Simon Van Ventersdorp. Because he was a model aeroplane enthusiast he was sometimes known as "The Flying Dutchman" – even though despite his name he came from Donegal and not the Netherlands or the Transvaal. But he was more commonly known among pupils as "Vents", "The Vent" or "The Dorp". And this neatly brings me on to my next rant. We were often told at school to never start a sentence with "but", "and" or "because". I'm not sure why as there is no rule of grammar which states this. Because of that I'm going to do precisely that. And because there's no-one to mark my work now I'm going to keep on doing it. Because it's my own book I'm writing I'll do whatever I like. And that's that. Indeed. Because.

The most important exams of our school career were just around the corner, yet we were being forced to go on this pointless overnight excursion which would be as much use as a pork butchers stall in a mosque. Anything we'd be told on this retreat we'd heard it all before. Even if you were one of the more pious boys who was into that sort of stuff there was nothing to stop you from doing it in your own time. All the local churches organised regular retreats anyway to Lough Derg or Knock, which you were free to go on and in the presence of much more willing participants – if you were that way inclined of course. And worse still we were being forced to pay (or get the money off our parents) for the privilege. It was supposedly compulsory, even though we had to pay for it, but that would be difficult to enforce in a court of law. Suffice to say, no-one took the school to court as far as I'm aware.

There was a three hour bus journey to the centre which was located on the northern outskirts of Dublin, but the bus broke down just a few miles from our destination. We were forced to walk the remainder of the journey. Actually we weren't, but it would embellish the story a little. The driver managed to fix the problem and we were (unfortunately) back on our way.

On arrival at the centre we were forced to get off the bus, but leave our bags on board for "inspection". This gave Vents the chance to search everybody's bag for hidden contraband. Many of us were over 18, so legally we were "adults" old enough to vote, go to prison, get married, drink alcohol or fight in a war, but we still had to capitulate to the demands of a smaller, but older man.

The Flying Dutchman's suspicions were confirmed when he struck gold, finding several cans of beer in Darren "Benji" Keogh's bag, which he duly confiscated. You couldn't get away with that nowadays. It would be an invasion of privacy. Vents would no doubt be dragged before the European Court of Human Rights charged with violating the fundamental human right of a schoolboy to drink beer on an otherwise boring retreat. Though apparently he did reimburse Benji for the cost of the beer. It would liven up the

116

story if I were to say that the Flying D was looking quite rough and dishevelled at breakfast the next day and that slurred singing had been heard coming from his room the previous night – but unfortunately this didn't happen.

I'll not go into too much detail about the blasphemous and sacrilegious behaviour which ensued, resulting in decapitated statues of Jesus and Mary, crucifixes defaced, intoxicated goldfish, water pistols that squirted holy water, pupils drunk on communion wine plundered from the sacristy, toasted communion wafers served for breakfast, the school minibus in flames... (Ok, I just made that last bit up – and a few of the other bits as well – ok, *most* of the other bits then - but I won't say which bits).

In between all this we had some recreational time. There were handball courts in the grounds. I remember attempting to play a game with Peter Meehan and Ciaran Curran (the latter was known to be rather good at the game) – till some immature and irritating tosser who shall remain nameless invaded the court and ran off with the ball in the tradition of Aesop's dog in the manger – and as I said earlier we were supposed to be "adults".

There was a trendy young priest at the centre called Jim who played the guitar, wore Joe Bloggs jeans and a t-shirt bearing the logo of the popular indie band James. There was also a youngish nun called Phyl, who like the others chose to forgo the habit and dress in civilian clothes. The sessions were all well-meaning, but of little value at the end of the day. I was actually glad to be getting back. To normality.

Or at least what passed for normality in for a school boy in Omagh.

-9-
Rhythm & Booze

Towards the later period of my school days drinking alcohol (or more specifically getting drunk) had become a popular hobby. There were mad parties when parents had gone away for the weekend, leaving their (or so they thought) very reliable, responsible and positively angelic sons in charge. Stories of such indulgence were the talk of the classroom on Monday mornings. They would usually be along the lines of:

"We had this brilliant party at Swiggsy's house. His folks were away for the weekend. And we all got completely slaughtered! That peach schnapps is lethal stuff you know. And Terry McCanny drank a whole bottle of Southern Comfort. He was on his knees in the bog all night puking his guts out! I don't even remember how we got home! It was a class night!"

So being violently sick and virtually incapacitated was supposed to be how to have a good time? It is indeed a strange, contradictory world in which we live.

I myself occasionally indulged. It's not something I'm proud of, and wouldn't recommend it to young people, but a rite of passage however misguided which many of us go through during our naïve youth.

I remember on a trip to the theatre in Belfast one weekday evening when our year group was taken to see a production of Sean O'Casey's *The Plough and the Stars*. During the journey there, Mr Muldoon the teacher in charge (a.k.a Larry) who was either acting on an anonymous tip-off or a hunch searched Stevie Conolly's bag to find several cans of beer inside.

"Sir they're not mine!" he protested rather unconvincingly. One was almost expecting him to back up his protests of innocence in the manner of Cockney villains in the 1970s cop show *The*

Sweeney who when caught red-handed with the jewellery in their pockets come out with tirades like:

"I ain't never seen 'em before in me bleedin' life. Guv! Straight up! I swear on me muvva's life!!!"

And the unimpressed Flying Squad detective as he clicks the handcuffs shut retorts:

"Shut it you slag! Your old mum snuffed it ten years ago. Move it, pal, you're nicked!"

Larry didn't quite use these words, but during the rest of the journey to Belfast a preliminary on-board inquest was conducted and continued back at school the next day.

We even have an entire culture based around various tribes and the type of beverages they imbibe. There is the 1980s phenomenon of the "lager lout" on the football terraces or the beaches of Ibiza, the stereotype of the bearded, jam-jar bespectacled "real ale twat" from *Viz* comic and in the upper strata of the society the Pimms brigade. The local pub is the social hub of a rural village or urban district, the source of gossip, where business deals are conducted, where friends and partners are made, but also where fights and arguments start and where lives are ruined.

When I was growing up in the 1980s alcohol advertising was all over the television, on giant billboard posters and on the shirts of famous footballers. This may still be the case today, but it seemed to be much more prominent back then. Although I grew up in a household where alcohol consumption was mostly confined to the odd glass of wine or sherry at Christmas or very occasionally to accompany the Sunday roast, had you asked the 11-year old Ciaran Ward back in 1985 how many brands of alcoholic drinks he could name, he could have reeled off about ten. Off the top of my head without resorting to Google the following slogans spring to mind which as an 11-year old I could have recited verbatim:

"Harp – Very much to a Viking's liking" (as seen on billboard poster and on TV ads circa 1985)

"Get into the good taste of Guinness/Have a Guinness tonight" (Various TV ads around the same period)

"Smithwicks at the heart of the night/Smithwicks – it's one great beer" (as above)

"Great stuff this Bass"

"Carlsberg – probably the best lager in the world" (spoken in a voice similar to that of Spock from Star Trek, but I'm not sure if it was definitely him)

"Fosters – the Australian for lager"

"Martini – anytime, anywhere"

All very disturbing when you consider the devastating affect alcohol has had on society.

Nevertheless, many of these ads were not surprisingly quite entertaining and innovative, given the fact that the drinks manufacturers spent and continue to spend millions on promoting their wares. One particularly eye-catching commercial from the mid-80s was for a now long defunct variety of lager known as Lamot. It featured an animated film of a knight in armour riding a tiger-like creature through a Tolkienesque fantasy sword and sorcery-type landscape reminiscent of an Iron Maiden album cover on a quest to seek out this bog-standard beer. Such imagery would appeal to a 12-year old hobbit obsessive, who may never have tasted beer, but would certainly be imbued with the desire to try this particular brand. You can even check the ad out on Youtube.

It would be several years before I drank my first pint – as a naïve, awkward teenager my early experiences were with cider, then graduating to lager with a shot of lime to make it more agreeable to my inexperienced palate. But repeated exposure to the apparent pleasures and thrills of drinking alcohol during my schooldays through ruthless advertising had certainly whetted my appetite. And a few short years later those clever chaps in the drinks industry came up with a solution to the "problem" of awkward teenagers like my younger self being unfamiliar with alcohol by producing "alco-pops", a cynical, almost criminal exploitation of the market for underage drinkers.

The impact of alcohol advertising on a pre-teen as described above is somewhat disturbing when one considers the culture of underage drinking and the binge sessions which occur throughout our towns, villages and cities on any Friday or Saturday night. And as if this wasn't enough, during freshers' week at universities up and down the country there are organised pub crawls and special offers of cheap drink.

Such has been the impact of alcohol on Irish society that we even have an organisation dedicated to abstinence, the Pioneers. I remember being confirmed at the age of 11 and taking the traditional pledge, along with all my classmates not to drink alcohol before my 18th birthday. I took it quite seriously at the time, but it fell by the wayside after a few years when I succumbed to peer pressure. I'd actually broken my pledge quite early on without realising it. One summer I got up in the middle of the night feeling thirsty. In the semi-darkness I saw a glass containing a dark liquid resting on the kitchen worktop. I assumed it was Coke. We didn't normally have Coke at home, but it had been someone's birthday recently, so we were allowed it as a special treat. I took a sip expecting to feel a fizzy chemically-enhanced cola flavour assaulting my taste buds. But I suddenly realised it was red wine, so I spat out what I could down the sink and felt really guilty about the fraction of a millilitre which had already gone down my throat. It wasn't long before any feelings of guilt I had about this dissipated and I stopped regarding as such a big deal. Nevertheless I salute anyone who kept their pledge of abstinence and indeed those who continued to live an alcohol-free life well beyond their 18th birthday.

"When we get confirmed we become a soldier of God" our teacher Mr Arthurs had told us in the run-up to the big event of our impending confirmation.

All these years later I ponder how naïve we were, being effectively conscripted against our will into the army of a questionable deity who's taken up spiritual arms against the army of an equally questionable anti-deity. Nevertheless, I will forever associate the day of my confirmation in the late spring of 1985 with the world snooker final between our fellow countyman Denis Taylor and Steve Davis, which Taylor won in a nail-biting black ball finish in the early hours of the following Monday morning. I was allowed to stay up late to watch it, as were it seemed most of my classmates.

The man who confirmed myself and my classmates was Edward Daly, the then Bishop of Derry, whose diocese we were under. He's probably best remembered for the iconic newsreel footage which was beamed around the world as the young priest waving the blood-stained white handkerchief while escorting a wounded man to safety on Bloody Sunday in 1972. This was before any of my class was born, but we'd already met him a few years before at the age of seven or eight when he had visited our primary school.

"Now remember to say "Good morning Dr Daly" when the bishop enters the classroom" our then teacher Mrs McArt had told us the day before the visit.

"But he's not a doctor!" was the inevitable response. Although my memories of the day aren't the most reliable I'm pretty sure it was Edward O'Reilly (now a dentist by profession) who said this.

"He's not a doctor of medicine, but a doctor of divinity. There are many different kinds of doctor you know".

I was vaguely aware of this at the time as I knew that the curly-haired fellow with the goggly eyes and the long scarf who travelled around in a phone box on Saturday evenings was called "Doctor", even though he wasn't really a medical man.

We were allowed to ask the bishop questions. I had mine worked

122

out the night before, but I'm not sure whether I asked it just for the sake of asking a question or if I was genuinely curious to know the answer.

The first few questions were fairly sensible and I suspect had been suggested by some of the teachers rather than conceived of the pupils' own volition.

"When did you first become a bishop?" was the first query.

"I became a bishop in 1973. I understand many of you were born that year. No, actually it was 1974. I'm sure quite a few of you were born that year as well".

"Did you speak Italian to the pope when you met him?" was another question.

"No, I spoke English to the pope actually. He was a very nice man, etc, etc...".

I don't remember what else the bishop said in response to this, although I know that John Paul II was an accomplished linguist and would have been able to hold a conversation in Italian or English (probably German, Spanish and Latin also) as easily as in his native Polish.

"Who makes your dinner?" was another question.

I think his grace must have said something about his housekeeper, but in my naivety I remember being puzzled as to why his wife didn't make the dinner. Then came my turn. I raised my hand and the bishop took up my offer.

"What age are you?" I asked him.

The headmaster burst out laughing at this. I'm sure the bishop must have laughed as well out of politeness, but I didn't understand why as I thought this a perfectly reasonable question for a seven year old to be asking.

"I'm 47" replied his grace with good grace, "So not that old - I hope!" Or words to that effect.

I didn't realise at the time that this was quite a young age for a bishop. Having been a priest in Derry during the worst days of what was euphemistically referred to as "The Troubles" he'd obviously impressed his superiors.

It seemed that from this point on the questions became increasingly flippant.

"What football team do you support?" was another one.

"I'm not really into football, so I don't have a favourite team. Who do you support?"

"Arsenal."

"Ach, sure they're rubbish! You should support a decent team!" said the bishop, demonstrating that he had a sense of humour. I think most of us laughed at this point.

Unlike a few of his contemporaries who have come across as arrogant men with an inflated sense of self-importance, more interested in preserving their own reputations than the welfare of their flocks, Edward Daly has always struck me as a thoroughly decent and modest man who had to take some difficult decisions in his time and showed great courage in the face of adversity. In his memoirs he even made the controversial, but welcome appeal for the celibacy rule within the Catholic priesthood to be abolished. He was criticised for not having said this while he was a bishop, but always better late than never.

~

After many years of compulsory government health warnings featuring prominently on tobacco products we now have similar warnings on bottles and cans, promoting the "Drinkaware" website. This is a move in the right direction, but in my humble opinion, not enough. The roots of the problem must be addressed. It may be an unpopular proposal, especially among those who wish to stem the influence of the "nanny state", but although I enjoy the odd drink or two myself, I personally believe that all forms of alcohol advertising should be banned. The manufacturers, distributors and the pub and off-licence trades would no doubt be up in arms at such a move, but in desperate times desperate measures need to be taken. The burden on an already struggling health service in dealing with alcohol-related injuries and illnesses is phenomenal. An all-out ban on alcohol advertising wouldn't stop those who already drink from continuing to drink, but if young children and teenagers were less familiar with well-known brands the desire to start drinking in the first place may well to a certain extent be quelled. We can still enjoy our favourite tipple down at the local without having to see it on TV, at football matches or on billboard posters.

Bizarrely we even have an "official beer" of the Olympics and the World Cup. A product which can have highly damaging effects on long term health sponsoring an athletics event? It's like having an official bacon of the World Jewish Congress or an official whisky of the International Muslim Federation.

-9-
Careering off the beaten track

We had careers classes in the third year of grammar school, at the end of which we'd be choosing our subjects for our GCSEs, the then new name for O-levels. Up to that point the concept of life after school had never occurred to me. The frightening thought struck me that one day I'd no longer be sitting in a classroom being told what to do. It suddenly dawned on me that I'd actually have to make an important decision in the not-so-distant future.

Being a grammar school, the emphasis was naturally on white collar professions.

Careers classes were taken by Mr Cathal Slipe (another one of the Golden Generation) who was for some reason known as "The Emperor". It may have been something to do with his complete lack of resemblance to the late Franz-Josef of Austro-Hungary. He spoke with a strong rural Tyrone accent. Yes, I know it's a big county, but for obvious reasons I'm not going to be any more specific.

The blue collar trades were frowned upon.
"Do you want to be stuck outside on some building site on a freezing cold wet winter morning?" he used to say.

There was a boy in the class called Hughes (one of my old roommates from the Donegal Gaeltacht the previous summer as it happened). The Emperor called him "Cues", a quirk of the local dialect. It became a running joke throughout the year that the boy Hughes harboured ambitions of becoming a plasterer.

"So Cues wants to be a plawstherer?" the Emperor would say somewhat disdainfully, although his tone was more one of banter than contempt.

"Up the plawstherers!" Hughes would shout with a raised fist in response to this.

126

Although at the time plastering wasn't such an ill-advised career choice. The popular TV comedian Harry Enfield was at this time famous for his cash-flashing tradesman character "Loadsamoney", a satire of the lucrative construction boom of the day.

In another careers class some years later towards the end of my time at the school a different teacher asked for a show of hands to see who was thinking of entering the teaching profession. A handful of hands (maybe this is a mixed metaphor, but I'll use it anyway) went up. Mine wasn't one of them. For some reason she seemed surprised by this. I didn't have much of an idea of what I did want to do, but I did know this was one career I wanted to avoid. Looking back in hindsight I don't think the teaching profession suffered any great loss by my decision not to enter it. The myth of long holidays, sitting with your feet up by 4 pm reading the paper in your t-shirt and jeans when the rest of the world's still stuck in the office, having the "unique opportunity" to "inspire and shape enthusiastic young minds" (subtle cough!) in the mould of Robin Williams in *Dead Poets' Society* just wasn't enough to persuade me. Having said that, a friend of mine at university told me that that particular film had such a profound effect on him that it inspired him to become an English teacher. Despite this he ended up becoming a lawyer instead.

Very few sons or daughters of teachers I knew followed in their parents' footsteps. I'm sure many of them were even actively discouraged by their parents from entering the profession.

One particular teacher used to boast about how he had insider intelligence on the bad boys who were up to no good:

"You see when I was at school I was no saint myself. I was a bit of a scallywag. So I know when boys are up to something. I've seen it all before. You name it, I've done it!"

He even seemed to be quite proud of this boast.

We also had a French teacher who once as part of the lesson went round the class and questioned us all in French as to what career we wanted to pursue.

«*Qu'est-ce que tu veut être dans la vie?*» she asked.

« *Je voudrais être professeur* » one lad answered.

"Don't!" came the half jocular half serious reply.

There was also a maths teacher by the name of Rory McVeigh who regularly told us the anecdote about a boy who he knew from a neighbouring farm. The story was a moral lesson which illustrated the differing levels of ability we all have.

"This boy wasn't what you'd call the sharpest tool in the box. He literally couldn't write his own name. But if you took a tractor engine apart and reduced it to wee small pieces, he could reassemble it part by part to exactly the way it was. So do you think he was clever or stupid?"

Despite the emphasis on pursuing a lucrative and rewarding career, pupils were banned from having part time evening jobs under the ridiculous pretext that it would supposedly interfere with their studies. This rule was largely flouted. The priority was academic achievement, rather than things that actually matter. Getting straight A's in your exams is all very well, but of little relevance to the real world. Having a job at least showed initiative and graft – even if it was just stacking shelves in a supermarket, doing a paper round or working the pumps at the local petrol station. Time management and juggling academic studies with getting your hands dirty shows resourcefulness which can benefit the pupil later on in life. This nonsensical rule was a very middle class one. Admittedly, many of us were indeed part of the small town *petit bourgeoisie*. Quite a few of us were the sons of teachers, nurses, small business owners, public servants, skilled tradesmen and farmers. But there were also lads from less privileged backgrounds, who like the rest of us had got a place at the school by virtue of having passed the much-maligned 11 plus exam. It's come in for much criticism, but is a good leveller when it comes to social mobility.

I didn't have a part time job myself except for a short term stint delivering phone books and a weekly TV review column in the local paper which lasted about a year and for which I was paid 5p a line. I had managed to secure this weekly column after submitting a piece on Christmas TV. The previous writer of the TV review section had just emigrated to Australia which left a gap to be filled.

Like most weekly local Irish rags the funniest section in the paper was (and indeed still is) the court reports. These typically involved defendants charged with drunk and disorderly conduct following brawls outside pubs on a Saturday night.

A typical story might read as follows:

"Grabbed publican by throat during high speed chase and threw gas cylinder through window"

A Ballykilbollocks man has been fined for being intoxicated in charge of an uninsured vehicle while being pursued at high speed by police on the main Drumgallykilderry to Killybastard road.

The court heard that Leo McFecker shouted "F*** off, youse bunch of f***ing c***s!" [a respectable local paper would never print such words in full] at the arresting officers and tried to headbutt one of them before throwing a gas cylinder and a pneumatic drill through the police station window. When questioned in court the defendant claimed to have had no recollection of the incident.

Mr McFecker's solicitor Adolf McAfortune pointed out that his client had no previous convictions, except one for mans laughter [sic – the proof-reading wasn't always up to speed either] in 1999, and was of good character and explained that on the night in question it was a Wednesday and his client had been heavily intoxicated after someone had poured methylated spirits into the glass of Coke he had been drinking at McStoutwaister's public house. And it was raining heavily, which explained uncharacteristic behaviour of the defendant who was definitely a lifelong non-drinker.

"He was in a bad way following the death of his hamster by suicide. The driving offences were motivated by the fact that my client had been disqualified at the time and had a drink problem for which he was undergoing counselling" Mr McAfortune told the court.

My dad used to complain that the local paper was full of pictures of people in pubs. There were indeed whole pages given over to the annual golf club dinner or someone's 21st birthday celebration in order to simply fill up space. A double page spread might be devoted to "Party time in Paradise" and have pictures of revellers at the not so aptly named local night spot. Other coverage included events of local interest in the outlying rural areas such as the annual Ballykilderrymore sheep dog trials or the Aughnadrumcrossbeg bull tossing festival.

In hindsight with regard to my own column where I almost always wrote stuff about the trendy alternative comedy shows of the day or cutting edge scientific documentaries, my articles were probably of as much interest to the average reader of a local paper as the *Who's Who of Reggae, Rap, Jazz, Soul and Motown Music* was to the average Ku Klux Klan member. Nevertheless it was a major ego boost to see my work in print as well as a bit of extra pocket money.

In any case careers advice at school was generally to be taken with a pinch of salt. Just like a lot of the books out there. Browse through the business or psychology section of any large bookshop and you'll find a multitude of titles on how to be an effective manager, how to improve your life in 293 easy stages, how to make the most of self-help books, how to sound clever by spouting meaningless management jargon, etc. ad nauseam. At a rough guess I'd estimate that 99% of these titles are pure unadulterated bullshit. There are even extremely patronising books on topics like how to look things up on the internet, many of which end up as bestsellers for fuck's sake!

Years later during my "working" adult life I was once invited by the training department of a supposedly professional association to attend a course on "paper management" ("a practical workshop for those wishing to take control of the paper they have to handle in the course of their work") - and (wait for it!) - pay over £200 (+ VAT) for the privilege! It sounded so ridiculous I almost thought it was a joke at first. I just can't believe how anyone would be prepared to part with this kind of money to be taught how to put e-mails and invoices into files, stick them on their desk or perhaps more fittingly in the bin – by which I mean the recycling bin of course. The aim of this one-day "workshop" was apparently to "reduce the amount of paper that arrives at their desk, and to deal with it quickly and effectively". The course included such learned skills as "the 'clear your desk' system", "golden rules of paperwork" and "General rules for filing".

What a load of total and utter bollocks.

I wonder if the consultancy firm dishing out this "invaluable advice" could cash in on their mountains of expertise by running courses in shit-shovelling management for pig farmers? Though, having said all that I'd be quite happy to conduct this workshop myself for £50 an hour or whatever the going rate is. If the people who run courses like this want to take the piss by spouting shite maybe they should be made to go on bowel and bladder management courses.

What's more we live in an age of bullshit terms like "knowledge management" and "human capital" invented by corporate wankers who think they're being clever, so they cash in on their so-called expertise by writing best-selling books.

I have two theories on this:

(a) That the writers actually believe in what they say and want to tell the world how great their ideas are, or

(b) They know it's bollocks, but also know they can make a lot of money by spouting it – as long as it's full of modern jargon and stupid meaningless diagrams involving bullet points, arrows and boxes.

In modern times we have also seen the dumbing down of academia. Certain universities are now offering Mickey Mouse degrees like golf management, equine studies or used car salesmanship. These are all noble career pursuits in their own right (except perhaps the latter), but do they really require three years of academic study as a substitute for serving a hands-on apprenticeship at a car showroom, stud farm or golf course?

Many graduates will end up as a call centre workers or bank clerks anyway – ie doing jobs they could have done straight after leaving school – so why not cut out the middle man and skip university altogether – think of all the debt you could avoid getting into. Earning money rather than watching daytime TV while nursing a hangover is surely a more attractive proposition.

We also still have a lot of snobbery in education. A degree in 3-D computer game design from University College (formerly polytechnic) of East Grinstead is probably of more practical and economic use than a degree in ancient Assyrian literature from Boatrace College, Oxbridge, yet the latter institution will have more prestige. A graduate from the latter will potentially have contacts in high places and is likely to end up as a merchant banker (deliberate use of rhyming slang there) or stockbroker, doing something which has absolutely nothing to do with their degree subject.

We have the growing trend of employees getting paid to sit at a desk and pretend they're working when in reality they're doing sweet FA. This charge has been traditionally levelled at civil servants and other public sector workers. Northern Ireland readers, for example may be familiar with the popular joke that the Department of the Environment (DoE) is an abbreviation for "Dossers only Employed". However it's equally rife in the private sector, particularly in big corporations where individual employees are effectively anonymous – cf Homer Simpson's non-descript job as some kind of safety officer at Springfield's nuclear power plant – very clever satire of corporate dishonesty and not as far-fetched as one might think.

Can sitting at a desk staring into a computer screen and taking the odd phone call for the best part of eight hours a day really be classified as a professional white collar job that requires a university education? Surely one is better off in the open air laying bricks or mixing cement or in a salon styling someone's hair. At least this is the real world – these employees may not enjoy the prestige or perks of the suited deskbound office worker, but at least they're not deluding themselves and not indulging in meaningless buzz words like "capacity building" or "knowledge harvesting".

I wonder what our would-be plasterer friend would make of all this. The last time I saw him was in a pub in the town several years ago. He was on a home visit from America where he was now based. And doing quite well for himself over there – but he was now a carpenter rather than a plasterer.

Here endeth my laboured rant. No pun intended.

9

Creatures unknown to Science

"Has anyone ever kissed a girl who smokes?"

It was an unusual question for a teacher to be asking his pupils, but it wasn't a witch hunt, it was simply illustrating the effects of smoking on human health.
Or maybe just an excuse for him to point out what a stud he'd been in his youth. In this case it was a biology teacher called Dermot Horgan.

"Honestly it's like kissing a bloody ashtray" he explained after no-one had raised their hand to admit such an experience.
The smart remarks inevitably followed.

"How do you know, sir – have you ever kissed an ashtray?"

Several years later long after my schooldays had ended I would get to test this out – ie by kissing a female smoker – not an ashtray. There is indeed a tobacco taste involved, but the ashtray comparison is somewhat far-fetched. My mouth didn't get clogged up with ashes and dog-ends.

In primary school the nearest thing we had got to science were schools TV programs which told us how beans grew or how a printing press worked. In grammar school we got to do the real thing.

It was combined science in first year, which would later in the third year be split into biology, chemistry and physics. On a Friday afternoon in the first week of September 1985, we naïve, innocent first years were made to congregate in the lecture theatre while the three science masters Mulholland, Thompson and Quigley decided who was to be in which class. It was an old-fashioned lecture theatre with wooden fold-up seats of the type you would have found in cinemas years ago. As we quickly found out the hinges of these seats were badly in need of oiling. It started with an accidental squeak. Then a few sneaky squeaks which were meant to sound as if they were made accidentally. This had a snowball effect. Before long there was a chorus of 60 chairs squeaking in unison and 60 amused 11 year olds. We were soon told in no uncertain terms to stop it.

Along with about 25 other lads I was placed in Mr Cedric Mulholland's science class. He was another one of those teachers who didn't have a nickname, but was simply known to pupils (among themselves that is – not to his face) by his first name. There was unlikely to be any confusion here as there weren't many Cedrics in the West Tyrone area.

"Does anyone have any experience of science?" he asked as an introductory ice-breaker in our very first science class.

"My brother's got a chemistry set" said the future biochemist Shane Rogan.

Another lad went one better and boasted:

"I've got a chemistry set".

And even better still was the classic line from Denis Tally:

"My brother squeezes stuff out of worms"

"What kind of stuff?" Cedric asked.

"Brown stuff".

Laughter.

"I don't think I'd like to meet your brother!"

"You already have, he's in 2B."

About a year later the worm-squeezer's brother came up with another classic, this time in Mr Thompson's science class. The topic of conversation was the chemical composition of agricultural herbicides.

"Some fella up by Ballygalduffy drank a bottle of etherium hypochloxite. And then he vomited this blue stuff."

A short pause followed.

"And died."

The last section of our textbook, the infamous Chapter 10 was on reproduction. On receipt of the book everyone naturally made a beeline for the back pages.

"Any questions?" Cedric asked.

"Sir, will we be dissecting rats?"

"Not this year."

Martin Fenelly was persistent and would ask at the beginning of each subsequent class:

"Sir, will we doing an experiment today?"

When we eventually got to do an experiment it amounted to boiling ink in a test tube.

Cedric wasn't one for physical punishment even when you were allowed to do that sort of thing. But he seemed to have an obsession for giving out lines as a form of retribution for minor misdemeanours. And the lines he gave were of a long, complicated nature like "I must endeavour to conduct myself in a dignified, civilised and respectful manner in Mr Mulholland's science class". Lines could be done twice as fast if you employed the old schoolboy trick of sticking two pens together with sticky tape and thus getting two lines written at the same time.
But this wasn't possible if you'd got into Mr Martin Walsh's bad books. He used a cleverer and more effective form of punishment.

He would make you write an essay of at least four sides of standard exercise book paper with a set title. Unlike lines which you could fly through without exerting any mental effort this technique forced you to think about what you were writing.

The science labs contained many collectable trophies like crocodile clips, pieces of wire, test tubes and gerbils, which were of no practical use in the "outside world", but still got nicked just for the sake of being nicked.

The teachers knew this was going on, but there was only so much they could do to stop it.
Jim Thompson was wise to what was going on and had had the foresight to count the crocodile clips in advance of handing them out. After an experiment involving electrical conductivity and circuit boards a number of crocodile clips had gone missing.

"We have six croc clips missing. No-one's leaving here till they're found" he said firmly.

At this point the bell for lunchtime went off.

Suddenly the missing clips all mysteriously and inexplicably reappeared in the oddest of places just like the apparitions of the Virgin Mary at Knock or Lourdes.

"There's one over here, sir" said one boy who had just "found" it in the sink.

"I've just found one on the floor, sir" said another after an undoubtedly long and difficult search.

Others miraculously reappeared under textbooks and on stools or desks.

Occasionally potassium permanganate, copper sulphate or borax crystals would go walkies. Rumour has it that some of the more entrepreneurial pupils would attempt to flog them in the seedier snooker clubs and bars of the town, passing them off as crystal meth or some new wonder drug which had just arrived in the sticks.

There was another science teacher called Pat Quigley who was known to the pupils as Penfold due to his apparent resemblance to a character of that name from a children's cartoon series. It wasn't so much that he was a soft touch. He was a highly intelligent man and knew his subject extremely well. He didn't suffer fools gladly, but he was a bit doddery and had the air of the absent-minded professor about him. But was basically a decent sort – as a contemporary of mine put it in a social networking site - "a civil oul' critter". Certain individuals even took the opportunity to have a sneaky smoke under the desks just before the start of class. Not a good idea in a lab full of gas taps and inflammable substances.

It was a Friday morning. He had his back to the class while he was setting up the experiment, which we were standing around watching. It was something to do with electrolysis involving (if I remember correctly) an electric circuit board and copper sulphate, the blue solution into which you could dip your locker key and it would comes out with a copper-coloured sheen which soon wears off.
There happened to be a box of crocodile clips on the table. When his back was still to the class one wag decided to discreetly attach one of the clips to Penfold's jacket tail without him noticing. This caused a few silent smirks. Another chancer rather cruelly decided to do the same and similarly got away with it. Before long there were five crocodile clips clipped to the tail of his jacket which he was completely oblivious to as he talked us through the chemical reaction and its significance to the scientific world while he continued to test the apparatus. By this stage it was becoming increasingly difficult to hold in the laughter.

"So the copper will now react with the sulphate solution to produce... Mr Loughry, what are you sniggering at?"

"Nothing sir"

A few minutes later…

"And as we can see... Mr Brannigan, what's so funny?"

"Oh...just a private joke, sir"

"Would you mind sharing it with us?"

"Er...well..."

"Come on Mr Brannigan, we all want to hear this really hilarious joke of yours, don't we?"

The rest of the class (who obviously knew damn well what he was really laughing at) responded with a unanimous chorus of

"Yes, sir! We definitely want to hear it!"

Brannigan turned bright red and slowly began to articulate.

"OK...sir...well, there was this neutron, like, who went into a pub and ordered a beer. So the barman poured him a pint and the neutron said "how much is that?" And the barman said "Don't worry, for you there's no charge!" Er, that's the joke, sir."

The rest of the class exploded with wildly exaggerated laughter. Even Penfold seemed mildly amused and forced a faint smile. Normality then resumed for a few more minutes. Then Mr Quigley was once again distracted.

"There's a boy behind me acting the cod. Is it you, Paul Mulroy?

"It is not!" young Mulroy (who in any case wasn't the loutish type) said indignantly, adding the caveat "I didn't do nothing!"

The rest of the class then jokingly said in unison:

"Well if you didn't do nothing you must have done something!"

As it happened Paul Mulroy's only crime was withholding

information, something we were all guilty of on this occasion.

It might have been easier just to say "Sir you've got five crocodile clips attached to your jacket tails. And some of us think it's quite amusing – but maybe not so amusing for yourself. And that's why we were laughing. It wasn't because of Brannigan's crappy joke about the neutron".

But because of the schoolboy code of omertà you never grassed up your mates – no matter how serious the crime was. If one of your classmates went down the town at lunchtime and robbed a bank in the high street or poisoned the town's water supply or went into the computer lab and hacked into the databases of the world's financial markets causing share prices to plummet and famine, disease and war to engulf the world you had to keep quiet about it if you still wanted to be considered "one of the lads".

I could just imagine our form teacher carrying out his investigation:

"Listen up, lads, we've just had a phone call from the branch manager of the Western Bank in town. They were robbed at peashooter point during the lunch break by a boy in school uniform who got away with £4.12, two paper clips and a bunch of post-it notes."

"The Wall Street stock exchange also think it was one of our pupils who caused their share prices to crash and cause chaos throughout the world."

"Right lads I know it was one of you who did it, so come on, own up. If you come clean now we'll be lenient. If you admit to it now you'll be lucky to get five years detention – probably out after two and a half years pending good behaviour."

Double chemistry immediately preceded lunchtime. As we exited the lab and buggered off to lunch with a spring in our step in joyful anticipation of the weekend ahead poor old Penfold must have walked through the corridors and possibly even entered the staffroom before someone (presumably another teacher) politely pointed out to him the presence of the clips attached to his jacket. Or maybe he'd suddenly noticed that his jacket had become slightly heavier than usual. An inquest followed. Even though I was wholly innocent of the charges I was summoned for interrogation along with a number of other prime suspects. This was probably because I'd got into his bad books a few weeks earlier for not paying attention in class and was therefore a potential troublemaker. On this occasion I was rightfully acquitted. From that point on I got on quite well with the man.

My short attention span was my Achilles heel. Even now when I'm attending conferences or training courses I tend to drift into a different world and begin to daydream just as I did in class (particularly maths classes) many moons ago. It was my short attention span plus my tendency to be easily amused which most often got me into trouble. It had been during another chemistry class about a year previous to the above episode that our regular teacher was off on a course, so we had a supply teacher supervising us. As he couldn't be arsed teaching the class we were basically told to get on with whatever work we had to do while he sat there quietly doing whatever he had to do – which by the looks of it was very little apart from staring into space. The thing was this supply teacher looked like he'd been on the piss all night. He had bags under his bloodshot eyes and his tie was loosely tied with the knot halfway down his unironed shirt. His face which had a permanently spaced-out expression was as white as two albino polar bears fighting in a snowstorm. It also looked like he'd been snorting coke or smoking whacky-baccy and was considerably the worse for wear. When one lad Martin Fenelly pointed out that this doped up, hung-over supervisor reminded him of Danny Kendal, a spaced-out boy from *Grange Hill* – and there was indeed a physical resemblance – this was it. I could hardly contain myself for the duration of the class. I was desperately trying to suppress the laughter which was bursting to get out of me.

I was attempting to draw a picture of him, which necessitated looking at him every so often.
Every time I made eye contact with this baggy-eyed Danny Kendal

lookalike I found it all the more difficult not to laugh.

"Wipe that silly smile off your face, it's annoying me!" Kendal finally snapped.

Not half as annoying as that man with the hammer inside your head who keeps banging away I thought. Even thinking about that incident now after 23 years I still burst out laughing. In the most awkward and inappropriate of places. By the way, the supply teacher was never seen or heard of again.

Biological Organs of Mass Instruction

"Take the earring out, Colm, it's not part of the school uniform!" Mr Horgan would scream at Colm Mitchell at the start of almost every fifth year biology class. By extension of that logic watches, glasses, contact lenses, socks, sideburns or eyebrows weren't part of the school uniform either, but he never asked anyone to remove any of these items from their person.

Then there were the legitimate scientific words like "organism" and "masticate" which sounded similar to words with sexual meanings. One lad Cornelius "Clarko" Clarke challenged his classmates to a bet that he would deliberately use the wrong terminology in a forthcoming exam paper. So he wrote about breeding micro-orgasms in a petri dish and masturbating food to break it down prior to digestion. He ended up getting the top marks in the class. Not surprisingly he's now a successful entrepreneur.

Sometimes even perfectly innocent words were singled out for special attention.
During the Horg's biology class on plant reproduction for instance:

"So the wall formed around the seed is called a fruit".

Giggles all round.

"They used to laugh at that fifteen years ago when I was at school.

142

Nothing's changed" said Horgs with a sigh and an air of resignation.

And the chances are that the schoolboys of today still laugh at it. Things really do go round in complete circles. Or in some cases incomplete circles.

What a bunch of creatures unknown to science (or C.Un.T.S for short) we were.

10

In Lands Down Under: From Omagh to Oamaru

I remember *Crocodile Dundee* being one of the big box office hits of 1986. Or was it 1987? The fish-out-of-water tale of an uncouth Australian bushman from the outback who ends up in the urban jungle of New York after meeting a spoilt rich American girl took cinemas by storm. But I didn't get to see it. Well not at the cinema anyway. I had to wait a couple of years for it to be shown on TV. My mum wouldn't let me see it as it had a 15 certificate and I was only 13 (or maybe 14) at the time. I later found out that the 15 cert had been due to the presence of the F-word, which was mentioned once during the entire film. A word that can be heard daily in any primary school playground for fuck's sake (I just had to gratuitously get that in somewhere). Oh and also the lead actress momentarily flashes a bit of flesh and there's a scene where a guest at a party snorts a line of cocaine – but apart from this it's wholesome family viewing. Really. Shortly afterwards the new "12" certificate came into being to cater for such situations.

It was one of those films from which a sequel should never have been made – just like *Jaws*, and *Psycho* before it. But one thing worse than making sequels to classic films is making re-makes of films which have no need to be remade – like *The Wicker Man* and *Alfie*.

Australia was cool at the time – the trashy soaps *Neighbours* and *Home & Away* were topping the viewing figures. Presumably because they provided a sense of escape for people in this grey, rain-lashed, windswept North Atlantic archipelago and glamourised the outdoor lifestyle of barbies and beaches. Australian Rules football was being shown on the TV – some might call it brawling by another name, but I've always preferred it to that horrible code the Americans call "football" where helmeted men dressed in heavily padded apparel crash into each other then stop every five minutes for a commercial break – a game which was also being broadcast to a new trans-Atlantic audience.

In Ireland we had a particular interest in the Australian version.

Due to its similarity with gaelic football an international compromise code had been devised under which the cream of Irish and Australian talent would ~~fight~~ play each other for what was effectively the GAA's equivalent of the Ashes, except a tad more exciting. But being more exciting than a neverending series of cricket matches isn't really saying much.

In 1987 it was the turn of the men from down under to brave the cold and wet of the Irish autumn. The Australians were set to face Ulster at Healy Park, Omagh, having already played an Ireland XV at Croke Park. The original plan was that we were supposed to get the afternoon off school to watch the ~~brawl~~ match. But on this day of all days it rained. It didn't just rain though. It pissed down very heavily all afternoon. In fact we had the worst flooding in living memory. The Campsie area of town and the neighbouring town of Strabane were particularly badly affected by the flooding as I recall. Apparently it was caused by autumn leaves blocking the drains. Or at least that was the Department of the Environment's excuse. The match still went ahead, but now because of the heavy rain we weren't allowed to go. I don't even remember who won.

The following year Australia celebrated its Bicentennial – ie 200 years since the native aborigines had their land invaded by convicts and overlords, were enslaved and decimated. This abuse of human rights struck a chord with me.

14 years later I would visit the country.

It was the autumn of 2002. Well, in the northern hemisphere at least. South of the Tropic of Capricorn it was the early spring. I had been awarded bursary to attend a law librarians' conference – the line of work I was in at the time - in New Zealand. I touched down in Auckland airport in the early morning almost 24 hours after I'd boarded the plane in Heathrow. During my youth I had always associated New Zealand with the succulent roast lamb we would have for countless Sunday dinners smothered in mint sauce and gravy accompanied by roast potatoes which invariably came from Cyprus. Looking back it seems bizarre that even though we lived on an island where spuds and sheep abound we still imported them from distant lands.

I've got a couple of hours to kill before boarding the internal flight to Wellington, so I venture into town for a quick nosey. There are familiar sights all around - blackbirds and sparrows, suburban housing with perfectly manicured lawns – and a large moorhen-like bird which I later identify as a Purple Swamphen or Pūkeko in the Maori tongue. The image of mockney TV chef Jamie Oliver on the back of a bus, an ad for his latest TV show, book or whatever jumps out at me. It was like a piece of Britain transported to a distant land.

Wellington's a windy place. And slightly wet too. I take a cable car up the hill where the former home of local writer Jane Mansfield is situated. There's a spectacular view of the horseshoe-shaped harbour. The building which houses New Zealand's parliament is shaped like a beehive. A short distance from here I venture into a delightful little family-run Cambodian corner café where I have an excellent curry.

The conference is being held at the Te Papa Museum. A Maori elder in tribal robes officially opens the proceedings by tapping a stick on the floor and rubbing noses with the convener, a time-honoured traditional greeting.

My only condition of receiving the very generous grant to get to NZ and back is to do a write-up of the conference. I gave it the corny title of where "Where Kiwis Dare" - you can now even buy it from the Cambridge University press website for £30.00 or "rent" it for 24 hours for the princely sum of $5.99 /£3.99 /€4.49. And in case you're wondering - the money goes to the publishers not to me.

From my experience of major ferry crossings around the world, I've noticed that you often have on one side a large vibrant city and on the other a poky one-horse town - Belfast-Stranraer, Dublin-Holyhead and Tangier-Tarifa all spring to mind. The crossing between New Zealand's two main islands is no exception. I board the ferry in Wellington, then a few hours later I find myself in an insignificant little town called Picton. The infrequency of bus times coupled with the unwelcome delay to the ferry's departure means that I'm regrettably forced to spend a night in Picton where there's very little to do for the passing traveller. I make sure I get plenty of sleep.

While waiting to catch the bus in the following day I decide to grab a quick bite to eat. After a long hard glance at the menu I decide on a "jumbo burger" – with a slice of bacon, cheese and a fried egg on top of the beef – in other words a heart attack in a bun – to take away. I sit down to eat it at a bench by the pond. All of a sudden I'm mobbed by about a dozen gulls and a couple of ducks who all want a piece. It's like a scene from that Hitchcock film about birds taking over the world. It gets to the stage where I have to physically push them away. I chuck the fried egg away as I never eat them, having had an aversion to them since early childhood. A mallard duck (in this case a drake with the unmistakeable shiny green head) attacks it. It's not quite cannibalism, but somehow this just doesn't seem natural.

I board the bus which heads down the east coast of the South Island towards Kaikoura. There's a view of a snow-capped mountain which looks positively Alpine.

One of the town's main attractions is the opportunity to go swimming with dolphins. In the hostel I get talking to a young English couple who have been backpacking around Asia and Australasia for the past year.

"I'd like to go on the dolphin trip, but I'm not sure about going into the water with them" I tell them.
"You've got to swim, mate, you gotta swim" he advises.
The next day I decide to stay on the boat rather than enter the water and mingle with the dolphins, something I end up regretting. They are curious creatures who swim up to the boat to investigate what's going on.

As the bus travels down the east coast of the South Island, it stops briefly at Oamaru, a town famous for its penguin colonies.

Unfortunately it doesn't stop long enough for me to see these feathered flightless curiosities. But to the locals these creatures are probably as much as a novelty as crows or starlings would be back home. But unlike crows or starlings the penguins at least bring in the tourists.

After visiting Queenstown (where it rains constantly and where the only kiwis (of the beaked variety) I see during my time in NZ are in captivity), Nelson, Greymouth and the spectacular Franz Josef Glacier over the next couple of days it's time to get the ferry back to the North Island.

Shortly after my arrival on the other side of the Cook Strait I get a night's accommodation booked at a budget hostel in Wellington. It's the third Saturday in September, which means that tomorrow is All Ireland final day. It's Armagh against Kerry on this occasion, a particularly significant event as although the Kingdom are no strangers to Croke Park, it's the northerners' first final for 25 years. An internet search and quick phone call reveals that there's an Irish pub in town showing the match. The only thing is it's at 3.00 in the morning. I set the alarm clock for this ridiculously early hour with the intention of going to watch the game. After a deep sleep my ears are eventually assaulted by an unwelcome series of electronic bleeps. I just can't bring myself to get up.
"Sod it!" I say to myself and go back to sleep.

The next day at Wellington airport I log into an internet terminal and find that the cup has gone north, an historic triumph for the men in orange who have just claimed their very first All Ireland title. A few days earlier during my brief overnight stay in Christchurch I'd notice a street called Armagh Street. An insignificant detail, but somehow fitting. A three hour flight later I find myself on the other side of the Tasman Sea in Australia.

Sydney Opera House is just as Clive James once described it - reminiscent of oyster shells sticking out of a typewriter. On the pavement just outside the building there are plaques commemorating various authors, one of whom, fittingly enough is Clive James himself. The opera house is perfectly located on the

148

harbour and just beside the botanic gardens. Hanging from a tree are huge bats. A few are flying around from tree to tree in broad daylight. They're fruit bats or flying foxes.

That evening while strolling through a trendy part of central Sydney I pass a restaurant specialising in aboriginal cuisine, which I presume includes kangaroo meat, emu and wichety grubs. But the only native Australian I see is a man in tribal paint dancing on stage as part of this tourist-friendly eatery's entertainment. Sadly, the only other Aborigines I've seen since arriving here have been a few down-and-out drunks in the seedy Kings Cross area, which in some ways resembles its London namesake. I get "invited" into a so-called gentleman's club by an over-friendly doorman, but I politely decline the offer.

I end up in a pub called the CBD in a different part of town, which I remember from geography at school stands for central business district, the main commercial centre of an urban settlement where the shops and offices are located. I'm almost expecting to find a pub around the corner called Ox-bow Lake or Christaller's Central Place Theory. It also has a casino. I meet two characters who work in the casino part and end up drinking with them for the remainder of the night.

The next day I'm on a trip to the Blue Mountains. Although it's still only spring in Australia the heat is quite intense. I regret having tried out the exceptionally strong Tasmanian beer which is allegedly brewed with pure spring water.

The highlights of the trip are kangaroos (eastern greys in this case) which seem to be as common in the local woods as deer are back home. And the roos are considerably less shy than their hooved counterparts.

On a branch of a tree there's a lone kookaburra, a local variety of kingfisher which apparently has a call similar to manic laughter. This particular specimen remains silent, but stays in the tree long enough for me to get a picture.

The tour guide Joe is of Italian origin and physically resembles a younger version of the TV detective Lieutenant "Just one more

149

thing" Columbo. He points out the primeval ferns which wouldn't look out of a place in a Jurassic landscape.

"I bet no-one's seen these before" he says to the entourage who are mostly foreigners.

"Yes , I have" I respond cockily.

I explain that I've just come over from New Zealand where ferns are almost everywhere.

The next day I'm on a Heathrow bound Singapore Airlines flight which briefly stops off at
Singapore where the passengers are forced to temporarily alight. It's the first time I've set foot in Asia. Several hours later I'm back in London early on a Sunday morning. My local park is resplendent in the colours of the fall and bathed in an eerie autumnal mist. It then occurs to me that Transylvania might be a good place to spend Hallowe'en at some point in the future.

-11-
From Castlederg to Castle Dracula

In the summer of 1987 the BBC screened a season of Hammer horror films. I was allowed to stay up late to watch them as it was the summer holidays. I became a Hammer horror nerd.

The poet and librarian Philip Larkin referred to the Hammer oeuvre as "tit and fang" films, encapsulating their quintessential mixture of soft porn and quasi-literary gothic horror plundered from the works of Mary Shelley, Bram Stoker and Sheridan le Fanu and endlessly recycled.

Some 21 years later I would visit Transylvania.
Better still some 23 years later I would visit Black Park, where the films were made, the piece of English Home Counties woodland west of London masquerading as the dark ominous forests of Mitteleuropa. It's a pleasant place for a mid-autumn stroll. Nearby are the famous Pinewood studios, a staple of the British film industry – and where that other great B-movie franchise the "Carry On" films were made.

I have an obsession bordering on the unhealthy with film locations. If I'm at the cinema I'll always insist on staying till the very end of the credits to find out where the film was shot. This isn't so easy though if the cleaner is walking in front of the screen picking up discarded wrappers and fragments of popcorn.

With my GCSE exams just around the corner I remember the run-up to Christmas of 1989 being dominated by the unfolding events in Eastern Europe where Churchill's infamous iron curtain was being spectacularly torn off its rail and tossed aside to the charity shop of history. One of the last was Romania. The deposed president Nicolai Ceacescu and his wife were being hotly pursued by the angry mobs.

What also fascinated me about Romania was that even though it was very much inside what we used to call Eastern Europe, its

151

language, unlike the Slavonic tongues of its neighbours was from the Romance Latin branch, a language much closer to French or Spanish than Russian or Serbo-Croat.

My interest in Romania was therefore threefold – horror film-related, linguistic and historical/political.
My Transylvanian excursion in the autumn of 2008 turns out to be a cheap and cheerful package. Most of the participants are Australian and Canadian backpackers in their 20s wending their way around Europe in between pulling pints in the boozers of Shepherds Bush, Acton and Earls Court.

For some reason the tour group meets up in Budapest. This would be my second visit to the Hungarian capital in the space of a year. I had been there for a weekend just before Christmas the previous year with two old friends Phil and Alexei...

(If this was a film my face would go all distorted and blurry to denote the coming of a flashback).

Budapest, December 2007
There's a light covering of snow on the ground the day we arrive – the evening of 14 December 2007 to be precise. And it was a bumpy landing as the plane landed at Budapest airport.

We venture outside the hostel to check out the local nightlife. There's a patch of grass adjacent to the apartment block with a statue of some bloke called Jokai after whom the street is named. As we venture up to take a look, curious as to who this character is we get interrupted by a well-dressed gent in a red scarf. We expect him to say something like "get off the grass!" - but instead he's touting for business on behalf of what would euphemistically be referred to as the local "gentleman's club" just around the corner.

"It's totally genuine – no plastics!" he reassures us.

He asks us where we're from and as soon as he discovers that we're Irish he launches into a bizarre tirade – "Ireland – Jackie Charlton – Belfast – Dublin – sex machine!"

We politely decline his offer and instead seek shelter from the winter chill by heading to the nearest watering hole where the conversation for some unknown reason ranges from the Roman slave trade to politically incorrect comedians in northern English working men's clubs. The chain bridge across the not so blue Danube looks well when it's lit up at night.

A cursory glance at Wikipedia about four years later reveals that the statue is of Mór Jókai, a 19th century Hungarian writer.

The next day we come across a Christmas market selling hot mulled wine (or *glühwein* as they call it in the original German) in those ribbed plastic cups you get in hospital vending machines, a welcome respite from the cold. Alexei quite accurately describes it as being like a "liquid mince pie".
There's a Scottish theme pub across the road from our hostel. We get talking to Astrid, a dental tourist from Åland, the quasi-autonomous Swedish-speaking, but Finnish-owned archipelago in the Baltic and Clive from Scotland - the quasi-autonomous English-speaking region just north of England who works as an IT contractor and is here on business...and judging by the way he's been eyeing up Astrid on pleasure as well.

The next day we bathe in the pleasantly warm waters of one of the city's famous spas. It had to be done.

Hungary/Romania, October 2009
Back to the present – or more specifically the past present if that makes any sense... In the spirit of Jonathan Harker, hero of Bram Stoker's Dracula, I'm keeping a journal of my sojourn in Transylvania. I've been single for almost a year now and the trip's been planned at quite short notice.

Day 1: October 26, 2009 – A bad day in Budapest
My alarm clock goes off at 6:15 on Sunday morning, but in reality it's still only 5:15 as the clocks have just gone back an hour. I'm woken up in the middle of quite a pleasant dream (for the record I have no recollection of what this dream was about, but I had noted

in my diary that it was "pleasant") by the tooting of the taxi driver's horn outside the front door and I'm not even dressed yet. I suddenly realise I've inadvertently set my alarm for 6:15 pm instead of 6:15 am and have slept in as a result. I'm not in the best of shape either, having been to a friend's birthday bash at a karaoke bar the night before and made the fatal mistake of mixing the grain with the grape, despite previous experience demonstrating that beer and wine don't make good bedfellows.

As I'm getting dressed the driver gets impatient and toots his horn violently. I rush down the stairs and into the cab. The driver seems to have a death wish and dodges red lights and drives up the motorway like a lunatic in his rush to get me to the airport, saying he has other passengers to pick up and is already running late. It's lucky for both of us that there's so little traffic around – but I get to the airport in good time and catch up on some lost sleep on the plane.

On arrival at Budapest airport I receive a text from my mate Jake Foxtrot asking if I fancy coming for a drink. I tell him I can't as I'll be in Transylvania all next week.

At the metro station en route to the hostel I get accosted by a less than friendly ticket inspector, a stern-faced middle-aged, curly-haired bespectacled woman. I've made the fatal mistake of not having put my ticket through the machine that punches holes in them. She seems to be choosing passengers at random to single out for inspection and I must stick out like a sore thumb in my leather jacket and kingfisher metallic blue striped shirt.

I try to play the ignorant foreigner, the stranger in a strange land, who's made a perfectly innocent mistake, but she's not buying it. I tell her I've only just arrived and don't have any money on me. She says the fine for having an unstamped metro ticket is 6000 florin.

"Euros?" she asks.

"No I don't have euros" I reply desperately, but unsuccessfully trying to bullshit my way out of this situation.

"Passport!" she then demands impatiently.

No that's one thing you're not getting off me, Mrs.

I keep insisting that I don't have any money, but she's still unimpressed. It would be less hassle just to send me back and get my ticket punched but oh no, this jobsworth harridan is on a real ego trip. She's not letting me go without a scalp.

"I call police!" she says threateningly

I shrug my shoulders.

She then produces a mobile phone and begins to dial a number. She's probably bluffing, but as the proverbial stranger in a strange land this is a risk I just can't afford to take. At this point in time I just don't need the hassle or the stress, so I admit defeat and reluctantly take the notes from my wallet and hand them to her with a pained expression on my face. Out of compassion she hands me back 2000 florin and tells me to go back to the machine and stamp my ticket.
She then has the cheek to ask me where I'm from. At this stage a friendly conversation with a wizened old battleaxe is not exactly what I need.
I'm tempted to say "I'm from a small village just outside Ireland called Gofeckyerselfyakont. Maybe you've heard of it?" But I decide not to.
When I come back towards her after having stamped my ticket she's giving some other poor bastard a hard time. I walk on towards the platform hopeful, but not entirely safe in the knowledge that I'll never see her again. It now occurs to me that it would have been cheaper to get a taxi directly from the airport to the hostel.

When I eventually reach the city centre, my wallet now somewhat lighter I notice there are many people walking their dogs. Just as I'm thinking things couldn't get any worse I step in a dog turd. One of the reasons I've always preferred cats to dogs is because of their superior personal hygiene. Cats may be aloof and look down

155

on their owners (sometimes quite literally if they're up a tree or sitting on a high wall or roof), but at least unlike dogs they don't just crap anywhere that takes their fancy. And they at least have the decency to bury it once they've ejected it from their bowels.

This is my third time in Budapest and I've always found it to be something of an oppressive intimidating city. Its long wide tree-lined streets are an unsuccessful imitation of the Parisian boulevards. Its grim grey sidestreets and alleyways are a riot of concrete.

When I finally reach the hostel, having given the souls of my shoes a thorough clean I find I'm sharing a room with a pleasant couple in their late 20s from Sydney, Julie and Dane. I then get a reply to the text I'd sent to Jake several hours ago. On hearing of my imminent visit to Transylvania he comes back with the witty riposte – "Have a fang-tastic time!"

We have a briefing in the lobby of the hostel. The tour leader is a young Romanian called Gheorge. With his shaven head, lean figure and dark goatee beard he bears a passing resemblance to the tragic Italian cyclist Marco Pantani during his glory days of the late '90s before he put on weight and eventually died of an overdose. His sidekick is a diminutive swarthy South African of Portuguese origin called Carlos.

The driver is a Hungarian known as "John" which is presumably the nearest English equivalent of his real name. With shaven head, gold hoop ear ring in each ear, multiple tattoos and built like the proverbial brick shithouse he looks like a cross between the infamous loyalist paramilitary leader Johnny "Mad Dog" Adair and a Caucasian version of criminal gang leader Marcellus Wallace from the film Pulp Fiction.

Gheorge asks a question:
"Do we have any vegetarians on the tour?"

A couple of hands shoot up.

"We don't like vegetarians in Romania. We say the best vegetable in our country is pork"

156

This quip gets a quite few laughs.

He jokingly denigrates the Hungarian language, the incongruous Finno-Ugric tongue related to Finnish and Estonian.

"This is John our driver. He's Hungarian. I don't speak Hungarian. It's a language for dentists."

John clearly hasn't understood this, but laughs anyway as everyone else is laughing. He speaks very basic English and not a word of Romanian, so I begin to foresee communication problems on this trip.

Day 2 – Budapest – Oradea - Cluj-Napoca
After a frugal breakfast of the usual European low budget hostel fare of muesli, a
crusty bread roll, salami and flat slices of processed cheese it's time to hit the road.

A list is passed around for everyone to tick their name off. It has details of everyone's date of birth, which is contrary to European Data Protection law now that both Hungary and Romania are fully-fledged members of the EU. But as I'm on holiday and don't want to think about work I turn a blind eye. I notice that almost everyone else on the tour was born in the 1980s, and there's even someone who was born in 1990, which makes me feel old. However, although I was born in the '70s, I'm relieved to find that I'm still not the oldest participant on the tour.

The Hungarian countryside east of Budapest is largely flat and monotonous – the area known as the "Pushta", a vast plateau. There are bungalows with gardens containing neatly planted vine rows, ploughed fields and yellow fields of stubble bisected by pylons with small groups of roe deer running across them in the autumn sunshine. Apart from the music playing on what sounds like one of those "Hits of the '80s" CDs that you can get for 10p in supermarkets the bus is unusually quiet. There are almost 30 travellers on board, but none of them seem to be talking. I put this

157

down to the fatigue of travel and partying.

We're now passing small patches of deciduous woodland. Buzzards circle over the fields as Billy Idol's *Rebel Yell* comes on. I spot a pheasant in a field.

Now it's *Atomic* by Blondie. Most of those on board won't recognise the tunes as they weren't born when they came out.

I notice the odd road sign warning motorists to be aware of deer as Duran Duran's *Wild Boys* is followed by The Human League's *Don't You Want Me Baby* and we reach the town of Kisujallas. It's like being on a nostalgic journey through both space and time.

It seems that every town we pass through has a Tesco, which despite its name is not a Romanian company. The music is getting tackier. Now it's that one hit wonder by the former topless model Samantha Fox from 1986.

All the houses in this part of rural Hungary seem to look the same – small rectangular bungalows with pyramidal roofs.

Soft Cell's *Tainted Love* comes on as we enter the town of Puspoklademy. This nostalgia-fuelled romp continues as we reach the Romanian border where there's an incredibly long queue of lorries. As the majority of the tour party are from Canada, Australia or New Zealand and therefore non-EU citizens there's a fairly long wait at the frontier. I get a text on my phone from O2 which welcomes me to Romania and tells me the costs of calls/texts to the EU. I put my watch forward by an hour as bizarrely we're now in a different time zone.

We spend the night in a hostel in Cluj, a city now probably best known for its football team who feature regularly in the Champions League.

Day 3 – Cluj – Sibiu – Sibies
Breakfast Time
At breakfast a bubbly blonde South African girl called Tracey, who's currently working as a teacher in London, but currently has a week off for half-term hears my accent and asks me:.

"Are you Scottish?"

I decide to play this for laughs.

"Close. I'm actually from an island off the coast of Scotland."

"Skye?"

"No, Ireland."

"You don't sound Irish."

I'm assuming her interpretation of an Irish accent is based on the likes of Bono, Ronan Keating, Graham Norton or Louis Walsh whose soft dulcet southern tones sound quite different from my harsh guttural Ulster brogue. So in an exaggeratedly broad Dublin accent I reply

"So oi s'pose ya wan' me to be talkin' loike dis den, do ya?"

This gets a laugh from some of the congregation.

Now that I'm on a roll I'm almost tempted to continue in the vein of "Ah bejaysus and begorrah 'tis a foine day to be sure to be sure" or better still "So what part of Zimbabwe are you from Tracey?", but decide to leave it.

For the time-being anyway.

Then we're on the road again. In many of the town we pass through there are statues of the legendary twins Romulus and Remus - the founders of Rome being suckled by the she-wolf who supposedly brought them up – with the inscription "MADRE ROMA" below. A legacy of Romania's Latin heritage. There are also monuments to the Transylvanian folk hero Avram Iancu, although I only find out who he is on my return home after consulting Wikipedia. In case you're wondering – no I don't have an i-pad.

The bus stops in Sibiu, the 2007 European City of Culture. A friendly stray dog takes a liking to our group and decides to follow us. It barks violently at a passing local walking in the opposite direction and gives him a fright.

For lunch I have a chicken salad which contains more cheese than I'm comfortable with.

After a stroll around the city centre taking in the sights we have a few minutes before the bus is due to leave, so we decide to have a coffee in the main square, a fine medieval German-style affair, a legacy of the region's Teutonic settlement. Gheorge joins us. I get to try out my Romanian in the cafe by ordering a milky coffee.

"*O cafea sie lapte*" I say.

And they even understand me.

"You speak Romanian?" Gheorge asks, a little surprised.

"A little" I say modestly.

Despite Romania's long-standing Italian and French influences its coffee still has a long way to go before it catches up with the standards of the cappuccinos and lattes made by its linguistic Latin-tongued kinsfolk.

We spend the night in the nearby village of Sibies set in pleasant countryside of rutted roads, fast flowing streams and overgrown fields. The local shop, the only one in the village does a roaring trade in alcohol sales that evening. They must think Christmas has come two months early.

The after-dinner evening entertainment includes traditional Romanian folk dancing. Accompanying the dancers is a two–piece band consists of a clarinettist and an accordionist.
I'm one of the first of the tour party to get dragged reluctantly on to the floor. The climax involves dancing around in a huge ring.
As the night wears on, I find myself dehydrated – obviously exhausted from all that dancing. There's a glass of clear liquid on the table which I assume is water. I grab it and down it in one. It

turns out to be vodka. I'm not looking forward to tomorrow...

Wednesday 29ᵗʰ October Day 4 - Sibies – Braşov

The only day of the week which has a football team named after it...

There are numerous delays due to road works on the route from Sibies to Braşov. On a more positive note it's a gloriously warm and sunny day with the colours of autumn in full splendour. Such a shame to be stuck on a bus on a tediously long journey on a day like this though.
Like many towns and cities in the local area Braşov's centre has a medieval Germanic style of architecture and layout reflecting its history of Saxon settlement.   Gheorge refers to the German community who settled here in the middle ages as we gather in the main square with its famous Black Church.
A dizzy Australian girl who seems confused asks "Are we in Germany?"
Gheorge rolls his eyes and points to the illuminated Hollywood-style sign which says "BRASOV" in big cut-out letters on top of the hill which overlooks the city.
Ironically the Romanian-German writer Herta Müller would win the Nobel Prize for literature the following year.

Thursday 30 October, Day 5 – Braşov – Bran Castle – Braşov
Word has got around the hotel staff that I'm a fluent Romanian speaker.
Today's outing is the nearest thing to a real life Dracula's castle. The story (probably apocryphal) goes that old Vlad had spent a night here in Bran Castle.
It's the former home of Princess Maria and Ileana Bran whose descendants now live in Switzerland and have no intention of returning to Transylvania now that the peasants have rights. And are actually allowed to vote, join trade unions, go out on strike and appeal against unfair dismissal.

The castle is now apparently up for sale.

I can just imagine Peter Cushing and Christopher Lee in mortal combat on the balcony.

There's a statue of Vlad Tepes himself. It's ironic that a sadistic mass murderer should become a folk hero and a major tourist attraction. But this is far from unusual. While many English people regard Oliver Cromwell as a hero many Irish people would see in as a murderous tyrant, a similar character to Vlad the Impaler. He still has a statue outside the Houses of Parliament. But let's not go down that particularly tricky cul-de-sac. The subject that is – not Whitehall.

Later on back at our Braşov base I go for an early evening stroll through the beech woodlands in the hills overlooking the city. The ground is under a carpet of golden brown leaves and it's pleasantly and unseasonally warm at 17°. A small bat flits its way through the trees, no doubt ready to feast on the fresh blood of virgins after transforming back into Christopher Lee.

The Romanian papers, just like the press everywhere else in the world have substantial coverage of the forthcoming US presidential elections. Barack Obama is described as *senatorul de Illinois, candidaţilor la Casa Albă,* which doesn't take a genius to translate, so it is quite a readable language.

In the early evening we get a bit of free time to take a leisurely stroll around the city. There's a covered market which has a fishmonger's stall. In the great tradition of discovering that certain foreign words for perfectly innocent things mean something rude in English, I find out to my considerable amusement that the Romanian word for carp is "crap". The fishmonger is gracious enough to let me take a picture of the fish with its side-splittingly hilarious label attached, but probably thinks I'm mad.

Friday 31st October, Day 6 – Braşov – Sighisoara – Carpathian Mountains

On the coach Gheorge gives us a poignant description of the end of communism in Romania.

Under the old regime there were only three hours of television a day. Looking at the amount of crap you get on TV nowadays maybe that's not such a bad thing though.

There was no contraception and exotic fruits were unheard of. He tells us the story of the first time he saw a banana at the age of 12 and left it on the hob until it turned black in the mistaken belief that this meant it was now ripe and ready for consumption.

But on the plus side there was no unemployment either. Everyone had a job. Even if you were sacked apparently it was up to your employer to find you another job.

The teacher would tell the class not to go to church on the orders of the communist authorities. Yet they would still see other in church that Sunday.

It's Hallowe'en and tonight the tour party is sleeping in a cluster of log cabins in the Carpathian Mountains. We have plum brandy as an aperitif before dinner. This is followed by a combination of local beer and wine. This turns out to be an ill-advised combination.
A large bonfire is lit.
It's time for the big highlight of the trip – the Hallowe'en fancy dress party. I'm supposedly in the guise of a vampire - dressed all in black with wild black wig and cloak from Tesco and a touch of eye shadow borrowed from one of the girls. I end up looking like a cross between a comedy Addams Family style vampire, a bad Alice Cooper tribute act and lead singer of The Cure, Robert Smith.

Most of the girls are dressed as witches with pointy hats and broomsticks, but there are a few creative exceptions. Tracey's

163

come as the bride of Dracula in a tight cleavage-enhancing shiny purple basque with a few fake blood stains in strategic places. Her Australian friend and teaching colleague Kelly has gone a step further in her corset and fishnets with a very short skirt. I'm not sure who or what she's meant to be though.

"If they knew what we got up to in our spare time we'd never be allowed to teach again!" Tracy admits.

Things have come a long way from the Hallowe'ens of my childhood of trying to bite apples on a string or apples in a basin without using one's hands, cheap plastic masks from the supermarket and fizzling sparklers and apple tart with coins hidden inside. But hey, nothing lasts forever...

Saturday 1ˢᵗ November Day 7 – Cluj
A speckled starling-like bird, the like of which I've never seen before is perched on the branch of a pine tree. With the help of Wikipedia I later identify it as a spotted nutcracker.
It's remarkably mild for the time of year. We arrive back in Cluj at around 2 pm.
There's a street called Boulevardul 21 Dicembre 1989, named after the date of the revolution – when I was studying my GCSEs in between playing handball and listening to various heavy metal and prog rock bands.
I notice that unlike back home where jaywalking is second nature to people, the locals here obey the traffic lights scrupulously, crossing only when the green man appears – no doubt a legacy of the communist era when people were used to being told what to do and no-one questioned the system.
Like many eastern European cities there's a sense of grim bleakness once you stray from the centre and head towards the residential suburbs of sprawling rusting apartment blocks which could do with a fresh coat of paint. Inevitably the city has a statue of Avram Iancu the Transylvanian folk hero.
On our last night in Romania we ironically end up dining in a Hungarian restaurant.

Sunday, 2nd November - Day 8 – Cluj – Budapest – London
Our last day in Romania and it's raining.

Horse and cart seems to be a more common form of transport for Romanian farmers than the tractor. It's just like it was back home half a century ago. There are conical haystacks reminiscent of those in Slovenia and Bosnia.

I spot a turkey in the garden of a house along the main road. It's of the glossy black variety with resplendent tail feathers and wattles – not the miserable looking factory farmed white-feathered birds you get back home who wait for December with resignation.

You know you're back in Hungary when you see a sign welcoming you to a town with an unpronounceable name. The coach passes through Berettyóújfalu. I set my watch back an hour, remembering the time difference between Hungary and Romania.

It's 16:42 and I'm about to board the flight for London. I'm still getting that rocking, swaying feeling from all those hours spent on the coach. Lucky I don't have work tomorrow…

Oh and by the way in case you're wondering about the title of this chapter - I've never actually been to Castlederg. But I'm sure it's not a bad place.

-12-

The Beginning of the End

The Zeitgeist

By the tail end of the 1980s the Berlin Wall had fallen, the old Communist bloc countries had embraced capitalism. Winds of change were blowing across Europe. The German heavy metal band Scorpions even wrote a song about this. On my first visit to Prague about a decade later that bloody song was going through my head incessantly. Only a few days previously I'd been in Vienna, where I couldn't get a certain Ultravox song out of my head. It meant nothing to me. A decade on from that I even got to see Midge Ure himself (now with even less hair) performing the song live at London's O2 Arena.

The Cold War was finally over. Nelson Mandela had recently become a free man and the cracks in apartheid were beginning to show. A few years later we would even be able to buy South African oranges in the supermarket without feeling guilty about it.

We were on the cusp of a new decade which promised exciting things. But more importantly my school days were gradually coming to an end.

I had once successfully persuaded my mum not to buy South African oranges from the supermarket. I spent the rest of the time keeping my head down in case any of my schoolmates were around so I could avoid the shame and embarrassment of being seen out shopping with my mother. No offence, Mum!

I even wrote a poem about South Africa back in 1986 and sent it in to the local BBC office in Belfast. Not a very good poem at that, but I was young and inexperienced at the time. Although some might say that my literary skills haven't changed much since then. Reading it now, it actually seems quite funny to me (in an Adrian Mole kind of way), even though it was meant to be serious at the time.

"South Africa" (by Ciaran Ward aged 12⅓)

Pretoria, Johannesburg, Cape Town and more

On the news it's getting to be a bore

Will Winnie and Nelson be united again?

Maybe not till 2010!

State of unrest in the Transvaal

Orange Free State and Natal!

Will the president ever be black?

When Mr Botha said so I was taken aback!

Will they ever put an end to apartheid?

There's a very slight chance that they just might.

Winnie and Nelson Mandela were eventually reunited a few years later, but ironically they got divorced shortly afterwards. However the poem was prophetic in its reference to 2010, the year the football World Cup was held in what came to be known as the "Rainbow Nation". Needless to say my poem didn't get broadcast. Something which I was disappointed with at the time, but now I'm thankful that it wasn't read out over the airwaves.

It was a laugh seeing South African politicians with names like Stoffels du Plessis and Kobus Van der Voordenheyden being interviewed on the news and coming up with classic lines like:.

"The Sooth Efrikan gevamint will not yield to unternational prissure and thrits from communists and tirrorists! One man one vite for the blecks is sumply not an ooption!"

The performers behind the satirical comedy show *Spitting Image* which mocked the politicians and celebrities of the day by caricaturing them in the form of grotesque rubber puppets even released a hit single called "I've never met a nice South African". Don't get me wrong; having lived in London for over a decade I've met many nice South Africans. Many of them even seem to have a guilt complex over the injustice meted out by their past governments.

The key words during this time of great transition of the late 1980s and early 90s were Operation Desert Storm, Maastricht, *perestroika*, *glasnost*, and CD ROM. Bands who were big at the time like Blur, The Charlatans, Inspiral Carpets, EMF, James, The Mock Turtles. That other Manchester band Oasis was still a few years away from stardom. Even now when I hear such songs on the radio memories of Friday nights, McElroys night club, the Clock Bar which looked out over the river and dry ice and early experiences with alcohol – usually cider or the much-maligned Harp Lager with a shot of lime added to make it more palatable – come back to haunt me. Similarly, every time Kate Bush's *Wuthering Heights* comes on the radio, I'm suddenly catapulted back to my A-level English literature classes and visions of Cathy and Heathcliff on wind-swept Yorkshire moors.

In the autumn of 1990 I commenced my A-level studies. Our academic workload was reduced now that we were doing only three subjects. There was a distinct feeling of freedom and elation in the air, a sense that this was the glorious beginning of the end. By this time we thought we knew it all, having been at the big school for five long years, but the reality was that we knew next to sweet FA about the real world. Sometimes I think of that idealistic, but naïve 17 year old, his head full of ideas on how to change the world, a small town boy with a big city attitude – and saying to him "catch yourself on, mate!"

We suddenly had "free" periods – as referred to in Gerry Black's head boy's speech in a future chapter. I was now a "senior" pupil. I'd spent the summer in the outer suburbs of North London flipping burgers, frying chips and mopping floors at a fast food joint belonging to a well-known chain – thanks to Aunts Martina and Siobhan. It had been an eventful summer. Iraqi forces under Saddam Hussein had invaded Kuwait. Belfastman Brian Keenan had been released from captivity having spent five years as a hostage in war-torn Beirut. And there were billboard posters all over London advertising a new American cartoon series featuring a yellow-skinned family which was about to be broadcast on this side of the Atlantic via satellite TV. They said it would never catch on.

We were now allowed to leave the school premises at lunchtime and go down the town– although many of us had already been doing this unofficially for quite some time.

From what I remember my penultimate year at the school was quite a relaxing one. A-levels were still a "relatively" long way away and I was only doing three subjects and we had quite a few "free" periods. I remember spending quite a lot of time in coffee shops after school (one of which I nearly burnt down accidentally after casually sticking a piece of a paper into one of the lights – just for a laugh of course) with mates getting high on caffeine and talking crap.

We would spend quite a long time in these establishments. We perfected the art of making a cup of tea or coffee last for the best part of an hour - and stay well after we'd finished our beverages.

One irate café proprietor who didn't like students would get pissed off with us if we dared outstay our welcome.

"Right, if you've finished your tea can you please go now!" he would bellow at us.

If you ordered a cup of tea it came with a teapot. Some of us attempted to get around this by ordering one pot and two cups and sharing between two. He was such a tight old sod that he'd refuse to sell tea with one teacup and two cups and would insist on you buying two separate pots. So we went to a different café where they weren't as strict.

A week of work experience was compulsory. Opportunities were fairly limited in the local area if you were ambitious or pursuing a glamorous career. If you wanted to be a molecular physicist, astronomer, astronaut, an ambassador or chargé d'affaires, actor, marine biologist or petro-chemical engineer you were rather stuck. The town had no particle accelerator or nuclear power plant, no telescopic observatory, no space aeronautics centre with rocket launching facilities, no diplomatic missions or consulates, no film studios, no coastline, no aquarium and it was a long way to the nearest oil rig.

Instead work experience destinations generally followed a predictable pattern. If you were doing science A-levels you'd be sent to the local hospital. If you weren't you would usually end up in a bank or a solicitor's office, where you'd be making the tea, sending faxes and doing the post runs.

My ambition at the time was to be a journalist. I suppose I'd always fancied myself as some kind of a writer. I can just hear the discerning reader at this point saying "oh you poor misguided fool". I was however too slow in asking either of the two local papers for a placement. Two of my contemporaries had got there first which effectively left me in the lurch.

For the record neither of them ended up as journalists either. By default I ended up with an organisation dedicated to the promotion of Irish traditional music...

I was travelling from one small village to another and recording interviews with elderly fiddlers, tin whistle players and accordionists to capture the oral history of traditional music in the area.

I developed a crush on the young woman I was working with. But it was never to be. She was 28, I was 17. I knew it was never realistically going to happen, but liked the thought of it all the same. But then I always had a bit of a thing about older women.

Moving swiftly on...

Shortly after my week of "work experience" (11-15 March 1991 – for some reason I remember the dates clearly), I was parachuted into the final of an all-Ireland inter-schools debating competition held at Trinity College, Dublin. I say "parachuted" as I was brought in as a last minute replacement for Kevin Nolan. Kevin

Nolan was a rare example of one of those annoyingly talented people who seemed to be good at everything. He was unavailable for the debate as he was playing the lead role in the school musical. He was also captain of the school football team and his girlfriend Roisin was particularly fragrant. As well as being able to successfully pursue these extra-curricular activities he was also a straight A student.

Not that I was complaining though. On this occasion I was a net beneficiary of Mr Nolan's multi-talented and highly successful persona. I'd reached the final of a national debating contest without having to do any work. I had of course been previously involved in more local debating contests, but now I'd hit the big time. So while I wasn't exactly a master debater I was still keen. Stop that sniggering at the back.

So it was a two man team consisting of Joseph Gorman and myself. Chairing the debate was the writer, statesman, newspaper editor, former diplomat, literary critic, master of the political U-turn and general jack-of-all trades (Kevin Nolan take note) the late Conor Cruise O'Brien. Although I wasn't a big fan of the Cruiser's politics I still saw fit to quote him in an essay on Franco-Algerian writer Albert Camus' *L'Etranger* while at university a few years later.

From what I remember there was one school from each of the four provinces taking part. Naturally we were representing Ulster.

I still have the hemispherical glass paperweight of the finest Waterford Crystal to remind me that I was a "finalist" (albeit a fraudulent finalist) in the 1991 Irish Times All-Ireland Schools debating competition. The motion was to do with European integration – something along the lines of "This House believes in a United States of Europe". We were opposing it. The famous Maastricht Treaty was just around the corner. I gave the usual argument about the erosion of sovereignty and the fusion of unique cultural identities into an incomprehensible mish-mash. It didn't necessarily reflect my personal views, but I had no choice. I couldn't help feeling out of my depth. Our opponents were too clever by half and seemed to have witty ripostes for everything. I kept thinking "Shit! Why I didn't think of that?" every time they came up with witty one-liners, which although ingenious were nevertheless glaringly obvious.

For this reason we didn't win. Nevertheless I enjoyed the experience. It had given me a small taste of university life and certainly whetted my appetite.

Shortly after my debating experience it was time for an A-level English lit trip to London with the two grammar other schools in the town. This involved an incredibly long coach journey from Stranraer to London.

We stayed in a hotel which was very centrally located at the back of Piccadilly Circus...

My memories of the trip are something of a hazy blur.

We had a few "free" evenings where we were free to sample the delights of the Smoke. On one of these nights two chancers ventured into Soho in search of some "entertainment" and were allegedly charged £50.00 for two drinks in a seedy joint – and encouraged to buy a drink for "the lady" from the next table who joined them. Apparently they escaped by climbing out of the toilet window from where they beat a hasty retreat, the baseball bat-wielding doorman in hot pursuit of them as they high-tailed it down the street. I won't name the chancers in question, but they're the same two characters who went looking for semi-pornographic holiday brochures as referred to in a previous chapter.

Some of us went to find more legitimate forms of entertainment and ended up paying through the nose to see films we knew were never going to be shown at Omagh cinema, such as *Cyrano de Bergerac* – starring Gerard Depardieu and Anne Brochet and the gangster flick *Miller's Crossing* with Gabriel Byrne.

As part of the official itinerary we went to see a Harold Pinter play starring Warren Mitchell famous for his ranting racist character Alf Garnet and Cheri Lunghi then best known for playing the female manager of a football club in the short-lived feminist Channel 4 series *The Manageress*. And a student version of Brian Friel's

Translations – even though neither Pinter nor Friel were on the syllabus of set texts.

I have vague memories of a cider bottle being thrown from a sixth floor window on the last night.

After we got back I wrote a rather smart-arsed article about the trip for the school magazine. While going through my parents' loft recently I managed to recover it. And here it is in a slightly amended form.

FIVE DAYS IN MARCH

Prologue

And this it was written in the stars above that one day an epic journey in search of great adventures and cultural fulfillment to satisfy an insatiable lust for literary bliss would take place; an adventure that knew no limits. Whatever this epic journey was it certainly wasn't the English trip.

Our story begins one starry night in March with a coach in a car park [incidentally the same car park where Barry Bennett picked a fight with a traffic warden a couple of years earlier – but I didn't put this bit in the actual article obviously] under the bright lights and carpeted corridors of metropolitan Omagh. The three schools hereafter known as the Academy, Convent and Christian Brothers' under the administration of five teachers from the aptly named English departments head the cast in this moving picture of mixed fortunes.

Very little happened between here and Larne unless the reader would prefer his/her/its sordid imagination to run away with him/her/itself and seek political asylum in a luxury villa in Tuscany.

After being blatantly ripped off by the various retail outlets of the Stena Galloway ferry bound for Stranraer and experiencing

the American Dream of good old Rocky (IV) winning the Cold War by defeating the Commie scum in vivid technicolour the enthusiastic band of students (hereafter known as "we" or "us") and teachers once again boarded the luxury coach. Travelling through rural south-western Scotland and seeing glowing sheep with five heads in Cumbria before traversing the broad majestic Pennines during the wee small hours in between watching *Crocodile Dundee II* was as you may have already guessed a tiring experience.

After passing through the Midlands we were soon into the sprawling conurbation of Greater London and eventually reached our destination of the Regent Palace Hotel at about 12:30 pm, Wednesday. The hotel to our delight was discreetly tucked away behind Piccadilly Circus in the sleazy part of London's fashionable Central London. The next significant part of the itinerary (there were many insignificant parts in between, but I'll not go into this) was the excellent performance of Brian Friel's *Translations* at Goldsmiths College. Authentic sets and an overture of traditional music plus the incessant and almost annoying cry of a curlew in the background provided an almost genuine atmosphere recreating rural Donegal. The acting was also quite good, but the pronunciation of "poteen" left a lot to be desired. An enjoyable production nonetheless. Had the production been staged in Deptford however we would have arrived considerably earlier and the trains proved to be a problem regarding tickets and actually getting on.... [A bit of an in joke there – you would really have had to have been there to get it].

THE MORNING AFTER...

A "guided" sightseeing tour of London was the order of the morning or for those on the lower deck of the coach, a guide to the famous pavements of London, none of which were paved with gold. Our trendy, chilled out, down-with-the-kids guide reliably took us to the cool parts of town, where we were told if we were lucky we might even see the odd authentic "punk rocker" (sic). Unfortunately we didn't. We were about 15 years too late.

On the Friday morning we embarked on a day trip to Canterbury where we travelled back in time through the Twilight Zone into the 14th century to discover the medieval tales of Chaucer in all the glory of Middle English. One of the poet's lesser known works was the *Manx Cat's Tale*, and of course there was also the recently discovered A-level *English Literature Student's Tale*, an extract from which I've reproduced below:

The English Literature Student's Tale

To Canterbury that is called Canterbury

Wente a grupe of stewdentes inne a hurrie

Inne a lukshurye koche ful to the brimme

Under the commaunde of the dryver Jim

On that gentil toune theye al sette foote

For aventures folwen oon greate route

The Canterbury Tales strukke them doune in awe

And the Cathedralle was the nexte thyng theye sawe

A gyded toore was the order of the day

Withe a learnede manne who had plentie to saye

There were gentil cloisters and windowes of stayned glasse

As the sonne bete doune on the freshe greene grasse

Then bake to the koche they alle wente doune

To savoore the delytes of olde Londonne toune

"My tale is nowe at an ende" quod he

The reste is ther foore thee to see.

Back in the 20th century things were hotting up as we took our last chance to see the bright lights and sights of London on the last precious night of our brief sojourn in the metropolis. With a heavy heart and a light head we departed early the next morning, exhausted from such little sleep the previous night. What happened the night before I'll keep to myself (and about three dozen other boys and girls from Omagh's three grammar schools) in the classic tradition of "What goes on tour stays on tour".

The journey home was the same as the journey over except that it was the other way round. Many interesting things happened along the way including the initiation of Seamus "You wouldn't let it lie" Conway through the ceremonial washing of the hair and the equally bureaucratic painting of Gavin "Dances with Wolves" McCarthy's face thanks to the artistic talents of Geraldine Daly.

EPILOGUE

Things have never been the same since and so it came to pass that one of us must air our views on the trip based on subsequent feedback. Sorry, where was I?

THE END (or is it?)

Prog Rock of Ages

Gaining entry to a certificate 18 film while were still only 17¾ was seen as something of a coup, but getting into licensed premises at this age was even more so. A summer's afternoon off following an exam was happily passed in one of the town's watering holes after you'd taken your school tie off in a pathetic attempt to disguise the fact that you were underage. Before that the only option had been to go to the local park or the river bank with a bottle of cider shared between a party of ten. The tallest boy in the group was assigned to go into the off-licence, having not shaved for a few days and put on a deep voice when ordering the offending liquor. Occasionally, if one of the party was a talented artist he would draw a fake scar down the designated buyer's cheek and a couple of realistic tattoos on his arms. That way no-one would dare refuse to serve him.

Certain pubs were known to serve underage drinkers. Of the ones that didn't get their licences confiscated, some then started asking for ID. Even after I'd turned 18 and could drink legally I would occasionally still get ask to prove it. As a result of this I got into the habit of bringing my passport to the boozer. It was as if the pub was a different country and the doorman was a border control inspector. The outside world was like North Korea, dull and regimented, but once we got into the pub it was as if we were in the decadent, free-for-all anything goes world of the "South of the Demilitararized Zone" Zone, the heart and seoul of existence.

By the dawn of the 1990s, the ridiculous '80s schoolboy fashion of wearing black shoes (often slip-ons) and white socks was gone. Major sportswear labels like Nike and Adidas were still very much in vogue then as they are now. But little did we know we were unintentionally contributing to global capitalism and the exploitation of young children in Bangladeshi sweatshops getting paid 50p a day to make our cool t-shirts and trainers for the western world – even though we still wear the designer labels now. As a backlash against the ridiculous 1970s fashions of outrageously vomit-inducing flowery-patterned wide kipper ties and flared trousers the schoolboy fashions of the mid-80s had been wafer thin ties and almost skintight trousers. The anorexic effect of the neck attire was achieved by tying one's tie using the thin end as the longer part and stuffing the thicker end into one's shirt. Looking back in hindsight this probably looked rather silly, but the folly of youth really knows no bounds.

In the '80s Skintight bleached jeans were considered cool. Then in the following decade one of the most ridiculous trends in fashion was jeans with holes in them.

During these heady days I was juggling driving lessons with inter-schools debating competitions, inter-schools "university challenge"-style quiz competitions and analysing commercial land-use in the town centre for my A-Level geography project while trying to make sense of Chaucer's Middle English in *The Canterbury Tales* or Celtic mysticism in Yeats' poetry and examining the colonial metaphors in *The Great Gatsby*.

Indeed, these were interesting times.

It was the early 1990s, but there seemed to be a retro phase of late 60s/early '70s music in vogue. The film *The Doors* (the bio-pic starring Val Kilmer as the ill-fated Jim Morrison had just come out), Jimi Hendrix, Velvet Underground and Bob Marley were all de rigeur in the sixth form common room among the school magazine editorial committee and the debating team – that is they would have been if the school had had such a common room, but since my departure I'm told it has now. The new extension to the school had been in the pipeline for years, but ironically only got round to being completed after my year group had left. '70s punk like The Clash and the Sex Pistols was also being listened to. But maybe this is true of every generation who yearn for times past which occurred before they were born. The aforementioned Morrison of The Doors and Hendrix of the imaginatively named Jimi Hendrix Experience had been dead for 20 years, but were still popular. I find the fact that these people are still being talked about now, and I've outlived them by over a decade somewhat worrying.

Around the same time as the heavy metal boom (or possibly shortly after it) there was an explosion of indie bands, many of whom came from Manchester. They usually had silly names like the Joyful Tuesdays, Petrified Violets, Inspirational Curtains and Nick's Nuclear Waste Disposal Unit or something similar. They were basically middle class boys with floppy fringes. Whereas the heavy metal crowd were middle class boys with mullets. Inevitably there was a bit of a cultural and tribal divide between the indie crowd and the heavy metal crowd.

But a new emerging band from Seattle called Nirvana, early pioneers of the so-called "grunge" scene, who appealed to both camps would change that. A few short years later their lead singer Kurt Cobain would blow his brains out – at the age of 27, thus joining the notorious "27 Club", of which Amy Winehouse has become the latest member. A tragic irony when you consider one of Nirvana's songs contained the lyric "No, I don't have a gun".

And no doubt I'll now be receiving bundles of hate mail from outraged Nirvana fans after that quip. Or in this modern age, gigabytes of hate mail would be more accurate.

On the more gothic side were the so-called "Cureheads". Many of them tended to be A-level art students for some reason. They would dress in black and wear eyeshadow.

But I was going down another avenue, preferring that much maligned musical genre from the late '60s/early '70s known as progressive rock. I listened to the self-indulgent lyrics and was transfixed by the elaborate artwork on the sleeves.

I got into the early Genesis under Peter Gabriel which roughly spanned the period 1968-1975. This was a bunch of former public school boys indulging in rambling compositions of long keyboard solos and silly voices. There were tales of giant killer plants, mythical subterranean worlds beneath the New York subway and unscrupulous property developers, East End gangsters fighting in forests. The then current incarnation of Genesis with the balding Phil Collins at the helm was terribly unfashionable – as was the Gabriel version – but at least the latter had some degree of intellectual sophistication – or so I thought – ok, or at least wanted to think so. Getting nostalgic about things that I had no memory of as that had happened before I was born was a tad bizarre I suppose.

It seems that Gabriel's gone all serious now with his pretensions to embracing "world music"– I sometimes think he would have made a good comedian. Similarly with Jethro Tull the novelty factor was a plus. The band's lead singer was a bearded wizard-like figure in long coat and codpiece playing the flute while standing on one leg – a classic quintessentially British eccentric. Then there was Rush the Canadian power rock trio with their sci-fi epics on future dystopian worlds spouting the right wing philosophy of Ayn Rand.

Whilst studying *Hamlet*, *Wuthering Heights*, the poetry of WB Yeats and Moliere's 17th century French farces, getting to grips with the existentialist philosophy of Jean-Paul Sartre, the French past historic tense, the economic policies of Brazil and the soil composition of tropical rainforests, Hendrix and Zeppelin, Pink Floyd and Jethro Tull…and Marillion kept me going. A whole CD borrowed from the local library would easily fit onto one side of 90-minute blank cassette tape, so I ended up with the strange combination of Led Zeppelin on one side and The Pogues on the other. CDs back then were still seen as the cutting edge of technology. Digital downloads were still the stuff of science fiction. Early versions of mobile phones were around, but they were usually about the size of a small car.

Doc Marten boots, previously the exclusive preserve of neo-Nazi thugs and football hooligans had now become a respectable unisex fashion. And now they came in a range of colours, some of which were even spotted or had flowery patterns on them.

In my year there were also a few devotees of underground music who were into bands no-one else had ever heard of and would come out with classic statements of pretentious self-pity along the lines of:

"I was listening to U2/Nirvana/REM/Ash/Spice Girls, etc [delete as appropriate] before anyone had ever heard of them. I saw them play at the Post Office Club in Omagh three years ago and there were only five people in the audience, but it still a great gig – really atmospheric. They really interacted with the audience. They didn't talk down to us or anything. Then they got famous and now everybody likes them. It's not fair. They've sold out. They're not interested in the music anymore, they just want to make money"

And inevitably someone else would counteract this statement:

"Sure I always knew they were going to be big. That's why I never liked them. I listen to The Mottled Albatrosses and they still churn out good music even though no-one's ever heard of them. Except me and a few others. In fact they could have been really big by now, but they turned down offers from all the major record labels because they didn't want to prostitute themselves to the big global brands. They don't even tour big cities, they only do gigs in obscure venues like pubs, student unions and council-run arts centre in unknown provincial towns."

I would attempt to prick the pretentions of this Mottled Albatrosses fan with a simple question.

"So how they break even let alone make any kind of a living then?"

Long pregnant thoughtful pause…

"They get by."

There's a perception among pompous pseudo-intellectual student types (ie people like I used to be during my younger more foolish days) particularly among that once a rock band, comedian or writer (especially if they were once considered to be a bit cutting edge or left-field) achieves mainstream commercial success they've "sold out" to the big corporations and are now mere "entertainers" rather than "artists".

In my infinitely misguided pomposity I considered myself to be morally and culturally superior to my classmates as I had posters of French actresses from sub-titled trendy pseudo-intellectual arty films about the deeper meaning of life like Juliette Binoche and Irène Jacob, both of whom I had a crush on at the time on my bedroom wall rather than well-known pin-ups or supermodels like Claudia Schiffer or Elle McPherson.

The same could be said of English soccer teams. The vast majority of pupils who followed sport supported either Liverpool or Manchester United, teams they had chosen to support from the age of 7 or 8 simply because they were popular and doing rather well at the time. There was also a smattering of Spurs, Arsenal and Everton supporters, but there was always someone who chose to support (or at least pretended to support) a less successful, less glamorous club like Hartlepool or Plymouth Argyll just so they could stand out from the crowd. Then there were of course the fairweather supporters who would switch allegiances at the drop of the hat. If Liverpool were going through a barren phase, they would quickly transfer their support to United or Arsenal. However if any of the Hartlepool/Plymouth supporters still remain loyal to their chosen clubs (which I very much doubt) I take my hat off to them.

Hard Core Geography

The soul singer Sam Cooke claimed not to know much about history, biology, science books, the French he took, algebra, trigonometry or geography. There were two of these subjects, French and geography (along with English literature) which I studied right to the bitter end of my school days.

Geography was one of the few subjects which required independent research in the form of a dissertation. A lad in the year above me advised me "Do your project on physical geography instead of human geography. For physical at least you can make the answers up".

I went against his advice - the fact that he'd come back to repeat after having failed his A-levels wasn't a particularly good omen - but I ended up making up some of the answers anyway. I did my project on land use in an urban area. Part of the research involved doing pedestrian counts in the town centre which required me to stand on a street corner on a Saturday morning

Naturally enough this attracted some bemused looks from passers-by. I was approached by a wino in his natural state who got curious and asked me what I was doing. His breath smelt like the forecourt of a petrol station. If I'd stuck a match at that moment both of us would have ignited.

"I'm recording a pedestrian survey to gauge how the central business district of an urban centre compares with the theoretical concentric circles models as drawn up by Burgess, Hoyt and Mann".

He seemed satisfied with the answer and staggered off to find the nearest licensed premises conscious that it was now getting dangerously close to opening time.

I don't think the findings of my research revolutionised the world of urban planning though.

As referred to above, any former student of geography will tell you, the discipline is divided into two distinct branches, physical geography (rivers, coasts, volcanoes, etc) and human/ social/ economic/ political geography (population, migration, urban land use, agriculture, etc). I preferred the latter.

I remember one GCSE class where we were studying industrial development or possibly something to do with trade deficits/imports/exports. One pupil seemed confused and asked Mr Martin Walsh

"Sir, is this not economics?"

"Economic geography" came the knowing reply

"Economic bollocks more like" muttered an unimpressed Shane Rogan at the back of the classroom, but not quite loudly enough for Marty to hear.

Teachers naturally like to propagandise their own subjects.

"Geography is all about the world around you" Mr Walsh once said to us. "And if you're not interested in the world around you, you might as well not exist". I don't think those were his exact words – ie I'm sure he didn't ram home the existential element quite like that, but you get my drift. He had a point. He was in fact quite a philosophical person and would sometimes use his subject to illustrate that philosophy.

"When you think about the mountains and the cliffs that have been there for millions of years and they move a fraction of a centimetre every year – a thousand years in geological time is no time at all – it's the blink of an eye – you realise just how insignificant we are. Long after we're all gone mountains and cliffs will still be there – and they'll still look the same – that's how little we matter" he used to say. I remember feeling somewhat reassured on hearing this – and bizarrely such thoughts continue to reassure me. I suppose it puts life into perspective.

In this modern age of global travel I would imagine that school geography field trips are to places like the Amazon basin or Antarctica where pupils go to study the effects of leaching in tropical hardwood rainforests or the impact climate change in polar regions. But our GCSE field trip was to a patch of bogland a few miles out of town where we measured the velocity of a stream. I wrote a humorous tongue-in-cheek account for that year's school magazine, which I include below in heavily edited form:

Correlative Investigation Into The Geographical Factors Of A Moving Body of Water By Means of theoretical and practical analysis and the collection of appropriate data
(OR "FOURTH YEAR GEOGRAPHY FIELD TRIP 1989")

Somewhere in the prevailing of time [sic – I think it should have said "prevailing **mists** of time", but don't remember if the mistake was mine or the printer's] of a small green minibus trundled along a dusty, winding road in a remote rural West Tyrone outpost...

Inside this seemingly inanimate mode of transport a collection of enthusiastic geographers prepared for an enthralling journey into the unknown.

In glorious May sunshine the expedition arrived at the legendary source of the Glencam burn after a pleasant, albeit lengthy ramble through squelching bogland.

The would-be geographers set to work with their first piece of practical analysis. A confused frenzy of surveying rods, clinometers [I don't even remember what a clinometers is now], tape measures, pebbleometers, orange peel and expletives (but not necessarily in that order) came into contact with the stream.

Trusty wellingtons waded through murky waters pausing here and there to take measurements or record any useful details pertaining to geography. Ingenious correlations and hypothetical statements of velocity, cross-sectional area, gradient at all [I think this should have read "et al" – again probably the printer's or proof-reader's mistake not mine] probed into the minds of the active researchers. After passing an endless series of interlocking (Tottenham Hot)spurs. Meanders and depositional and erosional features the party finally settled down to hearty meals of their choosing with stimulating drinks of carbonated water topped off with citric acid, sugar, E numbers and flavouring all in one handy recyclable aluminium can. A slight controversy over a missing surveying rod or two was soon remedied and any environmental damage was avoided during the much-needed lunch break.

The ozone-friendly, lead-free, recyclable geography class [all these terms were fairly new at the time, it being an era of increased environmental awareness] re-boarded the verdant vehicle and set off to another part some distance downstream.

The water was naturally somewhat deeper at this point and a slimy scum of algae manifested itself in the channel ready to pounce and wind its fearsome tendrils around the leg of an unwary student or teacher and drag him kicking and screaming into the uncharted depths. But a sharp prod with a surveying rod (the rhyming here was unintentional by the way) put paid to its evil ideas.

(The next few lines aren't worth including so I'm fast forwarding to the last bit)

The field trip terminated in style at Aghnamirigan Bridge where the last handful of pebbles was laid to rest, the tape measures were retracted and the instruments were put back into *l'autobus vert* , to await the next group.

Excess water was poured out of boots and although our socks had been dampened, our enthusiasm certainly hadn't. You've heard of historic occasions, but the expedition carried out by us, Section 1 of the then Fourth Year Division of the CBS Chartered Exploratory National Geographic Society was truly a geographic occasion.

There's little more that remains to be said – the more dubious [like the boy who attempted to impale a frog with a surveying rod, but was persuaded not to] and the boring events have been duly excluded.

The bedampened hydrological geographers indulged in a bit of friendly revelry as the little green bus trundled along in the searing afternoon heat. [If I remember correctly this involved a bit of banter with two lads in a car stuck behind the bus].

The bus drove on into the sunset even though it was only 3 pm, but it makes a good ending.

(Cue a chorus of "Kevlin Road far away in time" to the tune of *Echo Beach* by Martha and the Muffins repeated thirty-seven times before gradually fading out).

****

At the time my 16 year old self thought the article was a literary masterpiece of comic wordplay, irony and ingenious wit. But looking back in hindsight it now comes across a pretentious, self-indulgent piece of drivel – in other words a typical fifth form school magazine article. The discerning reader at this point may well be thinking to herself that it therefore fits in perfectly with the overall tone of the book. However I am proud to say it took up an entire page and a quarter in that year's magazine.

Creatures of Language

At an all-boys school languages were very much a minority subject. There was an emphasis on sciences – ie subjects that could get you a job other than teaching. But doing a language at A-level was often an excuse to hang out with dusky skinned continental female students or watch subtitled films with deep and meaningful plots containing some kind of underlying metaphor about the futility of life, usually shown late at night on Channel 4. Well, that was my excuse anyway.

Films of this nature were invariably along the lines of:

Young man of Algerian origin (possibly an illegal immigrant) from the ghetto stuck in monotonous dead-end factory job in some miserable industrial inland city in northern France where no foreign tourists ever go – joins trade union to demand better working conditions – meets beautiful, but unattainable young woman from respectable middle class background with a conscious on a demonstration – her parents disapprove – but they strike up a kind of relationship - police try to frame him on some trumped-up charge – he goes on the run -, etc, etc – inconclusive and not entirely happy ending which leaves you wondering what the film was all about…

And inevitably there was the odd bedroom scene with the obligatory nude shots. All very tastefully done of course for purely aesthetic reasons and completely integral to the plot. Allegedly.

How the young (almost always female) teaching assistants who were studying English at their respective French or Spanish universities ended up in Omagh was beyond me. With the whole English speaking world at their fingertips they seemed to have drawn the short straw and been sent to this one horse town. Most of them seemed to end up in a flat in the town centre opposite the offices of one of the local papers.

As part of the A-level French extra-curricular programme we went on an outdoor activities weekend at Lough Melvin, Fermanagh. This involved crawling through part of the county's famous network of limestone caves and canoeing during the day followed by language classes in the evenings. It was a strange combination. What all this had to do with the French language I have no idea. My memory of the weekend is somewhat hazy, but with the help of an old school magazine article by Seamus Conway I've managed to piece together a rough account, allowing for the fact that stuff written in the school magazine wasn't always reliable. And I've added in some of my own fictional snippets for good measure.

There was also a contingent from a young offenders centre near Belfast staying at the hostel. Presumably getting young people to take part in outdoor activities was seen as a way of getting them on the straight and narrow. This made our stay all the more interesting. On the Saturday night we all congregated in the TV lounge where one of the Rocky films was being shown. Our new friends watched with great enthusiasm as they cheered on the eponymous hero as he battled his opponents in the ring with shouts of encouragement:

"Go on Rocky, beat his fucking face in!"

This soon got upgraded to:

"Go on Rocky, beat his fucking lips in!" and so on.

Their attempts to chat up Valérie, our flame-haired French assistant were thwarted on hearing that her 6 foot 10, 25 stone rugby playing boyfriend Jean-Pierre, a scrum half with Stade Français was arriving imminently for spot of cave diving.

Nevertheless, by the end of the weekend we knew all about the finer points of house burglary, car theft and violent assault.

****

At this time a war was going on in Yugoslavia, the economy was in recession, it would still be a few years before the internet was to infiltrate offices and households by stealth.

It's a tragic irony that while old borders across the rest of Europe were disintegrating following the tumbling of the Berlin Wall and the process of increasing continent-wide integration, new borders across the former Yugoslavia were springing up. A decade and a half later I would visit a battle-scarred Bosnia with two old university friends. As we were to find out it was a society in the slow process of rebuilding itself, as my notes from the experience will testify.

I hadn't realised how big Yugoslavia was. One country back then – and now divided into six countries (or seven if you count Kosovo). In my youthful ignorance I used to get it confused with Czechoslovakia – two east European countries with long names which weren't particularly famous for anything. Except those surreal cartoons that would occasionally fill the five minute gap in the programming schedule before the main evening news - and the odd tennis player who would do well at Wimbledon. Oh, and the Czechs had a car which had a reputation for being crap (as it turned out an undeserved one) and was the butt of numerous jokes at the time. The Yugoslavs also had their own car – the imaginatively named Yugo, prices of which dropped suddenly when the war broke out, but the car never really caught on.

In a few years time both countries would cease to exist as they splintered into smaller fragments. And now people tend to get Slovenia confused with Slovakia. Or Moldova with Macedonia.

But ironically Prague and Croatia's Dalmatian coast would become two of the most popular European tourist destinations a few short years later. I would eventually visit the latter on a brief tour of the Western Balkan region several years hence...

-13-

A Kick in the Balkans

I first heard of the three Baltic states of Lithuania, Latvia and Estonia during a school history class on the First World War. They were then part of the old Soviet Union. In fact the terms "Soviet Union/USSR" and "Russia" were often used interchangeably back then – something which your average Armenian, Georgian or Ukrainian would not have taken kindly to.

When the USSR finally disintegrated at the tail end of the 1980s countries that we in the west didn't know had ever existed like – Moldova, Uzbekistan, Tajikistan, Turkmenistan and Custerslaststan– suddenly sprang up out the ashes of the once vast Soviet Empire. Countries which even today rarely make the headlines and being mostly famous for oil and mineral reserves, barren deserts where secret cold war era nuclear testing took place, cotton, vast dried-up inland seas and eccentric dictators.

In the summer of 2005 courtesy of a cheap and nasty low cost no frills airline I made my first trip to the former Soviet Union. Lithuania and Latvia had just joined the European Union a year earlier.

"What do you want to go there for?" my friend Alexei Simonson had asked, apparently bemused that I would be holidaying in such obscure spots well off the beaten tourist track.

A good question. I derive a strange pleasure and smug sense of satisfaction out of going to places few people want to go. The fact that they're there is a good enough reason in itself. And the fact that they're cheap and you can get there on low cost airlines for the price of a pint of beer. Or at least you could have done in those days.

Alexei went on to ask the same question about Budapest a few years later. The difference this time was that both of us were in Budapest at the same time, although Alexei probably thought he was floating on a cloud above the land of flying green-eyed monsters. He'd been drinking absinthe.

In 2006 we venture a little further south – to the other end of the former "Iron curtain" – the Balkans...

After an early morning flight from Stanstead I arrive in a humid Trieste with two old university friends Ian and PL, where it looks like a torrential downpour is about to erupt.

We get talking to a young Bulgarian woman on the plane who's living in Trieste, married to a local man and doing a PhD in psychology at the local university. She warns us that Trieste isn't the liveliest of places. Rather than being a vibrant town it's acquired a reputation as a coastal retirement home.

We have a much-needed lie-down on being shown to our room, but our sleep is interrupted by loud motorbikes driving up and down the street.

We discover the city's famous James Joyce statue purely by accident, which happens to be a stone's throw from the hotel. We have a look inside an Orthodox church which has no seats.

Then we end up in a German beer kellar for the night.

The next day we're bound for Ljubljana by coach. Such is the heaviness of the torrential downpour we take a taxi to the bus station, which would normally have been a 10-minute walk. The Slovenian border is a short distance away. The spectacular mountain and forest scenery compensates for the miserable day. Three hours later we arrive in Slovenia's capital city and it's still pissing down. We get a taxi to the hostel which we discover is well within easy walking distance from the bus station.

During our brief wet stay in the Slovenian capital we take a picture of a shop called "Ars" - as is the usual practice when in "foreign parts" to photograph things which sound rude in English.

A few days later, having got rid of our remaining tolars at the bureau de change and after a night in Zagreb where we stay in a hostel that has the look and feel of a prison about it, we find

191

ourselves travelling by train through the now peaceful and incredibly picturesque Bosnian countryside of green rolling hills dotted with the tall slender white minarets of mosques. A bizarre incongruity. I'm reminded of the dark days when doing my A-levels during the war, a war which continued long into my university days. Bosnia featured on the news every day throughout the early 1990s in much the same way as Iraq or Afghanistan in throughout the 2000s.

Pulling into Sarajevo train station as dusk approaches after a tiring ten hour journey from Zagreb, one could be forgiven for thinking it's not worth a stopover. Miles of sprawling ugly Soviet-style tower blocks so typical of the suburbs of many Eastern European cities do little to encourage the potential visitor. But once you're in the heart of the city, you find it has a rough charm which really catches the imagination.

Sarajevo is a curious mixture of east and west. For centuries this city has been at the confluences of two great cultures, at the western extremity of the Ottoman and the eastern extremity of the Austro-Hungarian empires.

It's been over a decade since peace returned to this region, but the scars of war are everywhere, albeit in a subtle way. Market stalls sell intricately carved trinkets – pens, ashtrays, plates – fashioned from spent bullets and mortar shells. It's not hard to find a building still pock-marked with bullet holes. Also on sale are Turkish rugs and ornately crafted metal coffee pots and pepper grinders. Mosques and churches rub shoulders in this proverbial melting pot of cultures, but the city has an unmistakable European flavour

Some women choose to wear the traditional Islamic head scarf and some young men sport Islamic-style beards, but their ethnic origins are most definitely white European and the majority of Sarajevans prefer the western dress style. The city's focal point is the Baščaršija bazaar, a Middle-Eastern style market place where there's a casbah style café in which you can smoke hookah pipes and drink the notoriously thick black coffee which is standard fare in this part of the Balkans. Ask for a coffee in Sarajevo and you get a tiny cup containing a dense tar-like brew – what's generally known as a Turkish coffee, ie black coffee with much of the water boiled off to strengthen it. Elsewhere in the former Yugoslavia you will be given a standard espresso as is the norm in most of continental Europe. Ubiquitous in Bosnia and Herzegovina is the Greco-Turkish style kebab of minced lamb in pitta bread.

Quite by chance we stumble upon a plaque which commemorates a historic event. The bridge where the Archduke Ferdinand, Emperor of Austro-Hungary was assassinated in 1914, the catalyst for the Great War which would rage for another four years and result in countless more deaths. Memories of third year history classes during the last period on Friday afternoon as we waited for the bell to go off so we could make a mad dash into the weekend come flooding back to me.

That night the beer flows. We're sitting outside the trendy Bar Havana in the old market place. Despite the rain, it's a lively, atmospheric spot. A talented chanteuse belts out cover versions of Tina Turner, The Police and Van Morrison songs.

Next day in the green area of parkland adjoining the grounds of the National Museum (unfortunately it's closed as we'd arrived too late in the afternoon) is the abandoned wreck of a military helicopter, presumably a relic of the old Yugoslav army, now a sort of unofficial museum exhibit come work of modern art sprayed with graffiti. We're along one of the city's main thoroughfares, a long wide road leading to the railway station where our adventure began. Just across this road is the distinctive yellow lego-like tower block of the Holiday Inn, where journalists from around the world lodged during the war.

The city is surrounded by steep craggy wooded hills, the perfect terrain for an army wanting to put a city under siege. At the railway station there's a battered metal sign, reminding all and sundry that this city was the venue for the 1984 Winter Olympics – the mascot of a cartoon wolf and the Olympic rings against a blue background liberally dotted with rust and what appears to be the odd bullet hole.

Our lodgings are in a private house owned by an entrepreneurial local who rents us a room for the sum of €10 a night. We're on a top of a steep hill which has panoramic views of the city. Further down the hill is the "Hotel Sarayevo" (sic), probably more luxurious than our lodgings, but considerably more expensive and no doubt with a less spectacular view. The Sarajevo skyline is dominated by apartment blocks and minarets.

As the evening sun casts long shadows over the streets, some old men are playing chess with giant pieces. It seems so peaceful here now. Swallows swoop low over the shallow narrow Miljacka river. It has the air of a sleepy provincial town rather than a capital city. I could easily spend the rest of the summer here.

Our next destination is Mostar.

The route between Sarajevo and Mostar on a bus that's less than half full takes in some of the most spectacular scenery in the Balkans, if not all of Europe – gorges and waterfalls, hairpin bends, wooded hills, amazing valleys and winding rivers – and major reconstruction projects funded mostly by the EU. It's an adrenaline sports junkie's paradise.

Mostar is of course famous for the iconic bridge which features on the front cover of so many guide books on the Balkans which was blown up by the Croats during the war. It doesn't take us long to find it. "Stari Most" is now a UNESCO World Heritage site. Just around the corner from our digs is a street with bombed out building on either side and a Muslim cemetery full of the graves of people both young and old who died in 1992 and 1993, a stark reminder of the carnage that went on in this city not so long ago.

The next day we get up early to catch the 7 am bus to go back across the border into Croatia to spend a few days in Dubrovnik. This time the bus we travel on is quite full. And there's quite a long delay at the border.

We manage to find the ubiquitous Irish pub in Dubrovnik's old town. It's got the imaginative name of "Irish Pub". On the TV is a hurling match between Derry and Donegal, but we decide to sit

194

outside. A torrential downpour accompanied by the odd burst of lightning suddenly occurs as we're on the terrace sipping our cold beers. Maybe it's a punishment from on high for our philistinism and narrow parochial outlook. The equally narrow streets are gradually beginning to flood and Dubrovnik's old town is beginning to look like Venice. Then after about 20 minutes the rain stops by which time our refreshing pints of Ožujsko are heavily diluted. Point taken. From now on we'll try and seek out places of genuine local culture rather than tacky faux Hibernian tourist traps.

We visit an exhibition dedicated to those who lost their lived during the shelling of Dubrovnik by the Serbian navy in 1991 – another poignant reminder of this region's troubled past which contrasts with the lively bustle of the tourists milling around the trendy bars and restaurants and the yachts in the harbour, which seems a world away from those dark days. Our plans to go hiking in the hills surrounding the city are put paid to when we hear that they're still full of unexploded landmines.

We end our two–week Balkan odyssey in another of the Adriatic's coastal gems. Split is a settlement founded by the Romans and steeped in historical and archaeological interest.

Not far from the famous Roman site of Diocletian's Palace there's a huge bronze statue of the medieval bishop Gregor of Nin. The big toe is considerably shinier than the rest of the statue due to the local superstition that if you rub your hand over this toe you can make a wish. Most of those rubbing the toe, not surprisingly are foreign tourists. I also make a wish. I won't say what is was, but six months later it would be fulfilled, so full kudos to old Gregor and his magic big toe.

It's a sweltering hot day as we browse the market stalls at Stari Grad. They're selling a vast array of souvenirs including plates, mugs, glasses, ashtrays, hats, t-shirts, statuettes, religious icons, towels, replica guns, knives, Croatian flags, football shirts, snowstorms and fridge magnets mainly advertising the glory of Split, Croatia and the Adriatic.

Walking along the quay we're greeted by the unappetising sight of a dead rat floating in the water. I don't think I'll have the ratatouille for dinner this evening, even though it's recommended as a must by the guide book at one of the local restaurants.

We find an enticing beach close to the port area. After a refreshing dip in the clear blue waters we find ourselves sipping cold beers as we watch the sun set over the Adriatic, the rugged flat-topped mountains in the distance, while discussing the merits of "Carry On" films. A not altogether unpleasant experience. Don't ask.

-16-
The Joys of the Velocipede

Ever since Stephen Roche became the first (and so far the only) Irishman (despite the valiant efforts of his contemporary Sean Kelly) to win the Tour de France in 1987 I've been fascinated by cycling's greatest event. In my experience no other physical activity leaves the participant in such a state of ecstasy and bliss (stop that sniggering at the back of the class, you lot!)

In fourth form as part of our GCSE English coursework we were asked to write a mock letter to a celebrity of our choice. Others chose to write to Slash or Axl from Guns N Roses or the Danish drummer from Metallica and one wrote to the then Soviet president Mikhail Gorbachev. My idol of choice was Stephen Roche. In the grovelling letter I asked for sponsorship to raise funds for the non-existent local cycling club which I wasn't really a member of.

"Dear Mr Roche
Grovel, grovel, I'm not worthy.
Our cycling club is raising funds for a local charity. If you could send us an autographed yellow jersey which we could auction off to raise funds for our club this would be so much appreciated. The council has cut our funding – hard times, straitened circumstances, austerity measures, blah blah, etc etc ad nauseam
"Who knows one day a member of our club could even be triumphantly popping the champagne cork on the Champs Elysée in his yellow jersey".

I got to learn the specialist vocabulary of cycling with words like "peloton", "soigneur", "grimpeur", "domestique", "maillot jaune" (and its Italian equivalent the "maglia rosa") and "contre le montre". I got to grips with the complex points system and the different coloured jerseys signifying different achievements. I reasoned that as road cycling was primarily a continental European phenomenon, it must therefore be glamorous and sophisticated – and was therefore something I should take a profound interest in.

How naïve was I, unaware of the disreputable nature of a sport tainted by drugs. The cyclist's lot seemed like a glamorous life to me. Whizzing past fields of tall sunflowers and up Pyrenean or Alpine mountain passes, getting kissed on each cheek by the luscious PR girls on the podium after winning the stage...

It was another Irish cyclist turned sports journalist Paul Kimmage who blew the whistle in his book *A Rough Ride*. But it had already been an open secret for some time.

Nevertheless the hills up to Glencordial for me became Alpine and Pyrenean slopes. I used to get back in time for tea just as the highlights of *le Tour* were on.

At the age of ten I had received a BMX bike as a Christmas present. It had high-tec plastic spokes – the ones spokes that never rust - and chunky yellow tyres. BMXes were all the rage back in those days. Many of my classmates had received the same. The year before that the big Christmas present to get was a snooker table (not a full-sized one of course, but a junior version aimed at those destined for a misspent youth). The following year it was computers – Sinclair Spectrums and ZX81s being the state of the art models back then.

During the BMX era I immersed myself in the art of wheelies, bunny hops and endos. Then couple of years later I grew out of this and graduated from the stunt bikes to the racing bike. I don't know why I didn't join a local cycling club at the time. Maybe I just wanted to indulge in my own private fantasies and didn't want any competition to get in the way. Or more plausibly, I probably just wasn't good enough.

Then one day my dream of wearing the yellow jersey all came crashing down on me. I fell off my (racing) bike one summer's evening in 1989 when I was 16 during a rapid downhill descent. There had been a screw or bolt loose which I wasn't aware of. As a result I was thrown over the handle bars on my way down the hill and hit my chin on the road. I didn't think much of it as I got up and brushed the dust off my hands. As far as I was concerned I'd just fallen off and was about to get back in the saddle and carry on.

Then I suddenly realised that the white t-shirt I was wearing was soaked in blood and had a big rip down the front. The front wheel was badly buckled and the bike was now unrideable, so I was forced to walk towards home.

I was picked up on the Gortin road and taken to the hospital by a kindly motorist whose car was full of Daniel O'Donnell and Hugo Duncan tapes. But I didn't hold that against him.

The doctor spent about an hour taking grit out of the wound before he stitched it up. For the rest of that summer there was a huge cut visible on the side of my chin. The scar remains to this day.

Usually at this point you would expect me to say "And I've never ridden a bike since that fateful day...."

But the truth is I got back into cycling in my very late 20s and have kept it up on an on-off basis ever since – and enjoy it immensely. Ironically it was Lance Armstrong's amazing comeback after suffering a near fatal cancer that inspired me to get back in the saddle – a comeback which eventually proved to be a little too amazing to be genuine. How the mighty fall.

Even in cold wet weather there's also something therapeutic about cycling along a wet tarmac surface on which you can see your reflection, with raindrops or sleet stinging your face. The prospect of stopping off at a cafe for a good quality coffee, before getting into a nice warm shower afterwards provides that extra incentive to pedal that bit harder. That combination of adrenaline, endorphines, caffeine and warm water from a nozzle provides an unrivalled feeling to brighten up an otherwise dull Sunday afternoon.

Nowadays I'm acclimatised to being in "the zone" once I've left the London suburbs and am cruising along the lanes of rural Hertfordshire on an Allez Specialised, unencumbered by traffic lights, with woods and fields in the background - sheer bliss for a man of simple pleasures. It's amazing how quickly the body heats up on a cold day during a short sustained burst of vigorous pedalling.

Cycling into central London is just so bloody dangerous and at times unpleasant, but nevertheless I gave it a go for a brief period during the summer when I worked in the city. Running the gauntlet with double decker buses and articulated lorries is not something you want to do on a daily basis. As a commuter I faced the choice of paying through the nose and taking the train into work and getting crushed in the melee of passengers, often having to remain standing for the entire journey clinging on to the overhead bars for dear life, spending prolonged periods stuck in tunnels - or taking the risk by biking it instead. Neither option is particularly appealing, but cycling gets the adrenaline going and is considerably quicker. The element of danger combines with the thrill of the chase and a cold shower afterwards is highly therapeutic – well during the summer months that is. The sheer satisfaction of reaching your destination unscathed is an achievement in itself. Unlike certain other cyclists ("allegedly" I hastily add just in case any sports lawyers happen to be reading this) I didn't take any performance enhancing drugs. Unless you count caffeine.

The adrenaline rush of downhill descents and the build-up of lactic acid in the lungs and thighs on the ascent is simply thrilling. It's not quite the same as racing past fields of sunflowers to match the colour of one's jersey in rural Provence with the multi-coloured peloton in hot pursuit or popping open the champagne on the Champs-Elysée, or the agonising ascent up the hairpin bend of an Alpine or Pyrenean mountain pass – but there's no other feeling like it. And of course, unlike the professionals I don't have to rely on pharmaceutically-enhanced "medication" to go faster. Having said that I've never been in a race or a time trial in my life. And not sure if I'd even want to be. I ride for pure pleasure.

And exactly a quarter of a century after its first Irish winner, an Englishman finally wins le Tour in 2012. And in twelfth place is a certain Nicholas Roche. Things really do go round in complete circles. I think that's the third time I've used that phrase now. Two mentions is probably enough to justify a book title.

-17-
From the Basques to the Berbers

Part 1: Trans-Iberian Express

Although I studied Spanish at school I'd never been to Spain or any other Spanish speaking country at that time, unlike some of my classmates who had been with their families to the Costa del Booze or Beniporn. The desire was there though. I grew up entranced by Sergio Leone's Spaghetti westerns in which the barren hills and plains of Almeria served as a substitute location for the US-Mexican border region.

While in my early 20s I would eventually have a brief stint as an English teacher in the former mining town of Puertollano in the Castilla-La Mancha region shortly after graduating.

On arrival at Madrid airport back in January 1997 my very first experience of trying out my Spanish (GCSE level) to a Spaniard in Spain ended up with me getting ripped off by a bogus taxi driver. After I've handed over to him about five times the going rate, expecting at least some change he adds insult to injury by telling me in perfect English that "the tip is not included". Ah well, you live and learn as I found out the hard way.

Prior to arriving my main point of contact at the school of English where I'd be teaching was West Belfast man Jed Mullarkey, a bit of a cowboy and an ardent bullshitter.

"When you arrive at the airport, just get a taxi to the train station" he had advised me over the phone. In hindsight it would have been just as easy (and considerably) cheaper to get the regular shuttle bus to the station.

A more memorable visit to Iberia was to occur in the autumn of 2011 when I travelled across the peninsula from north to south accompanied by the inimitable PL.

We start off in Bilbao.

The place easily lends itself to puns. I could say the say the city is a veritable basquet of curiosities or that we find a café terrace where we can basque in the glorious September sunshine – or that our plane landed at the correct ETA.

Don't worry - I won't be giving up the day job any time soon.

On the evening of the first day (a scorcher of a late September day at 33°) we find an inconspicuous and rather quiet Irish pub, a shady bodega called The Dubliners just off the city's main square at around 7 pm and find ourselves sipping Cruzcampo to the melancholic strains of Dido as locals drop in for post work refreshments. There's a framed cartoon on the wall entitled "Gilhooley's Supper Party".

The following day the post-modern Guggenheim, probably the city's most famous landmark is like no other art gallery I've ever been to. A giant metal spider and a giant terrier-like dog made of flowers dominate the outdoor exhibits.

Breakfast in a nearby bar consists of *pintxos* the local equivalent of tapas. Sandwiches made from submarine shaped rolls impaled with cocktail sticks and containing various fillings are laid out at the bar. You sit there and eat what you want, then pay for it after telling the barman how may you've eaten. There's plenty of scope for dishonesty here, but we do the decent thing and don't avail of it. I can't help thinking that if this system existed in Ireland or the UK the eateries would go out of business overnight.

On our second evening in the city we get roped into participating in a poetry reading at Café Teatro Mystik, a regular venue for such events. The organisers hand out small pieces of paper for the participants to write their lines on. For some bizarre reason the poem has to be about your feet. The night is a combination of poetry and live music. In between poems a singer/guitarist plays cover versions of Sting and Pink Floyd while in the background a slide projector pours out images of Ezra Pound, Federico García Lorca and numerous other lesser known Iberian and Mexican bards, including the local boy Miguel de Unamuno whose statue can be found in the city's Casco Viejo (old town) district.

When my turn comes around I produce the following "words of wisdom":

"Time catches up with us sooner or later
Space is what gets left behind
Under my feet..."

It's just like the type of pretentious, meaningless sixth form poetry you'd see in the school magazine – or exactly the sort of crap I used to write for the school magazine when I was in the sixth form.

Later on we end the night in another Irish pub with the ingenious name M'Ore O'rless, much more original than the usual Pogue Mahones or Molly Malones which you find dotted around the globe from Tokyo to Toronto.

On the third day we rise again and decide that no trip to the Basque Country would be complete without visiting Guernika, the town made famous by the Picasso painting depicting the aftermath of the aerial bombardment by the Germans as ordered by Franco in 1937. It's a short journey by rail to this ill-fated town, which now seems like a quiet spot surrounded by pleasant scenery and hills which could be a hiker's paradise. As the train trundles through swathes of pine forest and pampas grass I discover the completely useless fact that the Basque for "next station" is *hurrengo geltokia*. The announcements on the train's electronic message board above the doors in each carriage are in the two languages. And the Basque tongue is as different from Spanish as Japanese or Urdu.

After a walk in the hills above the town on our downhill descent we notice what appears to be a light brown twig in the middle of the road. On closer inspection it turns out to be a praying mantis, its huge compound eyes staring at us suspiciously like an alien creature from a distant world. Just as I'm about to take a picture of this magnificent insect a car whizzes past and crushes it. Last night's poem now seems so tragically appropriate.

****

Somewhere on the five hour coach journey from Bilbao to Madrid, shortly after crossing the provincial border into Castilla-y-Leon the landscape changes from the lush greenery of the north to the various shades of brown and yellow of the more arid centre where the woodlands are replaced with fields of stubble or shrivelled looking sunflowers.

We visit an old schoolmate in Madrid, Fintan Gavigan now a local resident who's teaching at a school in the city, who very decently offers to put us up for a couple of nights. On the Friday night following a fine curry in Lavapiés, the city's lively immigrant quarter we participate in a quiz at a pub frequented mainly by young, mostly English-speaking ex-pats. The questionmaster is a Scouser. The questions aren't easy, but we manage to come joint first, so the quiz goes to a tie-breaker. The decisive question is "How much money do I have in my pocket?" So it's down to a matter of estimating the amount of loose change on our Liverpudlian lounge lizard's person. My guess turns out to be well over the true figure, so we have to make do with second place. It's such an irritatingly overused cliché, but on this occasion the phrase "shit happens" seems fitting.

Back at base we sit out on Fintan's balcony and take in the atmosphere of the balmy Madrileño night. PL, not normally a smoker makes an exception on this occasion and lights up a Ducado, the notoriously strong Spanish cigarette with its characteristic black tobacco. A bat flits over the roof tops weaving its way around the TV aerials and satellite dishes. We have a relatively early start the next morning, but for now we chill out and savour the moment. Tomorrow we're due to head south.

****

On the train from Madrid to Granada we pass through familiar territory –my old stomping ground of Puertollano, the former mining town in La Mancha. Literally hundreds of thousands of foreign visitors will pass through this anonymous town on train journeys between Madrid and the vastness of Andalucía, but few will ever stop there. 14 years earlier I'd been one of those few. But not on this occasion – it's now just another anonymous passing-through town.

The hostel in Granada is full of young backpackers from Europe, the US and Australasia. Being there is like reliving my student days. The city's narrow Moorish streets give us a foretaste of what to expect in Morocco.

After a chilled out first day which includes an organised night time visit to bathe in sulphurous hot springs (it's too hot to do it during the day of course) about a half hour drive from the city, the following morning we go on a guided walk in the foothills of the Sierra Nevada. Our guide is a lively Mancunian with a colourful past called Wez, who regales us with tales of his travels around war-torn Algeria in the 1990s and his days as a bullet-proof jacketed doorman at a notorious Manchester night club. Our tour group is a multi-national affair consisting of Australians, Americans, a Moroccan and a Dutchman – and of course the two Irish drifters.

After a not too taxing walk along a river bank we return to the village and adjourn to the local watering hole and have a few *jarras* - large beers served in those thick chunky pint glasses with handles and indented squares which used to be commonplace back home in the 1970s, but are now rare on account of the damage they can do if someone's had too many of them. The first few glasses are frosted with ice.

We move on to another and then another bar in a neighbouring village situated uphill from our starting point. I suddenly that notice that my money belt containing my passport is no longer attached to my waist.

"Oh shit..." I begin to quietly panic.

We retrace our steps in the darkness to the previous bar we'd just

205

been in, but no joy. We then walk the mile and a half back to the village we started off in. I go into the pub and make enquiries, but no-one's seen it. It looks like the next leg of our tour in Morocco will have to be cancelled and instead we'll be hot-footing it back to Madrid for a visit to the Irish embassy.

I have a look on the ground outside. And there under the wheel of a parked car is my money belt still remarkably intact – and most importantly it still contains my passport. I breathe a massive sigh of relief as I manage to prise it out from under the wheel. Never has such relief been felt since Mafeking.

The plan for the next day is to get the bus to Algeciras and from then to head to Tarifa where we're due to stay the night before boarding the ferry to Africa the following morning. On arrival at the station we find that all buses to Algeciras for the day are fully booked, so we're forced to take the more expensive option of travelling by train.

We get talking to a father and son from Colorado on their way to Ronda for a spot of cycling. The son seems to be a bit of an artist as he's surreptitiously drawing a sketch of PL while we talk. We never get to see the finished product though.

The train passes through obscure Andalusian towns of whitewashed flat roofed houses – Gaucin, San Pablo, Paredas, Jimenez de la Frontera, Almoraima. Few tourists will stop here, but like Omagh they all must have their household characters and naïve young people dreaming of an idealistic future. Cacti are quite common along the route which is characterised by seemingly endless brown fields of olive trees.

A bunch of middle-aged cockneys (and a Norwegian woman who's part of their entourage) in smart casual summer wear get on at Benaojan Montejaque. Their bouffant grey-haired "leader", the loud one of the pack has the air of an ageing 1960s pop star on a comeback tour. He's constantly cracking jokes and reminiscing on lively incidents from the past, including a karaoke night during which they all sang Neil Diamond's *Sweet Caroline*. He tells one particularly crude joke and they all burst out laughing uproariously. Then they ring up a mutual friend and sing "happy birthday" down the phone before getting off at San Roque-la Linea, the nearest station to Gibraltar.

Tarifa – the Edge of Europe

On arrival in the ferry port town of Tarifa (famous for windsurfing and whale watching) at around 7:30 pm we take a sunset stroll along the beach, casting long shadows as we look across the water towards Africa. There are several wind turbines dotted around the local landscape, but because of the heat haze no visible sign of the Dark Continent. But it is quite breezy as the presence of these alternative energy conductors would suggest. Despite the fact that there are prominent signs along the beach saying "No Dogs" and "No Fishing", apart ourselves the only other people on the beach seem to be dog walkers and fishermen. The beachcombing excursions of my youth come flooding back to me.

We then head towards the old part of town for sustenance. Its narrow cobbled streets and whitewashed buildings are typically Andalusian, a legacy of the Moorish era. I'm tempted to order a pork dish at the restaurant as we won't be getting any of it in Morocco, but on health grounds (and also because we're on the coast) I opt for fish instead. It's a chilled out relaxed kind of town with a seemingly permanent breeze coming off the Atlantic making this balmy night more pleasant. I'd like to stay here a bit longer, but we've got a ferry to catch for the Dark Continent tomorrow...

From the Basques to the Berbers: Part 2: Moroccan Autumn

Prologue: On School Trips

School trips usually had an academic slant. There were history trips to Berlin and Rome or the battlefields of the Somme or A-level English trips to Canterbury and Stratford.

During my time at the grammar school there were also regular skiing excursions to Bulgaria, which was then still behind the Iron Curtain, but was managing to successfully market itself as a cheaper alternative to the Alps. Such trips had no academic purpose as such and were purely recreational. Unless you go along with the theory that travel of any kind broadens the mind. Having been on this planet for almost 40 years I've never skied in my life. I wouldn't go so far as to say I've no intention of doing it, but it's just never appealed to me. The idea of going somewhere cold for a holiday doesn't float my boat.

In the final year of primary school there was an annual week long residential trip. It was usually to "glamorous" locations which involved a ferry crossing followed by a long coach journey such as London or Edinburgh. But in my year the destination, to my great disappointment was the distinctly less glamorous location of Dublin. Dublin's a fine city, but I'd been there enough times on family holidays for it not to be much of a novelty. Plus it didn't entail a sea crossing, so wasn't sufficiently "exotic" for my tastes. However one of the attractions of the trip was bizarrely an air flight from Dublin to Shannon. It may have appealed if you'd never flown before, but the irony was that you'd spend longer queuing up in the departure lounge than you would on the actual flight.

I'd been saving up for months, using the financial gifts generously provided by grandparents, aunts and uncles whenever we used to visit them. This made me feel guilty for not giving enough of my money to the Band Aid fund which had been set up by a loud-mouthed Dubliner who sang in a rock band to aid famine relief in Ethiopia. I then decided to wind up the fund when it was announced that it wasn't going to involve my preferred destination. I finally did get to go on a school trip to London during the 1988 Easter holidays. It was officially designated as a history trip, but was basically an excuse for the teachers to have a jolly romp for free in the big smoke. There wasn't much about the itinerary that was historical, apart from a visit to the Imperial War Museum and the outside of the Houses of Parliament.

I made my first (and to date my only) trip to White Hart Lane to see Tottenham humiliatingly lose 1-0 to newly promoted Portsmouth. We were in the stand behind the goals. I was sitting beside a disgruntled Spurs supporter who gave a running commentary on the match littered with expletives in which he regularly referred to his own players as "facking useless cahnts".

On our last night of the trip, Easter Sunday we met two raven-haired German girls from Bavaria, Ruth and Doris who were staying in our hotel. They were a few years older than us and spoke good English - a damn sight better than our Germa – but not surprisingly they had a little difficulty understanding our accents. Our school didn't teach German, so we had to make do with what we'd picked up from old war films.
There were three naive 14 year olds in the room – plus Ruth and Doris.

"*Vorsprung durch technik?*" I said, using a phrase I'd picked from a TV car ad, but hadn't a clue what it actually meant .

They didn't understand.

Shane Rogan piped up and said:

"*Sprechen sie Deutsche?*"

They responded to this more enthusiastically.

"Ah! You speak German."

"Er, well a little bit"

"Bavaria, isn't that near the Black Forest?"

"Yes! Have you been there?"

"Er…no, but I've been to the Gortin Glens Forest."

The room fell into an awkward silence. No-one knew what to say next.

Then I looked at my watch.

"Shit! We should have been in the foyer five minutes ago for a briefing with Lenny and the Emperor about tomorrow"

"We'll be back in half an hour. We'll bring a bottle of wine."

For some reason the off-licence around the corner from the hotel wouldn't sell us a bottle of wine, so we had to make do with sparkling grape juice.

As I was good at languages (even though I knew about as much German as next door's cat – *"Deutschland über alles"* and *"Sieg heil"* were the height of my understanding of the Teutonic tongue) I was assigned as the ambassador to deliver the goods as part of this historic new chapter in Hiberno-Germanic relations.

I knocked on the door.
A very tall young man with very blonde cropped hair and round-rimmed glasses – every part the Germanic stereotype - answered the door. He was wearing a tight t-shirt which emphasised his muscular torso. Both arms were covered in tattoos ranging from Celtic artwork to dragons, wizards, elves and other strange creatures.

"Yes? Can I help you?" he said in a thick Bavarian accent in a tone that was both polite and menacing at the same time.

"Er, sorry we must have the wrong room" I said in a hurry before legging it.

From down the corridor I could just about make out the sound of female laughter coming from the room.

The topic of conversation on the train and ferry on the way home was inevitable.

"That Ruth one had the hots for me. Did you not see the way she was looking at me?"

"Aye, right! I think she was feeling sorry for you!"

"I preferred Doris actually."

"But did you see the way they reacted when I said "*Sprechen Sie Deutsch*"?"

Unfortunately we never got the opportunity to impress Frauleins Ruth and Doris with our heroic tales of bravado of living in a war zone and dodging the bullets on our way to school, having cleared the sandbags surrounding the garden gate.

Rewinding momentarily back to primary school I remember a conversation about school trips which occurred in the aftermath of the Dublin excursion.
"Why couldn't we have a trip to somewhere decent?"
"I wish there was a school trip to Morocco".

A colleague at work then told me he'd been on a school geography trip to Morocco in the 1960s, during which they visited the Sahara, after a journey which involved a long trek down the length of Spain followed by a short ferry crossing across the Straits of Gibraltar.

As far as I'm aware my old primary school has yet to organise an excursion to North Africa, but at least one of its ex-pupils went there in 2011.

Straits of Gibraltar, October 2011
The quick boat ride from Tarifa on the southernmost tip of Spain to Tangier on the northernmost tip of Africa lasts under an hour, but takes you to what is effectively a different world. I'm reading the autobiography of socialist Liverpudlian comedian Alexei Sayle in the hope of getting inspiration for a memoir of my own that I'm planning to write some day. Coincidentally Tangier even gets a brief mention in his book. It's my first visit to the African continent in 34 years. I'm wondering what took me so long to return.

It's frustrating that this ferry has no deck where you can go out into the open air. There's a silent Moroccan man, a chubby moustached chap in a casual checked shirt, but with no uniform or visible means of identification sitting at a desk at the front of the aisle with a laptop and two rubber stamps stamping passports. A long queue has formed along the aisle which I decide to join.

Just as it's my turn to get stamped he takes a wad of Australian, US and Canadian passports out of a plastic bag and proceeds to stamp each one as I patiently wait with gritted teeth. Then a chorus of electronic bleeps resounds around the ferry as several dozen passengers simultaneously receive texts from the national mobile telecoms provider welcoming them to Morocco and advising them of tariffs for roaming rates.

Although we're almost there the Moroccan coast still isn't visible because of the heat haze shimmering above the water. My travelling companion PL, not a big fan of boat trips is looking forward to disembarkation.

It strikes me that 300 million years ago we could have made this journey overland when Europe and Africa (along with every other land mass) were still stuck together as part of the supercontinent of Pangaea. But as there were no buses or trains in those days it would have been quite a hike.

During my time on this vast continent I'm constantly reminded of an incident from a few years previously. One of my younger brothers had arrived home for Christmas one year, but had stopped off in Belfast en route to visit some old university friends at whose flat he had apparently spent the night.

"Where did you sleep last night?" our mum asked.

"Africa" he replied cheekily.

This became a running joke for years afterwards. And still is now in fact.

Tangier (about an hour later)

A scrum of would-be taxi drivers, self-appointed tour guides, money changers and possibly even drug pushers greets the passengers as they get off the ferry.

"You need taxi?" one shouts out to us.

"No, we've already booked a taxi" we lie.

He is sharp enough to pick up on our accents, but doesn't get it quite right.

"You have accent. You are Scottish? Aberdeen?"

"Near enough" I answer, in an attempt to sound sufficiently disinterested that he eventually gives up and stalks some other travellers.

As there's no answer when I try phoning our hotel we reluctantly decide to take up his offer and pay €5 for the privilege, only to find that the hotel is a mere ten minute walk from the ferry terminal. It won't be the first time that we unwittingly pay over the odds in Morocco.

The medina in Tangier, the old part of town is a labyrinth of narrow streets, all of which are a hive of constant activity. There are men sewing dresses with painstaking skill, barber shops, cafes, kiosks selling all manner of things and halal butchers. The narrow streets ensure that you're in the shade and not at the mercy of the ruthless Moroccan sun.

After being made to wait in the lobby of the guesthouse (or "riad" to use the local terminology) for quite some, time we finally get to meet the proprietor, a Frenchman called Gilles.

When at long last we get to dump our stuff in our room we decide to explore the area. We're feeling peckish, so on the "recommendation" of a waiter we meet at one of the cafes, we end up on a restaurant run by his cousin. The restaurant owner bears a passing resemblance to the DJ Steve Wright of BBC radio's "Steve Wright in the Afternoon" fame. We're the only people in the place, which isn't surprisingly considering what they're about to charge for what amounts to little more than a light lunch of vegetable soup, a bizarre chicken pakora style concoction with icing sugar and cinnamon sprinkled over it, a meagre portion of couscous with chicken –and for dessert a tiny slice of shortbread with heavily sweetened mint tea to digest it all. This comes to the equivalent of £30 each. In Morocco you could probably buy a half-decent second hand car for this price. Ironically, a few months later I would find myself in a Moroccan restaurant in London paying two thirds the price for a much more substantial and superior meal.

As we finish eating the siren for the Adhan, the Islamic call to prayer goes off – something we'll be hearing a lot more of over the next few days. We look over the balcony on to the streets, but surprisingly people just carry on as normal.

That evening we sit out on the terrace taking in the atmosphere. The rooftops are dotted with rusty satellite dishes. Sparrows and the occasional dove perch on ancient TV aerials. Two chickens are strutting around the roof of an adjoining apartment, while the cat sits in the corner eyeing them up.

We go out of the medina to explore the Tangerine night life of the downtown area known as the Grand Socco. It occurs to me this city gave its name to the delightfully juicy citrus fruit sold in the supermarkets in wooden boxes and wrapped in purple tissue paper which provided many a Christmas stocking filler during my childhood – the tangerine. They came with a tiny diamond-shaped sticker bearing the legend "Maroc" in Arab-style lettering. But we simply knew them back then as "wee oranges". I made no distinction between tangerines, satsumas, mandarins, Seville oranges or Jaffas. As far as I was concerned there were only two kinds of orange – "big oranges" and "wee oranges". I preferred the small ones because they were tastier and much easier to peel. Attempting to peel one of the larger varieties of orange can be a nightmare, especially if you've got blunt nails. And if you dig your nail too far into the skin you can get squirted at full blast in the eye.

Just I'm nostalgically reflecting on the festive joy of citrus fruits an oldish man approaches us with a proposition.

"You want some hashish?"

Moroccan jails are not pleasant places according to the guide books. I very much doubt if there are any jails in the world which are pleasant despite some of the reactionary right wing British tabloids painting pictures of UK prisons as luxurious holiday camps where the inmates live it up at the taxpayer's expense, but I take the point. And we politely turn down his kind offer.

At the local cinema there's a film in French by the acclaimed avant-garde surrealist Spanish director Luis Buñuel playing – *Cet Objet de Desir*, a bizarre, but intriguing work in which the female lead is shared by two different actresses playing the same character. The curtain-raiser *Le Chien Andalou* is cancelled much to our disappointment, although the admission fee was cheap compared with cinemas back home.

As we exit the picture house, whose selection of refreshments doesn't extend beyond mint tea and orange juice PL seems quite desperate to have a beer.

"You can drink all the beer you want once you get home" I assure him, somewhat puzzled as to why he's so keen to imbibe in a largely dry country (in both senses of the word). In any case it's not like we didn't drink enough beer on our journey across Spain the previous week.

"I'm on holiday, I want to wet my whistle" he insists.

"Then go back home and become a football referee. With the amount of rain we get you'll be able to wet your whistle to your heart's content. Or you could be one of those killjoy jobsworths who patrol swimming pools [someone like Ken Blowtorch for example] and blow their whistle if they see young kids messing about. With the amount of water and splashing that goes on I'm sure they get their whistles wet all the time".

On our way back to the medina PL still hasn't given up his quest and enquires at one of the few kiosk style shops which is still open if they sell beer, but is disappointed. Looking for booze in the medina is like looking for snowballs in the Sahara.

A man in an Islamic robe walking behind us with his wife, presumably having heard the exchange mutters something in Arabic, mentioning the word "infidels".

The next morning – naturally a gloriously sunny one - we have breakfast on the roof terrace which overlooks the sea.

Train to Fes
The local train station is in the newer part of the city beyond the medina with its long tree-lined boulevards, a legacy of the colonial era is reminiscent of a French city. We're now heading south to Fes. My Arabic is limited to the standard greeting "السلام عليكم", a phrase I make sure to use on every conceivable occasion when new passengers get on and sit in our carriage, although I'm not sure if I'm pronouncing it right. Although Moroccan trains aren't as well maintained or clean as those in Europe, they are nevertheless efficient and (at least during our time in the country) they tend to run on time.

The only camels I see during my time in Morocco are on the beach at the resort of Asilah from the train window on the journey. Unless you count the camel's head we see in a butcher's shop in Fes medina. But I'm fairly sure it's not the same camel that Djibril Mohamed Sissoko Touré "Duffer" McElduff took on to the Omagh-Timbuktu Ulsterbus school express service all those years ago.

The ticket collector encourages us to move to an air-conditioned carriage. PL has carelessly left his ticket in the other compartment, assuming he won't need it again now that we've boarded. Later on we begin to wonder if the ticket collector had wanted us to move carriages as part of a cunning ploy.

Sure enough about an hour later when we're settled in our new cool and breezy carriage the same inspector comes round asking to see our tickets.

"I left it in the other carriage" PL is forced to admit.

"You can look for ticket. Maybe you find and I come back later."

We look high and low throughout the train, politely (if somewhat hopelessly) enquiring of the passengers in each carriage if they've by any chance seen a ticket lying around. But our quest proves to be fruitless.

PL is forced to give up the search buy a new ticket at the inflated price of 120 Dh, 15 Dh more than the original price. Despite this setback, rail travel in Morocco is still dirt cheap compared to what you'd pay in Europe for a similar journey. On the Spanish tickets they make it clear with the words "CONSERVE SU BILLETE HASTA EL FINAL DEL VIAJE" in large font. On Moroccan rail passes it's not so obvious, but out of common sense I've decided to keep my ticket till the end of the journey just in case.

The stations we stop at have names like Gare Tletta Risanna and Ksar El Kebir, Michra Bel Kirsi and Sidi Kacem and are signposted in both Arabic and western script. I later learn from

Wikipedia that the town of Sidi Kacem had been known in colonial times as "Petitjean", which when translated into English is coincidentally the nickname of one of my old teachers.

We pass salt marshes and melon fields with egrets in abundance.

Towards the end of the journey two young men sit in our carriage. Amin, a very chatty fellow is an estate agent now based in Canada who's visiting his family in Fes. He invites us to join him and his friends at a trendy bar situated close to the main railway station that night. It's apparently one of the few places in the city where alcohol is served. The other much is a much quieter fellow called Tayeb who's working as a pastry chef in France.

~

Fes
We arrive in Fes. There's a fellow in the main station building holding up a sheet of paper with my name on it. It's Mustapha the taxi driver. He takes us the relatively short distance to the hotel (or "riad" to be precise) for a price which we later find out is about three times the going rate.

There's a very pleasant young woman at the reception desk called Fatima, dressed in traditional Islamic headscarf. She's studying English at the local university and speaks the lingo flawlessly.

Over glasses of teeth-rottingly sweet mint tea (the genuine article with a sprig of real mint in the glass rather than those teabags you get at home) and pastries she confides in us that the riad owner Mohamed is an unscrupulous character who has a habit of ripping off his guests by recommending restaurants and local guides whom he's in cahoots with –and who then charge extortionate prices for their services. This sounds suspiciously like the fate which befell us in Tangier.

"If you ask him to recommend a restaurant he'll send you to one his friend owns and they will charge you very high prices. But please don't tell him I said this" she tells us.

218

Instead she advises us to go to her brother Kemal who runs a barber shop in the medina and will find a reasonably priced guide to show us around.

When we venture out into the medina the place is full of life on this balmy late September evening. We look for the Salon Royal barber's shop owned by Kemal as recommended by Fatima.

A scruffy slightly built man with a single tooth protruding from his upper gum approaches us.

"You want guide? I show you round."

"We're looking for the Salon Royal barber's shop" I tell him hopefully.

"Ah, you want haircut? I take you to good place."

"Yeah, I really need a haircut!" PL says taking off his sweat-encrusted baseball cap to reveal a shiny bald head.

"No we don't want a haircut, we want to see Kemal the owner" I explain.

"I know Kemal! I take you there!"

We suspect that he doesn't know Kemal at all, but we decide to go along with him as we have no idea where this place is.

True to his word he takes us to a barber's shop, but somewhat unsurprisingly it's not called the Salon Royal. The shop is empty as apparently the owner has gone off to the mosque, but will be returning soon. He does return a few minutes later, but his name isn't Kemal and he certainly isn't Fatima's brother. Frustrated, we beat a hasty retreat with our would-be guide in hot pursuit.

Two 12-year old boys come running after us as we exit the medina's walls.

"You want haircut?" they shout.

After being eventually very kindly escorted to the Salon Royal by a very helpful middle-aged woman and her son, despite encountering various imposters only too willing to "help us out" along the way, we get to meet the real Kemal. Paradoxically Fatima's brother speaks French, but not English.

Enter Youssef, our guide. Young man, mid-20s, wearing a Rastafarian-style woolly hat, a Popeye t-shirt and jeans. After a short tour through the winding streets which our guide clearly knows like the back of his hand by night we announce our desire to dine.

Youssef has assured us that this restaurant has beer. However the fact that we're the only customers in the place isn't a particularly good sign.

The waiter approaches our table ready to take the order.

"A beer please!" PL shouts up to the waiter.

"Sorry, no beer" replies the waiter.

The disappointment of this fatal blow cuts through him like a blast of icy arctic wind.

"OH, FOR F…" he explodes like a spoilt child about to throw a tantrum after Mummy's just run out of sweets, almost banging his fist on the table. But I manage to cut him off in mid flow and diplomatically order two mineral waters.

This restaurant turns out to be another rip-off. No wonder we're the only diners there.

But then maybe it's worth paying a few extra dirham to avoid getting diarrhoea or stomach pains, as has befallen some our fellow guests at the hotel.

When we mention to our guide the fact that Kemal's sister had provided us with some useful local knowledge his face lights up with enthusiasm.

"I know Fatima so well" says Youssef, "she is like sister to me" he assures us.

When we get back to the hotel that night Fatima tells us she doesn't know anyone called Youssef.

The next day we have an early morning tour of the medina with a 7:30 start. Our first port of call is a school of handicraft with examples of fine Islamic tiling. We're then taken by Youssef to a blanket/carpet factory/shop to "sample" the wares on display. Our satin-ist heavy metal-loving friend from the "Metalmania" chapter would have been in his element here. My first experience of haggling over steaming glasses of the ubiquitous local mint tea ends up with me buying an azure blue blanket crafted from cactus fibres and a natural dye. It's a beautiful blanket, but I can't help thinking I've paid well over the going price for it.

After that it's a tannery. We're introduced to Mohammed whose gums are somewhat lacking in teeth. He shows us around the premises. There are various rooms full of handbags, belts, jackets, wallets and shoes. To prove the supposedly high quality of the leather, he strikes a cigarette lighter and holds the flame to the belt which stubbornly refuses to burn.

"Feel the quality" he urges us, "is the skin of young camel - is real thing. This is not Chinatown" he adds.

Sure enough the lighter has left no mark on the belt. Presumably it's not the skin of the same camel which ran amok in my imagination on the Omagh to Timbuktu bus all those years ago.

On finding out where we're from Mohammed suddenly gets excited.

"Ah, you Irish! You know Colin Farrell? I meet him when he come to Morocco to make film *Alexander*. I get picture taken with him!"

Presumably he had offered Farrell a specially discounted price for the privilege of having the picture taken.

We end up buying a belt and a pair of leather slippers each. As I type these words I'm wearing those very slippers. They're a bright orange colour, handy for casual wear in the home, but probably not worth what I paid for them.

When we finally manage to escape from this extortionate world of leather, our wallets now somewhat lighter, Youssef seems very pleased to have made our acquaintance.

"We are all brothers – we just have different mothers" he tells us.

He's apparently half Berber and half African. His father came from Timbuktu. At this stage I begin to wonder if he ever got the Ulsterbus express service from Omagh to Timbuktu, calling at Casablanca, Madrid, Paris and Ballygawley (as alluded to in an earlier chapter).

Youssef goes on to explain to us the supposed easygoing nature of Moroccan society.

"If you want to go to the mosque you can go to the mosque, if you want to drink beer you can drink beer."

"Is there anything else you want to see in Fes?" he asks.

"I read in the guide book about the ancient Persian remains at Basrajani." I reply

"Yes, I can get you taxi to go there. I show you round. We go tomorrow?"

No doubt he has a friend who drives taxis who he's done a deal with. And the taxi driver has no doubt done a deal with the local self-styled archaeologist who will be able to give us a history of the Basrajani empire. The only problem is that Basrajani is a fictitious place which exists only in my head. And as far as I know the Persians never even got this far west. No doubt they would have driven us a few miles out of town and taken us to a pile of rocks in a patch of dusty scrubland and said it was the remains of the ancient Persian citadel of – "what was the name of the place again?" – and charge us a Premier League footballer's weekly wage for the privilege.

"We'll think about it" I tell Youssef, trying hard to keep a straight face.

At this point the batteries in my camera have just gone flat. Not surprisingly as I've been clicking away all day. The taxi driver directs me to a street vendor selling batteries. The batteries turn out to be more expensive than what I would have paid back home.

Obviously delighted with having ripped off another naïve foreigner, the vendor tries to push his luck.

"You want case for camera? I got one – good quality leather!"

Maybe he'd then want to sell me a bag for the camera case, no doubt made from the finest camel skin and about the same price as a Saudi thoroughbred racing camel.

"No thanks" I tell him through clenched teeth.

When we're in the Jewish cemetery a young Spanish couple approach Youssef and ask him where the synagogue is. He clearly has no idea, but doesn't want to admit it, so tries to invent a story around it. It's obvious to us now that our guide is a bit of a cowboy and a natural born bullshitter. But to be fair if we were in his position and had the opportunity to persuade gullible foreign visitors from affluent western societies to part with cash for things they didn't really want to buy we'd probably do the same.

In any case we've been in Morocco three days and we've been ripped off left, right and centre. We decide to cut loose, dispense with Youssef's assistance and go it alone. We pay him off and assure that if we need him again we'll give him a call. I remain philosophical about our predicament. We're not the first and certainly won't be the last foreign tourists to be ripped off here. It's all part of life's rich tapestry – in this case a tapestry woven with cactus fibres which you end up buying for three times the retail price.

We have a look around the newer part of town, then sit on a terrace drinking coffee and watching the denizens of Fes go about their daily business The café looks quite a fairly plush place form the outside, but when I go inside I discover that the toilet has neither a seat nor paper.

On the pavements there are roadworks going on – a big gaping hole in the footpath, but no warning signs or barriers as you would get back home. Morocco is certainly chaotic and disorganised compared with Europe where everything seems to run like clockwork. But PL who's been to India comments "Compared to India this place is like Scandinavia"

That evening we pay our first visit to Bar La Chemineé which as luck would have it just across the road from the café. Despite its central location the place doesn't seem to attract any foreign visitors, apart from ourselves, which I suppose is a good thing in a way. And at least they're not ripping us off. Each round of drinks we order comes with a complimentary snacks ranging from olives to battered sardines to lambs livers. A beer including comestibles is reasonably priced at 15 Dh, the equivalent of £1.25.

That night back at base a gecko crawls around the ceiling. It's a tiny creature, almost transparent. It does a circuit of the smoke alarm. At least we won't have to worry about flies or cockroaches in the room assuming our little scaly friend is hungry and fancies a midnight feast. I feel a sense of déjà-vu from my last visit to Africa all those years ago when these big-eyed, sticky-footed lizards prowled the walls of our house in Nigeria by night.

224

~

The next morning we get to meet Mohammed the hotel owner, (not to be confused with Mohammed from the tannery) who looks like a fatter, balder version of the Iranian president Mahmoud Ahmadinejad. He oozes charm and as Fatima has warned us does come across as a sharp operator.

We decide to spend the day visiting the nearby city of Meknes.

As we walk across the main hall of the railway station, having just bought our tickets we hear a voice shout from the other end of the station:

"Hey Irish!"

And I'm thinking "how the hell does he know?"

But it turns out to be Amin our estate agent friend from the train, the one we'd failed to meet in Bar La Cheminée a few nights earlier. Although he seems pleased to see us, he makes clear his disappointment at us not having joined him and his friends for a beer.

"You didn't come to La Cheminée!"

"Oh…yeah, well we are a bit tired."

"How about tonight we go to bar, we have a few beers and then I take you to my uncle's tannery."

The first part sounds good, but as I'm all leathered out from our previous experience I'm not sure I want to visit another tannery.

We have about twenty minutes to kill before the train is due to depart, so we decide to have a coffee in the station café. The sachet of white sugar on the table is labelled in various languages. Curiously the English translation is misspelt as "wight sugar" as in the island off the south coast of England. Western pop blares from

225

the café's speakers in contrast to the traditional Moroccan or Arab music which seems to be played everywhere else.

We bump into Amin again on the train. It turns out that he's also going to Meknes, but his main port of call is the market there. He negotiates with a taxi driver on our behalf to take us to Volubilis. Volubilis is an ancient Roman settlement about 20 km from Meknes. It's set in what looks like a patch of scrubland in a rural spot in the middle of nowhere. A thin scruffy chap in a stained orange t-shirt and jeans with bad teeth called Hassan is, despite having no visible means of ID or uniform our official guide. He turns out to be very knowledgeable and gives the tour in a mixture of French and English, gliding effortlessly between the two languages.

From the road Volubilis had just looks like the ruins of a few pillars and arches, but there's much more to it than this. There are numerous restored mosaics, including an athlete riding a donkey backwards, Medusa the snake-haired creature of ancient legend and the labours of Hercules. There's even the remains of the local brothel with an appropriately carved sculpture of the male genitals pointing the way. There's the triumphal arch built in honour of the Emperor Caracalla, the Houses of Orpheus, Dionysius and Ephebus.

We do go to Bar La Cheminée that night, but this time to our disappointment Amin doesn't turn up. The two-man band and young female dancer from the previous night are again in full swing. The keyboard player bears a striking resemblance to Billy the Fish, Fulchester United's amazing half man, half fish goalkeeper from *Viz* comic. One of the punters, having had one or two beers too many gets a bit carried away with the festivities and ends up trying to imitate the belly dancer by dancing on the table – which is not a good idea as he's on crutches. He ends up accidentally kicking another customer on the head, as a result of which the gaffer has a few sharp words with him.

On the Sunday we decide to take the risk of entering the medina without a guide. To avoid getting lost we walk in a straight line the whole time and avoid side streets like the plague. Fes medina is after all listed as the main highlight of Morocco in many of the guide books – clearly a "must see" attraction. Apparently the medina has 9000 streets, many of which are narrow and winding, which is why the travel books advise you to never enter the place without a local guide. We beg to differ, anxious not to get ripped off again, but equally anxious not to get lost. And we succeed on both counts.

It's a treasure trove of curiosities – or at least what we in the west would consider to be curiosities – but maybe not so appealing to animal rights campaigners. There's a camel's head hanging on a string outside a butcher's, chickens in cages with their legs trussed up, live tortoises in crates and caged songbirds, including goldfinches, canaries and a crossbill. As the streets are too narrow for the passage of motorised vehicles the refuse collection is done by men on donkeys with huge loads strapped to their backs. There are shops selling countless varieties of herbs and spices, local sticky confectionery on display with honey bees flocking around them in droves, hand-crafted curved daggers, leatherware, crude replicas of football shirts (mostly the big European clubs like Barcelona, Real Madrid, AC Milan or Manchester United), paintings, pottery, fruit and veg, including stalls selling grenade-shaped prickly pears which taste quite similar to regular pears.

Not surprisingly we receive a great deal of attention from the locals, much of it unwanted.

"Hello Texas!" a young lad shouts.

It's a reference to the broad-brimmed hemp hat I'm wearing, invaluable protection against the relentless North African sun.

"*Dzien dobry!*" another lad shouts to us. Do we really look Polish I wonder.

We then receive an invite from yet another young boy who wants to show us around his father's tannery.

"We're just going to have a look down this street, but we'll be back up this way later on" is our attempt to politely fob him off, but although he's not naive he decides to give up all the same.

"OK, see you never!" comes his reply.

Despite the city (Morocco's third largest as it happens) giving its name to the celebrated item of headgear as seen on stereotyped caricatures of North Africans and popularised by the entertainer Tommy Cooper we don't see anyone wearing a fes. PL then points out that he did see a man in the medina wearing one – probably a tourist trying to "blend in".

We continue our walk in a rigidly straight line.

That evening we decide to have a pizza in the pizzeria just across the street from our hotel. We're escorted to a table on the roof terrace. If it wasn't dark there would probably be spectacular views of the city. My seafood pizza of calamari, prawns and what I presume is some kind of fish seasoned with dried parsley is filling, but distinctly lacking in taste. The goat's cheese base though has quite a strong flavour. We're the only diners in the place until a middle-aged British couple sit down at the next table. There's that moment of semi-awkwardness as we feel obliged to initiate a conversation. I break the ice with:

"Are you enjoying it so far?"

They've both been to Morocco before and seem quite streetwise about the place. He's quite a funny-looking chap, balding and bespectacled with one of those moustache-less Abraham Lincoln-style beards – suggesting that he's possibly an engineer or an academic. His wife does all the talking, while he hardly utters a word. "Mrs Lincoln", who's originally from Edinburgh points out that while the Moroccans are good micro-entrepreneurs they seem to have a lack of awareness of globalisation. There's apparently a Moroccan shop near to where they live in Devon which sells all manner of leather goods, rugs and ceramics at a fraction of what they charge you in Fes.

Suddenly a large cheer erupts and reverberates around the city. Morocco are playing host to Tanzania in the qualifiers of the 2012 African Cup of Nations. It sounds like the home side has scored.

The next morning (or afternoon to be precise as we leave it quite late after a prolonged lie-in) we get the train to Taza in the hope of going hiking in the foothills of the Moyen Atlas mountains. It's another scorcher of a day.

The railway map controversially includes the disputed territory of Western Sahara, which the Moroccan government sees as an integral part of its sovereign territory. As a result, Morocco's eastern border is shaped like a flight of steps.

On arrival in Taza we seem to be the only Europeans around. Even though we stick out like a sore thumb no-one seems to bother us, unlike in Fes. A man even gives us helpful directions and doesn't ask for any money. We go for a hike in the hills on the edge of town. There's an unidentified bird perched on top of a tall cactus. I don't want to get too close in case it flies away, so I zoom my camera in to the maximum capacity. The end product is quite blurred and although it's never going to win wildlife photographer of year I'm still able to identify it as a great grey shrike, also known as the butcher bird due to its habit of impaling its prey on thorns.

After a short walk it's time to head back. We have about half an hour to kill before catching the train, so we decide to grab a quick bite to eat. We sit outside on the street. A cat with runny eyes prowls around under our table in search of titbits, literally miaowing for its supper. I throw a few chicken scraps its way which it gratefully accepts. An old guy in ragged clothes, possibly of Berber origin sits down at the table next to us and proceeds to eat the leftovers of the previous diners. The staff don't seem to mind.

On arrival back in Fes as night is falling we find that the city's main downtown area is lively and atmospheric. It's all open air cafes and restaurants and bright neon lights. We've now sussed out all the outlets in the city that sell beer. This time PL has an excuse as he's celebrating his birthday today. Number 38 to be precise.

The man who was outside the Cinema Rex follows us across the road.

"You want restaurant? You come with me. I find you good place!"

"We've already eaten" I tell him. He leaves us alone and stops following us.

It's our last night in Morocco, so we make our third and final visit to Bar La Cheminée. Now that we've been indoctrinated as regular punters we receive a warm welcome from the staff with handshakes all round. And we're still the only non-locals in the place. This establishment must be one of Fes's best-kept secrets.

The slightly-built bespectacled middle-aged man in the silver suit with the pock-marked face and the slicked back hair is on vocals once again alongside the organist "Billy the Fish". The highlight of the evening is another belly dancer in the full belly-dancing regalia who dances around all corners of the room and even gets on top of one of the tables to strut her stuff.

We decide to try out the Ibis hotel right next to the station, another one of only three establishments in the city which we know serves alcohol. We sit at a table outside next to the pool. There's a group of young English people at the table next to us who are staying at the hotel. After getting one of them to take a picture of us we strike up a conversation. The inevitable topic of what we do for a living crops up.

Rather than saying what I really do I decide to be creative.

"I'm a taxidermist," I tell them in a casual matter-of-fact way.

"Wow!" Vicky says quite clearly impressed. "Have you read *Under the Skin* by Dr Richard Henderson?"

"Of course" I reply knowledgably, "one of the classics of the trade. If you haven't read Henderson you're not a real taxidermist."

The conversation suddenly begins to get interesting. But then PL feels the need to shatter the illusion by throwing a spanner in the works.

"He's winding you up. He really works in – "

"No, I really am a stuffer of creatures" I want to say, but there's no point now. If I had really been a taxidermist I'd want to stuff PL at this present moment. I want to tell him to get stuffed, but that would be taking corniness to a whole new level...

Nevertheless we enjoy shooting the breeze with our new found friends.

As we board the taxi for the airport the next morning Mohamed is keen for us to return soon.

"Don't forget – you now have family in Fes! Come back any time!"

We'll certainly bear his invitation in mind, but we'll be considerably more streetwise should we ever choose to return.

-19-
The Coming of Age Years

One of the big hits of the summer before our very last year at school had been Bryan Adams' awful sentimental ballad *Everything I Do* from the soundtrack to the film *Robin Hood* starring Kevin Costner. I saw it in France where I was the guest of a local family as part of an exchange visit. Over there it was called *Robin des Bois*. Unlike Bryan Adams' summer of '69 the summer of '91 didn't seem to last forever. Suddenly it was autumn and we had entered our very last year of school. It was a year of 18th birthday parties, driving tests and university applications.

I passed my driving test in the autumn of 1991 on a weekday morning. This obviously meant taking the morning off school, but I made sure not to tell anyone in advance, apart from my French teacher whose classes I'd be missing. She was good enough to keep quiet about it. It was my first attempt, although it had taken me a lot of lessons before I was ready to take the test. I had one final lesson with my instructor on the evening before which hadn't gone too well, so I wasn't terribly confident.

I rolled into the industrial estate to be met by a gaunt, pale examiner with the demeanour of an undertaker who spoke in a flat monotonous voice.

"Right I want you to turn left down this next road" he said robotically.

It was like having a zombie in the passenger seat.

"Carry on past the graveyard and then turn right".

I was almost expecting him to tell me to stop at the graveyard, so he could be at his resting place.

The roads were all familiar to me after the numerous lessons I'd taken. Driving through the town centre I had to brake suddenly at a zebra crossing to avoid pedestrians who were crossing at the time. From this point was almost convinced I would fail.

When we got back to the test centre at the industrial estate I awaited the verdict with baited breath.

"Right, you've finished your test and I'm pleased to tell you…"

I was dreading the next bit. He seemed like the type who would take great pleasure in failing someone. I waited with baited breath for him to finish his sentence and was relieved to hear the next two words...

"...you've passed"

It was obvious though that I hadn't exactly passed with flying colours.

"It wouldn't do any harm to have the odd look at your Highway Code now and again though" he added.

Two years later I would be driven by a New York taxi driver with a similar demeanour. I needed to get from the bus station to the hostel I was staying having just been on an epic Greyhound bus journey from Michigan through Ohio, Pennsylvania and New Jersey. He confounded the stereotype of New York taxi drivers. More like the grim reaper than Travis Bickle he didn't utter a single word on the journey.

About a week before my driving test Down had just been crowned All-Ireland champions, the first team to bring the Sam Maguire cup across the border since, er Down 23 years earlier. My mum, being a Down woman was naturally pleased by this and saw it as the perfect opportunity to gloat. Coincidentally one of Down's players Mickey Linden worked as a driving test examiner in the Omagh area. He wasn't the same examiner who took my test, but two of my friends were examined by him. For the record one passed and one failed – apparently for not looking over his shoulder at the beginning.

That year Serbian forces shelled Dubrovnik harbour. A decade and a half later I would visit this famous port, but assuming you've read that chapter by now, you already know that. The perils of writing about chronological events out of sequence.

From Carl's Berg To Hamlet's Castle

In hammering home the point how deep and meaningful Shakespeare's best known play was, our A-level English teacher suggested that you could almost study *Hamlet* as an A-level subject in its own right.

Some twenty years later I would visit the Danish castle which inspired Shakespeare to write his tragic masterpiece. It was a wet Saturday morning in late spring. Accompanied by Alexei and PL I took the short train ride from Copenhagen passing through the flat fields and silver birch woods of old Zealand.

But that's another story.

Oh, what the hell, I'll tell you it anyway, I've still got another 10,000 words to write to finish this bloody book off.

Having spent Friday exploring the Danish capital and its numerous watering holes we decide on an out-of-town day trip for the Saturday. During the brief journey where the train track runs parallel to the coast we stop at a station called Louisiana. But it's a far cry from the bayous and swamplands, French-speaking Cajuns plucking guitars and eating jambolaya pudding. In fact it's the setting for a renowned outdoor modern art and sculpture exhibition, but unfortunately we don't have time to visit. A great pity as the effervescent blossoms on the trees are looking positively Japanese.

Not long after this we reach our destination, the town of Helsingor from which Shakespeare obtained the name Elsinore, the setting for Hamlet. But the actual castle is called Kronborg.

The train station is beside the ferry terminal from where you can make the very short trip across the sound and over to Helsingborg in Sweden. Helsingborg is quite clearly visible and in fact you could almost swim across if the water wasn't so bloody cold.

It's a dull grey drizzly day. Sinister hooded crows are perched atop the bollards on the waterfront – the perfect setting for a Shakespearean tragedy really. My own personal tragedy is that the batteries in my camera have gone flat. Batteries in Denmark like many other things don't come cheap, so my dilemma is whether to buy or not to buy. I decide not to, as Alexei's camera is working so he can be the designated photographer for the day.

Just outside the castle a row of cannons pointing at the coast towards Sweden man the ramparts. Beside them are cannonballs arranged in neat triangles.

"Bloody hell, they must have big rabbits round here!" Alexei remarks.

We go into the castle and have a look. It's impressive. There's even a bust of Shakespeare carved into the wall at the exit. Deep in the castle's bowels is a series of dark underground chambers which once housed its military personnel when it was used as an army barracks up until the 1920s.

We exit the castle and make the short walk over the town centre where we come across a memorial commemorating Denmark's role in the Sino-Icelandic War.

I've never heard of this war, so I google it on my return. The only article I come across is in an obscure blog called "The Screaming Aardvark" or something equally stupid written by some chancer called Crasson Wand who's clearly got too much time on his hands. The relevant extract reads as follows:

"The Institute of Asio-Nordic Studies has called on academics all over the world to recognise the significance of that long-forgotten naval conflict the Sino-Icelandic war of 1902. This obscure maritime feud between the two great sea-faring powers of the early 20th century, Iceland and China evolved from a

235

trade dispute related to tax duties imposed on the export of plastic dinosaurs for distribution in cereal packets. Other Scandinavian powers including Denmark soon became involved.

In fact the war has been almost airbrushed completely from the history books and is no longer taught in either Chinese or Icelandic schools. Both Beijing and Reykjavik have played down the impact of the war such is their embarrassment about its causes.

The only known expert on the war is the discredited academic Dr Paul Lawkins of the Faculty of Sino-Scandinavian Warfare at the University of the Faeroe Islands. Lawkins, an alleged expert on Scando-Asiatic plastics-related trade wars was sacked from his previous post at Carrickmore University for suggesting that 90% of the world's pollution was caused by the emissions from cat yawns.

However Dr Lawkins has achieved significant progress in his efforts to bring the Sino-Icelandic War to public attention. During an archaeological dig in Iceland's barren volcanic interior he unearthed the long lost grave of Joov Beanhad, commander of the Icelandic naval fleet which launched the unsuccessful attempt to shell Shanghai harbour.

The inscription on the gravestone carved in ancient Icelandic rune script provides a fitting epitaph. According to Dr Lawkins' translation it reads:

"HERE LIES CAPTAIN JOOV BEANHAD...AND HE NEVER WANTS TO SEE ANOTHER PLASTIC DINOSAUR AGAIN"."

The war supposedly came to an end on 1st April 1902.

I'm not sure if this bit actually happened or whether it was just my imagination. Or maybe I just made it up. Who knows?

The next day we cross the bridge across the Øresund (or in Swedish the Öresund) by train for a day trip to Malmo in Sweden. The bridge wasn't there the last time I visited back in 1998. On the train we get talking to two hungover Swedish nurses returning home from a night on the tiles in Copenhagen, having taken advantage of the cheaper Danish booze. We bid them farewell as we alight and wish them a speedy recovery. Then we get to sample the delights of Malmo. Now this really did happen. But that really is another story. Time to go back to school now I think.

The School Magazine and the Great Belgian Crisps Caper...

The school had its fair share of "celebrity" alumni. One such example was a comedian called Kevin McAleer who was relatively popular at the time. He would ramble on about times past in an exaggeratedly broad country accent, juxtaposing reminiscences of life on the farm in a rural backwater of mid-Tyrone with psychedelic narcotic-induced trips and a twisted nostalgia for 1970s music and popular culture. He enjoyed the label of "Ireland's funniest man" at one point, (or so it used to say in the posters and the local papers), a tag attributed to about 40 other comedians of the day. McAleer even followed in the footsteps of Anthrax by doing a gig at the GAA club in his home town in (I think) early 1992. But unlike the American thrash metal outfit he didn't get spat on. Some of his old teachers even came to have a word with him after the show. And unlike the Anthrax gig, I actually kept my ticket this time and attended – with Noel McGowan and Aidan McCrystal in tow.

Another old boy made good was the writer Benedict Kiely – who returned to the school in the early 1990s as a guest speaker at the annual prize giving ceremony.

There were also the actors Gerard McSorley and the late Patrick McAlinney. The former is probably best known for his one-off appearance in Father Ted as a con artist priest, who starred in films such as *In the Name of the Father*, *The Boxer*, *Braveheart*, *The Constant Gardener* and the version of *Robin Hood* starring Russell Crowe. I should point out that Crowe was not a pupil at the school though. But by pure coincidence the other well-known New Zealand actor Sam Neill was born in Omagh.

Few people born after 1960 will have heard of Patrick McAlinney, a familiar face on the big and small screens from the 1950s to the 1970s. He actually wrote an article in the school magazine not long before his death in 1990, recounting his experience of ball games played during his school days.

Richard Meyler a former member of the pop group Luv Bug who represented Ireland in the Eurovision song contest in 1986 before going on to run a piano shop in the town was another school old boy. But the best known former pupils tended to be the numerous Tyrone gaelic footballers, notably the county's most successful manager Mickey Harte who led the team to three All-Ireland titles. There was also the sports journalist Jerome Quinn who had become a regular face on regional TV sports programmes towards the end of our tenure at the school.

Apart from these few exceptions any given year would normally churn out its fair share of doctors, lawyers, teachers, architects, engineers and accountants. Joining the rat race, although never one's ideal vision of life was always preferable (not to mention more financially rewarding) to the cop-out of finding spiritual enlightenment in a remote Himalayan monastery... ..or living in a beach hut in Goa, making a living selling beads, pieces of driftwood and henna tattoos to Australian backpackers and gap year students or hippy commune in California. It does beg the question of which is the braver option though.

Most of us ended up living the middle class dream with a safe, but dull white collar profession – detached house in leafy suburbia, or build your own house in the god-forsaken townland in the middle of nowhere where you grew up, 2.4 children. A world of Volvo estate, holidays in the south of France, perfectly manicured lawns, a conservatory looking out on the fields, cappuccino makers, oak-panelled kitchens, vegetable steamers, fine wines, self-assembly furniture from a Scandinavian department store, coffee percolators, health insurance, gold-plated pension plans...and all that other stuff which I won't go into.

In our final year at the school, a small group of us, the usual suspects fulfilled our long-held ambition which we'd aspired to since first year by joining the committee of the annual school magazine. We thought we were the proverbial dog's bollocks, but the truth is we were a bunch of cocky little bastards who probably deserved a good hiding. The membership of the magazine committee consisted almost entirely of the same boys who had been in the school's Dr Who ~~fan club~~ appreciation society some five years previously. Not entirely a coincidence. Most of us were also involved in the school debating society and none of us were particularly good at sport. And to identify a further pattern, down through the years the boys on the magazine committee had generally been to the same primary school in the town and had played lead roles in that school's annual pantomime, as referred to in an earlier chapter. Occasionally there was the odd annoyingly multi-talented all-rounder who would bridge the gap by being both sporty and into the more literary intellectual pursuits – again as referred to in an earlier chapter.

During my early years at the school I'd looked up to the senior boys who ran the magazine and wanted to be like them with their clever, witty articles, sophisticated sense of humour and sarcastic quips. Several years later when school was but a dim and distant memory one of my proudest moments occurred. I was in a pub in Omagh with a bunch of old schoolmates. I got talking to a younger lad who had been a few years below me at school. To my shame I don't even remember his name, but he said he remembered my contemporaries and me from the school magazine and the articles we'd written and told me – "I used to look up to you boys – I wanted to be like you".

In any given year the magazine would have articles on the previous year's school trips, the excruciatingly bad fourth form adolescent

239

angst-ridden poetry of the "I'm so depressed and misunderstood" variety, cartoons invariably plagiarised from Gary Larson's "Far Side" collections, quirky humorous pieces, short stories, reports on the mixed fortunes of the school's various sports teams and other extra-curricular activities, the occasional feature on successful past pupils, (particularly those who had bucked the trend by becoming something other than a doctor, lawyer, teacher, engineer, accountant, dentist or architect) and similar such odds and sods.

One magazine featured a staff picture taken in 1974 and caused much mirth. Teachers who were now cleanshaven and short-haired (or in some cases lacking hair) sported flowing locks, dense beards or horseshoe moustaches and wore jackets with huge lapels and ties the size of manta rays.

The quality of material wasn't always top rate, but if nothing else it was a great ego trip to see your own handiwork in print.

I myself wrote my fair share of bad poetry during my folly-ridden youth. For the local parish yearbook I also wrote a poem about handball called "The Kill", a reference to the technique of "killing" the ball by hitting it to the intersection of the front wall and the floor, so that it stops dead and can't be retrieved by your opponent. Not wanting to offend the parishioners' sensitivities they changed the title to the less suggestive, but totally unimaginative "The Ball", which somehow lost the impact of what I was trying to say and took away the violent imagery. I was using the game of handball as a metaphor for life. And with death being the only inevitability in life "The Kill" was therefore an appropriate title. Somehow I think all this was lost on the magazine's readers.

In order to recruit more writers for the magazine we put up a publicity poster featuring a warrior from a sword-and-sorcery "Lord of the Rings"-type graphic novel, glistening sword in one hand with his other arm around a comely young wench, the wind in their hair with the legend "Many are the pleasures of writing for your school magazine". But inevitably some "comedian" had to deface the poster and change the word "writing" to "riding".

Hilarious.

Another poster was a DIY cut-and-paste photocopy job of a fluffy white seal pup with big dark innocent eyes, but with a gun pointing to its head below the headline "Write for your school magazine – or the baby seal gets it!" Cruel perhaps, but an effective way of garnering attention.

Yet another somewhat controversial poster depicted Clint Eastwood as Dirty Harry holding up his Magnum revolver with a speech bubble containing some undoubtedly witty variation on the famous line from the film. I don't recall the exact wording, but it was something like "Do you feel, lucky, punk? If so write for your school magazine!"

A middle-aged female teacher (let's just call her Mrs Maguire) witnessed us sticking up the poster and rather bizarrely to our bemusement chastised us for the insensitivity of the firearm imagery considering the level of violence which was going on at the time in the north of Ireland. It was a connection that funnily enough we had never made as fortunately we knew the difference between fiction and reality.

We also tried to slip a few risqué pieces in, some of which successfully made it. The editor Joe Gorman, had been on a short trip to Belgium after having won an inter-schools essay–writing competition on the European Union. To his (and our) great delight and amusement he discovered that the leading Belgian brand of crisps, (their equivalent of Walkers or Tayto) was called Corky. He wrote a witty account of his Belgian experience for that year's magazine. At the end of his piece he included a cheeky afterthought. I don't recall the exact words, but it went something along the lines of:

"…and finally no trip to the low countries would be complete without a mention of Belgium's favourite junk food – Corky crisps!"

Accompanying this paragraph was a photo of a packet of the fat-saturated potato-based snacks bearing the distinctive "CORKY" logo in large letters. It's probably a safe bet that the crisp manufacturer's namesake was well aware of young Gorman's intentions here, but sensibly he chose to turn a blind eye.

Whatever happened to the Film Club?

Naturally enough the local cinema tended to show mainstream Hollywood films rather than Fellini or Bergman retrospectives, despite the extension which created two extra screens. Subtitled new wave French surrealists wouldn't exactly have drawn the crowds in Omagh.

Towards the end of my school career I remember going to the flicks fairly regularly with a bunch of mates. Popular films of the time included *Thelma and Louise*, *Dances With Wolves*, *Goodfellas*, *Cape Fear*, *JFK*, *The Field* and *Silence of the Lambs*.

At the behest of our English teacher, a Derry man called Mr Lawrence Muldoon, but known among the pupils as "Larry", a small group of us attempted ("attempted" being the operative word) to set up a film club. The idea was to hire a film projector and show selected films of the more artistic type like *Casablanca* or *Citizen Kane* and profound subtitled European films from the likes of Buñuel, Pasolini and Truffaut rather than the standard current Hollywood blockbuster to an audience of appreciative younger pupils.

We managed to procure some used film posters from the local cinema and stuck them up at various locations around the school to publicise the imminent formation (ahem!) of the club. Inevitably they were defaced. On the *Steel Magnolias* poster two drawing pins had been strategically stuck through each of Julia Roberts' breasts, and another one further south.

Due to a combination of apathy and logistical problems the film club never saw the light of day, even though about 20 pupils (mostly gullible first and second years) had already paid the £1 a head membership fee. Where that money ended up remains a mystery to this day.

Larry Muldoon, like many of that particular generation of teachers born roughly between 1940 and 1955 was a bit of a character. Being from Derry he saw himself as a sophisticated city slicker, whereas we were the primitive savages from the rural backwater. Too many of us all too often failed to see the irony here and regularly rose to the bait. He also had nicknames for virtually all of his pupils based on agonisingly bad puns.

During my early days at the school before he got to know us all, he would occasionally supervise us if we ever had him for a free period he would go around the class asking boys their names. A typical exchange would go like this.

Larry: What's your name, boy?

Pupil A: Sir, Liam Duffy.

Larry: Sir Liam Duffy? Have you been awarded a knighthood?

What's your name, son? (Pointing to Pupil C)

Pupil C: Otis McAleer.

Larry: So what do they call you then? McAlnose?

Pupil C: No, they call me Curly because I've got curly hair.

Larry: Where are you from?

Pupil C: Ballygawley.

Larry: Is that Ballygawley, Tyrone or Ballygawley, Zambia?

Pupil C: Zambia.

Larry: What's your name, son? (Turning his attention to Pupil B)

Pupil B: Mark Teague.

Larry: I just asked your name, not your religion. (To Pupil D) What's your name?

Pupil D: Martin McTosser, sir.

Larry: Are you from Ballykilbollocks?

Pupil D: No, Killybastard.

Larry: I didn't know there were any McTossers in Killybastard. Sure McTosser's not a Killybastard name.

Pupil D: My da's from Ballykilbollocks.

Larry: Is your da called Pat?

Pupil D: No, sir.

Larry: Mick?

Pupil C: No.

Larry: What the hell is his buckin' name then?

Pupil D: Frank.

Larry: Frank, the butcher?

Pupil D: No, he's an electrician.

Larry: You mean electricity has actually reached Ballykilbollocks?

Pupil C (Unamused): I wouldn't know, I'm from Killybastard.

Larry: You didn't have a brother at the school a few years ago?

Pupil D: No, I don't have any brothers.

Larry: And what's your name?

Pupil X: Sergio McBastard

Larry: You're not one of the Drumgallykilderry McBastards are you?

Pupil X: No, I'm one of the Castlegorfinmorebrack McBastards

Larry: You McBastards don't half get around…

And so on...

There would be situations when certain troublesome pupils were making a nuisance of themselves in class. Larry would pretend to get angry and bang loudly on his desk, then say: "Get yourself down to Brother O'Loscan's office now!" The miscreant in question would go out the door down the corridor and on his way to receive a bollocking or perhaps much worse from the Great Satan only for Larry to shake his head with a sigh and reveal his bluff, ordering a designated pupil to:

"Run after that buckin'eejit and bring him back here!"

He would also indulge in the occasional spoonerism – If someone had left the door open he would bark at them - "Fose that cluckin' door!!" Or he would occasionally briefly disappear from the classroom with the reassurance that he would "be back in a mock of linnets".

Head Boys at the Top Table

At the annual prizegiving ceremony the boys who had left school the previous year were invited back to receive certificates of distinction. The guest speaker would usually be a distinguished past pupil who had excelled in his chosen field, whether it be academia, business, law or the church. It wasn't necessarily anyone we'd actually heard of though. He would made the usual speech about aesthetic values (but with some of the less inspiring speakers "anaesthetic values" would be more appropriate) and the importance of education – and of course how his time at the school had taught him the core values of life. I don't think there's much chance of myself being invited to be guest speaker any time soon, especially after some of the stuff I've written in this book. But I continue to live in hope.

One year towards the end of my school career Gerard Black the head boy from the previous year gave the customary previous year's head boy's address and saw his chance to have a not so subtle dig at his old headmaster. A popular lad during his time at the school, a few years earlier he'd played the title role in a production of *Jesus Christ Superstar*.

The messianic Gerry was enjoying his first year of higher education.

"I don't know who invented the expression "Your school days are the best days of your life", but whoever it was obviously never went to university!"

"During our final year at school we used to have free periods – or "study periods" as Brother O'Loscan preferred to call them. I have no idea why, because during these periods we did anything but study! What we did get up to I'll keep to myself!"

The rest of his speech contained various details of the high jinks he and his classmates got up to, incorporating subtly disparaging but essentially harmless good-humoured criticisms of the school administration. There were tales of skipping class to go down the pub, thefts of traffic cones and shopping trolleys and conducting clandestine scientific experiments in the clump of trees at the back of the school yard.

He concluded his speech and walked off the stage to a standing ovation.

"If you believe that you'll believe anything!" said Corky as he resumed his MC duties, quite obviously pissed off, but trying very hard not to show it by saying it in a half-heartedly humorous way as if to imply he was half going along with the joke, being aware that there were parents present.

"No, I think he had a fair point actually" most of us thought.

"I actually wanted Patrick McGurk to be head boy" the Corker continued. You were almost expecting him to say in his annoying nasal whine "but we got this wanker instead" pointing contemptuously at Gerry.

Pat McGurk, who went on to become a doctor was a studious boy, a decent sort, but not quite the cheeky Jack-the-lad type of character that Gary was. Pat would have made a safer, much more respectful speech which would have met with Corky's approval. Not surprisingly Gerard Black is now a teacher.

Elections for head boy were democratic in theory. Although I suspect the principal could overrule the pupil's nomination. I have vague memories of the whole year of about 100 boys being summoned to the lecture and made to do a secret ballot by writing the names of their three preferred candidates.

I was a senior prefect which meant very little, except for the fact that I got to wear a metal-plated badge with "Prefect" on it. Our responsibilities included keeping order in the corridors and making sure the junior pupils went outside as soon as they'd finished their lunch. We were also given tape measures to make sure the first year's haircuts corresponded to the required length and a colour chart to check that their shoes were the right level of darkness.

I also helped out in the tuck shop during the 11am breaktime slot. It was a bit of a mad free-for-all with the clamour for the sugar or saturated fat fix craved by dozens of adolescent boys. The caretakers Kevin and Seamus did their best to keep order, but it was like King Canute battling the sea or like a frog trying to herd cats. A curious aspect of school etiquette was that we had to call the teachers by their formal titles (ie Mr, Miss, Brother, etc – as of course is the case in most schools), yet we were allowed to address the caretakers and the admin staff by their first names. We also got paid a small wage for our troubles – cash in hand, so there was no danger of the taxman coming after us.

While I'm on the subject of tuck shops and junk food, it's worth taking a nostalgic look back at the kind of rubbish myself and my classmates recklessly indulged in during our foolish days of youthful excess. Rewinding back to primary school for a brief moment I remember liquorice flavoured chewy sweets called Blackjacks which would turn your tongue black. Then there were "UFOs", flying saucer-shaped wafer casing (of an unnatural sky

blue colour) which had both the texture and taste of polystyrene –
but with sherbet inside. Ice pops were semi-frozen fruit-flavoured
slush with more Es than a 1990s rave party contained in a foot long
transparent tube from which you sucked out the contents and
invariably cut the side of your lips on the sharp edges of the
plastic. There were also the pear flavoured ice lollies which stuck
to your clothes like industrial glue.

It was as if the confectionery manufacturers had some kind of deal
going with the tobacco companies as candy cigarettes, chocolate
cigars and liquorice pipes were all popular items – a cynical way of
encouraging young children to start off with pretend tobacco
products before moving on to the real stuff . Or maybe I'm
reading too deeply into it.

For a brief period there were nettle flavoured crisps manufactured
by a local producer which probably went out of business years ago.
They had a pleasant spicy taste with a kick and were actually quite
addictive, so it's probably a good thing that they were
discontinued. My dad used to recall eating nettle soup during his
youth, a country delicacy which has now largely died out, but
something which I imagine would be quite tasty. At the risk of
sounding dangerously like those homespun rural Irish memoirs I
remember summer walks through the field in short trousers and
nettles would come up to my waist. I emerged with my legs
covered in stings. So probably the only thing nettles are good for
is eating them, either in crisps (although I very much doubt there
were any actual nettles in the ingredients), soups or stews. But no
doubt some biologist has written a paper in an obscure scientific
journal which concludes that without nettles the human race would
be wiped out. It's rather ironic that rabbit or nettle on the dinner
table would have been considered nothing special a couple of
generations ago, but now they've become the stuff of exclusive
gourmet restaurants.

Swords & Saucers

A minute ago I was in the classroom, but now I suddenly find myself in a windswept barren landscape. Like the cover of a 1970s progressive rock album. There are huge sand dunes and curious rock formations everywhere, but no sign of the sea. So I'm pretty sure I'm not in Donegal.

A giant wasp is buzzing around my head. I reach for my mobile phone from the pocket of my pinstripe suit jacket to call an ambulance – or an undertaker. I find it's now a sword. I manage to fend it off for a few seconds which gives me time to dig into my pocket and fish out an orange which I throw with great force towards the nearby pile of rocks. Seduced by the scent of orange crush on the rocks my striped assailant makes a beeline (or in this case a waspline) for this juicy citrus feast.

I carry on walking as pterodactyls and pteranodons screech and soar overhead, hoping that I'll die soon so they can scavenge my corpse. Talking of scavengers, an army of jorbs is feasting ravenously on the decaying carcass of a greepo. Or maybe it's a bypo - it's hard to tell the difference. Greepos have stripes whereas bypos have spots, but on this putrefying flesh I can't make out any definite skin pattern. Some of the jorbs are even nibbling at the dead creature's horns with their tiny, but razor sharp teeth.

The jorbs flee as they see me approach and hide behind the rocks, their six pairs of eyes darting in all directions ever alert for danger or the possibility of scavenging another free meal. On closer inspection the greepo/bypo has a huge bitemark in its side. This couldn't possibly have been made by the jorbs as their teeth just aren't big enough. Maybe it had got into a fight with another greepo.

I'm wondering what any of this has to do with nostalgic reminiscences of school days in the 1980s. And presumably so is the reader.

It seems like I'm trapped inside an unpublished comic memoir hemmed in by solid walls of twisted nostalgia reinforced with unreliable memories and barbed wire surrealism. There's no obvious escape route except to sell out my principles.

I look up to see a giant mouse with a Mohican haircut and sunglasses smoking a joint while rowing a boat in the purple clouds dotting the yellow sky above. It fixes me with a hard stare before blowing smoke in my face and giving me a rude two-fingered gesture (or the nearest approximation it can give with its rodent claws) and rowing off into the sunset. Just before reaching the sun both mouse and boat explode spectacularly and shatter into millions of tiny pieces which rain down on me.

Meanwhile from a pool of steaming lava steps a Spanish footballer in an all white strip. He has the body of a man, but the head of a fish – a bit like a reverse version of Billy the Fish from Viz *– and is kicking a giant hexagonal ball made up of thousands of tiny bubbles all fused together. It dawns on me that he must be the centre forward with Surreal Madrid. He suddenly vanishes and on the spot where he stood tumbleweeds are blowing in the wind and the eerie silence is broken by howls of sarcastic laughter coming from all directions and gradually rising to a crescendo.*

My eyes glance downwards. There's now a giant watch where my belt used to be. This is what you might call a waist of time.

Suddenly I'm ankle-deep in a shallow, slow-moving body of water with words bobbing up and down and floating past me. It must be my stream of consciousness. A trap door opens and I fall through the gravelly bed into a giant vat of lukewarm custard. The yellow creamy liquid is quite deep. It goes right up to my neck and it's that thick it's bloody hard to swim through. A labrador with a shark's dorsal fin growing out of its back is swimming round and round in circles. If this is supposed to be a dogfish then it's someone's poor idea of a joke. I'm desperately trying to keep my head above water – or in this case – custard, but I'm slowly sinking. I try to clutch at a strand of rhubarb in much the same way as the proverbial drowning man will clutch at a straw...

250

...but my arms and legs have given up. I'm going down...

Then I wake up. I'm back on dry land. My tie has just transformed into a python and is gradually tightening its grip around my neck. I tickle it in an attempt to make it laugh and loosen its stranglehold, but it doesn't work. And now the ground beneath my feet has turned to quicksand and is rapidly swallowing me up...

Then I woke up - again. I'd been having this weird dream that I'd written a memoir about my schooldays, effectively an autobiography of a nobody with a few tenuously linked travel stories thrown in for padding and the critics panned it for having this totally irrelevant chapter on sword and sorcery fantasy tinged with surrealism and stream of consciousness prose just to stretch it out to the required word length, accusing me of having nothing further to say and all major publishers and agents had turned it down, saying that it was not commercially viable as there really is no viable market for non-celebrity memoirs. I was so relieved when I realised it had just been a dream.

The bit after the beginning of the end which still isn't quite the end

Just a Formality?

But this bit certainly isn't a dream.

Although sometimes it feels like it was...

The big event of any pupil's final year at the school was the seventh year formal. The other two grammar schools in the town also had theirs –and there was naturally considerable overlap in the attendance. In this particular year it turned out to be something of an anti-climax. In America the equivalent, I believe is known as the "high school prom". This is the occasion so beloved of hackneyed, clichéd Hollywood rom-com movies where the underdog triumphs over the golden boy. The finale inevitably features the typical scene of "making out" in the back of the Chevy after the underdog; the weedy bespectacled guy has outwitted his butch gridiron football-playing rival and won over the glamorous girl.

But this wasn't California. For most of us in the real world of Omagh's ostentatiously named Royal Arms Hotel (not quite as plush as it sounds – and sadly no longer there) on a mild night in late January1992, this was a distinctly unromantic affair. Thanks to an old schoolmate who recently posted a picture of the ticket on Facebook I can confirm that the event took place on 23 January 1992. But there was no Marge and Homer moment. The young woman I took already had a boyfriend. I was aware of this, just as he was aware of the arrangements on the night. Being the decent fellow that he was he didn't mind. This wasn't a big deal in any case. My first and second choices were already spoken for and the formalities were more or less made at the last minute. The main topic of gossip from the beginning of seventh year was about who was taking who to the formal – or who was being taken by who to the Convent School's formal. Going on your own without a "companion" and being the proverbial spare prick was a non-starter. This boyfriend was an accomplished athlete and Gaelic footballer and if I remember correctly was on the Tyrone minor team at the time. I could provide very little in the way of competition. The sum total of my playing career had consisted of about four matches (two as a sub) for the Omagh St Endas under-12 reserve team, all of which we'd lost quite heavily. However as he was in the year below he was ineligible to attend, the formal being for final year pupils only.

One individual in our year group was adamant that he wasn't going, claiming that it was a waste of money. And to his credit he didn't go. Looking back in hindsight he did have a point. It was quite an expensive night – for a schoolboy anyway. On top of the costs of the two tickets and the hire of the tuxedo it was customary to buy flowers for your escort and chocolates for her mother. Any drinks purchased on the night were of course another added expense. However as I was driving I was strictly teetotal on the night – unlike more than a few others.

Only a few years earlier the secondary event, the annual school disco had been abolished due to drunken pupils going on the rampage and causing trouble. This would reflect the shape of things to come.

The formal was usually held on a Friday night for obvious reasons. Nursing a hangover in class the next day and throwing up all over your desk wasn't a pleasant prospect. However this year, due to some booking error or similar twist of fate it was on a Thursday.

My night didn't get off to a great start. While picking up my companion I crashed the car by reversing into a gatepost causing a crack in the rear light. I never mentioned this to my dad and although he probably knew damn well what had happened he never mentioned it either.

It was a spectacularly unremarkable night – until something totally unforeseen happened. I have vague memories of the band playing *Las Vegas in the Hills of Donegal* by Goats Don't Shave, a lively humorous song which advocates the idea of turning Ireland's most

253

northerly and most neglected county into a giant casino and to hell with both the north and the south – which had recently been a big hit in the Irish charts. Ironically enough during the short-lived so-called "Celtic Tiger" years this concept wasn't too far from reality. They played it twice - at the beginning and at the end of the night. But there was to be no Las Vegas in the hills of West Tyrone either – although someone did take a bit of a calculated gamble, which was to define the night and the year and would still be talked about 20 years later.

Before the main meal the boys had formed their own little cliques and the girls had formed theirs in which they chatted amongst themselves. Apparently this happened every year. That is until the bombshell was dropped.

After the unexceptional meal of roast chicken and the usual lukewarm, overcooked vegetables (although I do remember the pavlova for dessert was particularly tasty), the traditional mock awards ceremony took place. My memory of the night is hazy given that it was over 20 years ago, but if I remember correctly young Mick Cunningham was master of ceremonies, rather appropriate given that his initials were MC. So he was in effect "MC the MC". The prizes awarded were generally jokes directed at the personality of the recipient or in reference to a memorable incident in which they'd been involved. One lad, for example was known to be an ardent Celtic supporter, so the plan was to present him with a Rangers shirt on the night. But for reasons soon to become apparent this never happened.

It started off fairly innocently with a game in which a male and female participant were plucked from the "audience" and made to say "fluffy ducks" with a marshmallow in their mouths.

Following this less than inspiring start a young lad – to preserve his anonymity I'll call him Gavin McCarthy – was called up to the stage and invited to say his piece.

I should point out here that it was customary to invite the school principal to the event.

McCarthy walked up to the microphone somewhat unsteadily and addressed the crowd in a slightly slurred voice.

"Is there any teachers out there?"

"No!" lied the congregation who by giving him this illusion were inviting scandal.

McCarthy in his alcohol-fuelled innocence saw this as an opportunity to speak his mind more freely than would have been advisable under the circumstances. His next words have since entered into folklore.

"Who here agrees that Corky's an asshole?"

This was followed by a very awkward, uncomfortable period of eerie silence, which lasted about five seconds, but seemed more like five hours. In the meantime thousands of metaphorical pins dropped to the floor.

In his advanced state of inebriation he has been blissfully unaware of the presence of the object of his character assassination himself in the very room – along with a number of other teachers.

A Facebook discussion between a group of past pupils from the "Class of '92" project almost two decades later shed some more light on the incident:

"It was surreal...we were like...did he just say what we think he said? Everyone just sunk into the seats waiting for the shouting to start" one observer commented.

Naturally, there are varying eyewitness accounts.

Apparently an authoritarian voice with a southern accent could be heard saying in a calm, but firm manner "Gavin, step away from the microphone" followed about a half a minute later with the words "Gavin, I repeat, step away from the microphone!"

But my memories of the event are slightly different. From what I recall, this blip was ignored for the moment. The proceedings continued despite this dark cloud hanging over them like the proverbial elephant in the room. Things gradually degenerated into anarchy as the MCs started pouring beer over McCarthy's head as part of some kind of traditional game.

Corky had had enough by this stage and decided to intervene. He purposely strode up to the stage and called the whole proceedings to a halt. From that point on the atmosphere was somewhat subdued. I was pissed off as I'd been told I was going to be the recipient of some award and was looking forward to getting up on stage and making a witty speech. To this day I still don't know what award I was up for.

Later on in the gents – or so the story goes – McCarthy in conversation with an unnamed individual was supposed to have expressed a sense of betrayal, claiming "The bastards told me there was no fuckin' teachers there!"

Rumour even has it that Corky was waiting at the school gate the next morning to check on any late arrivals.

Needless to say young McCarthy never came back to the school. Four months of intense exam preparation (among many other things) later it was all over for the rest of us as well. In the words of Alice Cooper, school was out for the summer, school was out forever. Except for the poor sods who'd fucked up their A-levels and had to come back and repeat.

That summer I was in that no-man's-land of a twilight zone between school and whatever lay ahead, be it university, the dole queue, pulling pints behind a bar, going back to school to repeat, or pulling off a major insurance fraud and travelling the world with the proceeds. Gap years were virtually unheard of in those days. And there was a recession on, so times were hard.

I had a summer job of sorts. For a brief period I even had two jobs. I had a short-lived second job as a washer-upper up in a new bar-restaurant complex. It was on an on-off/as-and-when-they-needed-me basis. After two shifts at the place they never asked me back for some reason.

My main summer job was as a door-to-door salesman for a

256

company called Ultra-Kleen attempting to persuade people to buy household goods which they didn't need. The monotony of travelling around soulless suburban estates in the intense heat and rhyming off the same spiel over and over again wasn't my ideal summer occupation, but it did pay.

"Hello. I'm sorry you to disturb you, but I'm an agent from Ultra-Kleen. You might have heard of it – "

"No, can't say I have."

"Ok, well anyway it's a company that sells household goods at bargain prices and if you're interested by any chance you might want to have a look at this catalogue – there's an order form inside it – and I'll call back tomorrow".

Being cut off in mid-sentence and having the door slammed shut in my face by suspicious pensioners was disappointing, but understandable. In contrast it was often heavily tattooed burly young men who did want to order stuff and accepted the catalogue quite gracefully.

Nevertheless this approach was roughly 60% successful, considerably greater than the measly 20% commission I would receive for selling the crap.

After I'd taken the orders the next stage would be delivering the shower squeegees, ice cube trays, feather dusters to the buyers.

The art of being a good salesman revolves around the gift of the gab – or in plain terms – being a good bullshitter. This was a gift I didn't really have, although I did manage to sell more stuff than I'd hoped -and not all of it to members of my own family. And on the plus side knocking on a door and being barked at by a small dog on the other side as it jumped up to the letter box in a pathetic attempt to assert its credentials, while its elderly owner was out could be quite satisfying. Putting your fingers against the glass to make the little bugger jump up and try to bite you through the glass before pausing to relaunch itself into another frenzied and utterly futile bout of yapping, growling, gnashing of teeth and clawing at the door in between gasps for breath did provide some much-needed entertainment to what was otherwise an unfulfilling routine.

It was during this time I began work on an untitled semi-autobiographical novel about life in a dull provincial town. It gives an insight into the naïve and idealistic thinking of my 18 year old self, although you couldn't really tell that by reading the short extract below, which is the only part worth reproducing:

> "It was as if I was playing a capitalistic game of supply and demand in the suburban jungle, the world of tarmac and concrete, satellite dishes and leafy gardens of gimmicky neo mock tudor dwellings in which armchair corpses brainwashed themselves in front of the TV."

To Pastures New

Among its many purposes the school magazine served as a sort of swansong for the final year students who would go on to pastures new the following autumn. Not surprisingly any given year's edition was dominated by articles, poetry, stories and artwork created by the seventh year boys. These "pastures new" ranged from the genteel setting of medieval cloisters and grassy quadrangles to the plastic and plateglass campuses (or should that be campi?) of the newer seats of academia to the less glamorous environment of mould-ridden bedsits decorated with traffic cones, tatty Che Guevara posters and empty bottles - or for the even less fortunate - the dole queue.

The post-school destinations of any given year group did however tend to follow a general pattern. The bulk of the school's leavers usually ended up at one of the two local universities, Queen's and the University of Ulster or their affiliated teacher training colleges. This was effectively the safe option, admittedly one which I myself took. This way you could get the bus home every weekend with a big bag of dirty laundry and return on the Sunday evening with freshly ironed clothes and a large food hamper.

Of those who crossed the border or the water a handful would go to Dublin and a few would attend English, Scottish (and occasionally) Welsh institutions. The most popular cross-channel destinations were usually Liverpool and Manchester due to their close proximity to the main ferry crossings, the relatively low cost of living compared with Southern England and possibly even the popularity of the local football teams.

There were always one or two who took the brave step of going somewhere no-one else from the school went like Wolverhampton Poly or the University of East Grinstead. Sometimes this was out of choice, maybe a deliberate attempt to cut loose and make a fresh start. But other times it was accidental as in the case where they hadn't achieved good enough grades to reach their first, second or in some cases third choice seat of learning. This could often prove to be beneficial however, sometimes even a sort of blessing in disguise. Freed from the baggage of your old school and your home town in a new environment where no-one knew anything about your past you could effectively re-invent yourself and enter a completely new social circle where your friends didn't piss off home to Mummy and Daddy every weekend. This was in complete contrast to sitting in a lecture hall or the student union bar on the first day of term in Belfast or Coleraine and finding yourself surrounded by a dozen of your school mates (some of whom you weren't especially thrilled to see), especially if you were doing a popular course like business studies or IT.

One particular year produced a bumper crop of medical students. "It's going to be a healthy town" one teacher remarked on hearing the news.

Then there those unfortunates who hadn't done very well in their exams and were now repeating either at the school or at a local further education college. They were euphemistically referred to in the school magazine as "continuing A-level studies".

Whenever I hear the song "Born to be Wild" by Steppenwolf I'm reminded of the day my A-level results came out. A bunch of us were returning from the school where we'd just received the good news/bad news (delete as appropriate) and got a lift off a mate, Aidan McCrystal in his car (or more precisely his parents' car) and the song came on the radio just as we were passing the local library. We did a couple of circuits of the town for no apparent reason, other than it was the thing you did back then. We hit the town that night – and a rather enjoyable night it was too.

It was the end, but the moment had been prepared for. Nerdy anoraks will no doubt know where that quote comes from.

And the beginning of a new chapter – in life that is, not this book.

Then about a month later as the leaves turned various shades of brown, yellow and russet came university, an entirely different experience…

I had wanted to escape from the parochial narrow-minded confines of provincial life and experience the cosmopolitan vibe of a modern, lively, energetic city.

Despite this, I chose to study in Belfast.

But that's another story entirely. Maybe one day I could even write a book about it. I could maybe call it something like *On Square Routes: The Memoirs and Travels of an Ageing Student.*

Or maybe not.

I don't know.

THE END?

About the Author

Ciaran Ward was born in Co Tyrone in 1973. He has worked in various jobs including call centre worker, teacher of English as a Foreign Language, librarian, taxidermist and local government information manager. He lives in London.

He has also authored "The Dreaming Armadillo" blog since 2005, best described as a whimsical commentary on the state of the planet, the life forms which inhabit it and what they do in their spare time – plus anything else which may spring to mind.

His spare time interests include amateur drama, long distance walking, cycling, birdwatching, crocodile farming, early '70s progressive rock bands, falconry, camel racing, researching the Sino-Icelandic war of 1902, deep sea diving and blatantly lying about what he does in his spare time.

"In Complete Circles" is his first book.

http://dreamingarm.wordpress.com/

CPSIA information can be obtained at www.ICGtesting.com
Printed in the USA
LVOW06s0509030315

428941LV00025BA/813/P

9 781475 046359